Applied Anthropology: Theory and Practice

Applied Anthropology: Theory and Practice

Paramveer Bhatia

CYBER TECH PUBLICATIONS
4264/3, Ansari Road, Daryaganj, New Delhi-110002 (India)
Ph.: 011-23244078. Fax: 011-23280028
E-Mail: cyberpublicationsdelhi@yahoo.com

APPLIED ANTHROPOLOGY: THEORY AND PRACTICE

Paramveer Bhatia

First Edition 2009

Published by :

G.S. Rawat for **Cyber Tech Publications**
4264/3, Ansari Road, Daryaganj, New Delhi-110002 (India)
Ph.: 011-23244078. Fax: 011-23280028
E-Mail: cyberpublicationsdelhi@yahoo.com

Printed at : Asian Offset Printers

Preface

During the past decade, processes associated with what is popularly though perhaps misleadingly known as globalization have come within the purview of anthropology. Migration and mobility—and the footloose or even rootless social groups that they produce—as well as the worldwide diffusion of commodities, media images, political ideas and practices, technologies and scientific knowledge today are on anthropology's research agenda. As a consequence, received notions about the ways in which culture relates to territory have been abandoned. The term transnationalisation captures cultural processes that stream across the borders of nation states. Anthropologists have been forced to revise the notion that transnationalisation would inevitably bring about a culturally homogenized world. Instead, we are witnessing a surge of greatly increamsing cultural diversity. New cultural forms grow out of historically situated articulations of the local and the global. Rather than left-over relics from traditional orders, these are decidedly modern, yet far from uniform. The discussion and research engages the idea of the pluralization of modernities, explores its potential for interdisciplinary research agendas, and also inquires into problematic assumptions underlying this new theoretical concept.

—*Author*

CONTENTS

1

Introduction to Anthropology

Anthropology is the study of humans in all places and at all times. The term itself comes from the Greek (anthropos=man, logos=the study of). Both literate and non-literate peoples are of interest to anthropologists. The field includes many aspects of sociology; however, anthropology reaches much more deeply into prehistory, the humanities, and the physical sciences. Anthropologists study modern humans and their direct ancestors whom we will refer to as hominids.

Anthropology is a recent discipline originating a little more than a hundred years ago. The first course in the field was offered at the University of Rochester (New York) in 1879.

Modern anthropology has its roots in the European expansion and colonization of the New World. The appearance, beliefs, and customs of the Indigenous peoples in the Americas excited European intellectuals in the Age of Discovery. Reports of the 'savages' challenged the thinkers of the Enlightenment to formulate rudimentary theories about what distinguishes humans from the animals. The contact with native peoples forced examination of the very issue of what it means to be human. It took a papal bull in 1537 to declare that "the Indians are truly men."

INQUIRY

If you saw the motion picture, The English Patient, you saw the many references to Herodotus, The Histories. Sales of that ancient book increased dramatically after release of the film. The written work by Herodotus was literally, an inquiry. Written in the fifth century B.C.E., it was one of the first historical accounts in the ancient world. Inquiry is what anthropology is about. It is a search, an investigation into what we are now, from whence we came and how we got to be the way we are today.

EMERGENCE OF CULTURAL ANTHROPOLOGY

A crucial stimulus to many early anthropologists came from The Golden Bough. Some comprehensives survey of world mythology and religion written by the Scottish scholar, Sir James Frazier. He inspired a generation of anthropologists to go out into the world to do fieldwork and develop the methodology that has established anthropology as a rigorous scientific endeavor.

That interest came at an opportune time. At the beginning of this century the perception was that indigenous peoples were changing and that many faced extinction.

This was nowhere more true than in America where Native American Indians were rapidly fading into legend. Ethnography, the study of culture flourished as a result. The Yanomamo of Venezuela and Brazil have captured popular attention in our time as the last large unacculturated people on earth when reported in Chagnon's The Fierce People.

PHYSICAL ANTHROPOLOGY

Physical anthropology focuses on the place of man in nature. It emerged as a search into the ancestry, development, genetic, and other characteristics of the human species. In contrast, social or cultural anthropology examines the way in which people live.

Physical anthropologists view humans as a biological phenomenon, dissection our species with all the tools of anatomy, physiology, and zoology. For much of this century, they have concentrated on the way physical traits differ from population to population. Ultimately they seek evidence of our origins and the way humanity has come to populate the Earth.

Much about our past has been learned since Darwin's Origin of Species was published in 1859. Neandertals, Cro-Magnon, and the first 'Pithecanthropus erectus' were found in succeeding decades. The Taung child was found in 1924 and 'Lucy' by Johanson in 1974. The methodology, the number of fossil finds, and the body of knowledge about human evolution has grown enormously since Darwin. New finds in anthropology now are frequent and often become headline news.

FRAUD AND DEBATE

Anthropology has had its share of controversy both within the discipline and with critics outside of the field. Some cynics have said that 'anthropologists dig up bones so they can hit each other over the head with them!'

The discipline's most notorious fraud is the well-known Piltdown Hoax, a cleverly crafted assembly of an antiquated cranium and the jawbone of an orangutan. It was not fully dismissed until absolute dating tests around 1950 revealed it to be just trickery.

The evolutionary model for human origins has been vigorously debated. Milford Wolpoff (University of Michigan) is the proponent of the Multiregional Hypothesis. A different model is the Population Replacement Hypothesis proposed by Christopher Stringer (Natural History Museum in London). Both are articulate and powerful thinkers and each can cite compelling evidence for their case. The rancorous debate continues amongst their supporters and critics.

Cultural anthropology has had its own debates. Some fifty years after her pioneering work was published, Margaret Mead's Coming of Age in Samoa was challenged by both methodological and factual grounds by Derek Freeman, igniting a controversy that still has not been resolved in any definitive way.

Cultural anthropologists doing fieldwork at times have been at odds with missionaries and the people being studied. Native American Indians no longer tolerate indiscriminate digging by anthropologists.

Dispute with 'creationists' who oppose the theory of evolution is an ongoing contentious issue. Article 1.7 examines this issue in depth.

My own view is that the debates in anthropology reflect the intellectual vigor of the discipline. Discussion and difference of opinion are the price we pay for inquiry in the broadest possible sense.

THE SUB FIELDS OF ANTHROPOLOGY

Four distinct branches or sub fields of anthropology are recognized in current textbooks. There are also other more specialized fields which we will mention as we go along.

Physical Anthropology is the study of people from a biological perspective. In its work, it draws liberally from the biological and physical sciences. A. One of its broad interests is in evolution and human origins. The study of fossils is paleontology. More specific to our interests here is the study of the fossils of modern humans and human ancestors, namely paleoanthropology. While we are at it, let us mention two other terms so that we can agree on their meaning now. Hominids, a term we will use frequently, refer to modern humans (Homo sapiens), the Neandertals, Homo erectus, and the many Australopithecines/Paranathropus. They are our most direct ancestors. 'Lucy' is the most famous of the Australopithecines. Hominoid is a more inclusive term for all the hominids and their closest primate relatives, the apes (gorilla, chimpanzee, orangutan, and gibbon).

A second area of interest to physical anthropologists is human variation. This is an examination of how and why physical traits vary around the world.

Measuring human physical characteristics-anthropometry-was the main research activity of the first anthropologists early in the 1800s. A major focus for the early anthropometrists was the skull. Cranial capacity, jaw structure, the angle of the brow, and other criteria were analyzed in great detail. Although the focus and application of physical anthropology have changed from its early days, anthropometry remains a useful research tool for paleontologists engaged in the search for the origins of the humans species. Variations in skeletal shape and bone structure are vital clues to our prehistoric roots. Some obvious traits are skin color, body size, and eye color. Less obvious, but more easy to quantify are biochemical traits such as blood type and genetic differences. Late in this course we will look at human adaptability to extremes of heat, cold, and altitude.

Primatology is a third broad area of study. Jane Goodall has achieved world fame for her study of the chimpanzee at Gombe in Africa. The late Diane Fossey (Gorillas in the Mist) studied the mountain gorilla. Least well known, and still active, is Birute Galdaikas who works to rehabilitate captured orangutan in Borneo.

Primates are studied for their implications in evolution and the insights they provide into human behavior. They are our closest relatives and as such have had a crucial role in medical research. Nearly a million rhesus monkeys were used in the research for the polio vaccine. Today, many primate species are endangered and such a study would be impossible

Research on primate social behavior in the 1960s by the Harlows has important implications for human psychological development. Infant rhesus monkeys raised without maternal warmth and comfort revealed a wide range of abnormal behaviors: they would sit and stare, were inadequate parents, and were often aggressive. Maternal care is important for proper emotional development in monkeys as it is in humans.

Studies of primates have also given insight into the incest taboo, a world wide cultural universal amongst human societies that restricts mating with close relatives. Observation of anthropoids reveals that many primates have an inhibition against mating with close kin. Thus our feelings about incest that we relate to law, religion, genetics and psychology may be a part of a more universal embedded inhibition shared with other primates.

Forensic anthropology is a specialized area of physical anthropology. It is the identification of human remains for legal purposes. Teeth are especially important for several reasons. They tend to be the most enduring body part, as in a burial or a plane crash. Teeth contain many details, especially when they have been restored. This brings up another reason for the importance of teeth: dental records are extremely common. Here in Illinois, they must be retained for at least ten years after the patient's last dental visit. Sorry, forensic dentistry is not a part of this course.

Dental anthropology is a major focus in this course. Very briefly it is the study of teeth as recorded in casts of living mouths or as seen in the skulls of archaeological and fossil collections. A subsequent section will formally introduce this subject to you. This completes our discussion of physical anthropology. The next three sub fields of anthropology are considered to be cultural anthropology. Even for the physical anthropologist, a knowledge of cultural anthropology is considered important.

Culture is believed to date back at least to the origin of the earliest stone tools, some 2.5 million years ago. As hominids appear closer to us in time, the evidence for culture increases. This is evident as stone tools become more complex, fire is harnessed, and as hominids spread out of Africa into more challenging environments. With the arrival of modern humans about 40,000 years ago, the pace of cultural evolution overtook that of biological evolution. With domestication, metallurgy, and population growth, the rate of culture change has steadily increased at an exponential rate. The pace of cultural change today is now driven by technology. The Internet, personal computers, and compact discs were undreamed of just a couple decades ago. Your challenge when you leave school will be to continue to adapt new ideas, methods, and know-how into your life.

Some anthropologists think that we live in a modern, changing world equipped with Stone Age bodies. These ideas have spawned new disciplines such as evolutionary psychology, evolutionary medicine, and medical anthropology--which we will mention late in this article.

Archaeology is the study of human cultures and behavior through material remains--called by some material culture. Some authors call archaeology the science of rubbish! The archaeologist is interested in how people live their daily lives, how people understand the world around them, how they adapt to the surrounding environment, and how and why cultures change. Answers do not 'leap out' from the artifacts: developing a theory or picture from the physical evidence is a painstaking process.

We usually associate archaeology with prehistory--before written history, but some of archaeology's most spectacular finds involve writing. One is the famous Rosetta stone, found in 1799 by Napoleon's troops in Egypt. Written in hieroglyphic, demotic and Greek, it made possible translation of ancient hieroglyphic text. Another 'find' from 1947 is the Dead Sea Scrolls, many of which are now on display at the Shrine of the Book museum in Israel. Written nineteen hundred years ago, they contain much of the earliest text of books in the Hebrew Bible. Other texts give crucial insight into religious life in 100 AD.

Archaeology is no stranger to unusual personalities. 'Indiana Jones' of the movie Raiders of the Lost Ark has a real life counterpart in Vendyl Jones, a self-trained adventurer in search of the Ark of the Covenant. Sir William Flinders Petrie discovered that pottery types could be dated according to the layers in tells (mounds) where they are found. He also was the first European to measure the pyramids. An old man with a full white beard and blazing blue eyes, he did his work wearing a ballerina's frilly tutu, thus sparing himself from stoning by local religious fanatics.

Technology has been incorporated successfully into many aspects of modern archaeology. Landsat satellite images have located ancient Indian roadways in the American southwest. Radiocarbon C14 and other absolute dating techniques have made date in time much more precise than was possible a few years ago. Use of this technique revealed the famed Shroud of Turin to be a medieval fraud. (My note: the Shroud of Turin again made a world news comeback in April 1998; it is now on public display.)

The 'Iceman' mummy found in the Italian Alps a few years ago was dated at 5,000 years using C14 absolute dating. After years of political and scientific wrangling, it is now on display in northern Italy.

Some archaeologists literally study garbage. The most famous of this genre of study is the well-known Arizona Garbage Project. What we discard tells much about our lives. As an aside, the researchers found that hot dogs after thirty years in a dump were still edible. Does that say something about what is in hot dogs?

One final cautionary note: archaeologists primarily study material culture, not fossils. That is the province of the paleontologist. While we have mentioned writing and historic events here, do remember that archaeology is the one scholarly area that systematically focuses on prehistoric cultures.

Linguistics is the discipline that studies speech and language. Linguistic anthropology studies contemporary human languages as well as ones from the past. What relevance does it have for us here?

Anthropologists regard language as 'conservative'. It is retained by people when they move. They may move to new areas, adopt new foods, take to guns and horses, but their language stays with them. Vocabularies are the clues, much as words in the English language today contains many cognates from Latin, German, and French. Linguistics is useful worldwide, but it has been especially valuable in tracing the migrations of prehistoric Native American Indians. Navaho and Apache Indians are considered to be Athabascan--Indians who migrated to the south from Western Canada and who retained their linguistic origins as a New World immigrant group more recent than the 'first Americans' who came across from Siberia 12,000 years ago.

Ethnology concentrates on the cultures of the present. It is the study of human behavior as it can be seen, experienced, and discussed with those who live in a particular culture.

Ethnology is the study of many cultures from a comparative perspective. Earlier we briefly remarked about the incest taboo. The observation that it is a cultural universal is based on a cross-cultural perspective--the study of all known cultures.

The intensive study of a single culture is called an ethnography.

Napoleon Chagnon's study of the Venezuelan Yanomamo mentioned earlier is a classic in contemporary ethnographic study. It was not an easy task. He lived for five years amongst the Yanomamo as a participant observer.

The study of culture in its indigenous setting is difficult and challenging. Contemporary anthropology asks us to be culturally relativistic. This means to look at each culture in its own right and to step beyond your own personal bias, which we call ethnocentrism.

People in many cultures consider it appropriate to have more than one wife (or husband) at the same time. Many prefer to marry a first cousin--illegal here in Illinois. Some people eat dogs and cats: when tourists get off the plane in Hong Kong, the Cantonese guide will tease by telling them that they will 'soon have a new meaning to the term hot dog!' Do you get it?

Within cultures there are many subcultures. For example, within mainstream American culture, the Old Order Amish in

Pennsylvania is a subculture. They intrigue us because they eschew telephones and automobiles, yet seem to embody the best of what we admire: close family ties, integrity, and hard work. Did you see the Harrison Ford film, Witness?

There are subcultures in dentistry and especially in dental schools. When I teach freshmen dental students, I find them earnest and innocent. They respond strongly to messages of life success and learn very well off of prepared handouts. They are strongly focused on what they are to learn and have a defined goal: a degree and a state license to practice.

College students, in contrast, are more eclectic and much more liberal in outlook. Rote learning doesn't work, but discussion does. Students in an orthodontic program exhibit distinctively sub cultural traits. Can you discern them in this class?

This course will be primarily physical anthropology, but will make frequent references to the three cultural disciplines that we have described: archaeology, linguistics and ethnography. The subfields of anthropology are not mutually exclusive: in practice, they tend to overlap a good deal. That overlap or sharing is best illustrated by a new, emerging field, that of medical anthropology.

It can best be described as the study of the interaction between culture, health, and disease In anthropology, we call this biocultural evolution. As we conclude this unit, consider this vignette about an Italian-American community living in Roseto, Pennsylvania. Thirty years ago, medical researchers went there to study a contradiction in medical logic: Rosetans seemed virtually immune to heart attack. The men smoked and drank wine freely after days working in slate quarries. Evening meals were laden with large quantities of Italian food rich in fat: they fried their sausages and browned their meatballs in lard. Yet, their hefty bodies contained very healthy hearts.

The reason was cultural. It was a close-knit community that showed that people are nourished by other people. Recently, that closeness has faded and heart attacks occur as they do elsewhere. Similar effects have been verified in Israel and Borneo. Biology and culture interact; therefore, much of human adaptive change is a product of biocultural evolution.

LIFE ON EARTH

The Concept of 'Deep Time'

The unifying theme of this course is evolution. An immense amount of time was necessary for the evolution of life on earth. Historically, the great age of the earth was only slowly appreciated. When geology became a systematic science, the incredible age of the earth was fully revealed. With that understanding, evolution became not just a possibility, but a necessity in order for life on earth to adapt to a restless and changing planet.

Understanding the great span of time for life on earth will illustrate the possibilities and requirements for evolutionary diversity.

Let us first compare the age of the earth to the twenty-four-hour day. We will assume the age of the universe is about 15 billion years.

Consider the following: if we imagine the time since the origin of the universe as a calender year, the imprint of life on earth would begin on September 25th. Dinosaurs would emerge on December 24th. Humans, latecomers upon the scene would at last arrive on the final day, December 31st.

We present here linear time in three dioramas.

The first diorama covers 4.5 billion years, the approximate age of the earth itself.

The second diorama covers 4.5 million years of hominid evolution. It is a story of bipedalism and brains.

Finally, the last diorama covers 45,000 years to include the last of the great 'Ice Ages' of the Pleistocene, the modern peoples of the Upper Paleolithic, the last of the Neandertals, and finally, the events of the Holocene.

Earth History Diorama

The earth formed about 4.5 billion years ago. How did life begin? According to the 'soupy mix theory' suggested by Urey and Miller, the first building amino acids emerged for the early atmosphere of ammonia, methane, nitrogen, steam, and lightening. Others think that life arose from heat-loving archaeobacteria or perhaps from outer space by way of meteorites. The Murcheson Meteorite of Australia is cited for this theory.

Cyanobacteria appear and begin to produce oxygen. For nearly two billion years, bacteria rule the earth. The earliest organisms reproduce by cloning; change is possible only by mutation. Stromatolytes document the earliest imprint of life on earth some 3.6 billion years ago. Photosynthesis makes sunlight a source of energy.

Organisms with functionally differentiated internal parts including mitochondria, sexual reproduction, the exchange and recombination of DNA lead to runaway complexity. Multicellular organisms and the sexual exchange of genetic information open new possibilities. True runaway evolution begins.

With the beginning of the Cambrian, a riot of body diversity appears. The body plans of today's major phyla had their beginnings in the Cambrian explosion.

As life flourishes in the sea and invades the land, great waves of successful species flourish and fade away. Extinctions and environmental change drive along evolution. Five major extinctions are known; they are at once loss and opportunity. A progression of vertebrate life flourish: the fishes, amphibians, reptiles, birds and mammals. Primates and ultimately we emerge after the fifth extinction 65 million years ago.

Hominid Diorama

This diorama begins late in the Cenozoic era in the Pliocene epoch. It is a time of larger mammals, climactic cooling and mountain building. Hominid origins begin in the Pliocene.

Hominid origins are known only from Africa. The first group of 'gracile' Australopithecines include anamesis, afarensis, and africanus.

The second group is the 'robust' hominids identified as Paranthropus from both east and south Africa. Some persist into the Pleistocene, living contemporaneously with early Homo. Their name comes from their powerful chewing capability and the massive size of their cheek teeth. The 'robust' hominids appeared to have been side branches.

In the third group is Homo habilis, 'handy man' is the first of the hominids associated with stone tools of the Oldowan type. They have an increased brain capacity compared to the chimp-like brains of the Australopithecines and Paranthropus.

Hominids in the first three groups are known only from Africa. But, Homo erectus of group four is taller, bigger brained, and now literally 'walks out of Africa' to colonize new territories in Europe, West Asia, and East Asia. Homo erectus is now known as heidelbergensis in Europe and ergaster in Europe (but retains the name erectus in east Asia). These are the first users of fire and their distinctive Acheulian tool kit.

Group five are the Neandertals. They possessed a more diverse tool kit known as Mousterian. Their brain size overlaps ours; in Europe, they became a distinctive adaptation to the cold of the late Pleistocene. They are contemporaneous with modern humans; the nature of their disappearance is a major debate in anthropology.

Modern humans comprise group six. They appear suddenly in Europe with a rich artistic tradition, and an inventive and diverse material culture. With modern humans, cultural evolution overtakes biological evolution. The origin of modern humans, like all of the hominids appear to be in Africa.

Modern Human Diorama

This diorama begins in the late Pleistocene during the last great glaciating. In Europe, the Neanderthal present with robust skeletons, a high frequency of skeletal injuries, intentional burials occasionally with grave goods, worn anterior teeth, and all having strong brow ridges.

Modern humans burst upon the scene with blade tools, painting, sculpture, elaborate burials, a broadened subsistence base and abstract engravings. The first cave/rock art is known from Australia, where also the tradition survives today. As the Ice Ages come to a close, humans enter the New World.

At 11,000 ya, the climate changes and the megaphone die out. Human subsistence changes to a more broad-based diet in anticipation of revolutionary changes in human life.

People begin to herd their animal prey instead of hunting them. Farming with domesticated plants increases the harvest. The environment is intentionally altered. Culture is transformed.

Metallurgy begins; this initiates new technology and social stratification with enormous changes in culture. Agricultural surplus leads to life in cities, with urbanization comes science, mathematics, a mercantile class, armies, money, and congested traffic.

Population increased exponentially as exploration, industrialization, and the information age finds us as we are today. Where to next?

HISTORY OF EVOLUTIONARY THOUGHT

How it all Began

The origin of evolutionary thought has had a long, well-documented history. Like human culture, it went through many stages, each one laying the groundwork for the next. And then, in the nineteenth century, like many roads coming together in a central intersection, the idea of evolution was the inevitable result. Here we will briefly trace those historical steps leading to the independent development of the theory of evolution by two naturalists, Alfred Wallace and Charles Darwin.

Four Intellectual Hurdles to the Theory of Evolution

There were four serious barriers to acceptance of the theory of evolution.

(1) *The age of the Earth.* There were, of course, the two creations accounts in the Bible. Variations of these accounts appear also in Babylonian mythology. Incidentally, most societies on earth have creation stories and many begin with 'In the beginning... ' The great depth of time you accept as fact was not conceived of even a few hundred years ago.

(2) *Possibilities of change.* For many reasons, species were considered fixed. After all, dogs give birth to dogs, not cats. Species were considered immutable. Yet, domesticated plants and animals were testimony to change. Pigeon fanciers could easily produce new varieties in a few generations through selective breeding.

(3) *Scripture as absolute truth.* Before the printing press, the Church controlled the Book. But after printing made books cheaper and more people were literate, religious authority diminished as learning became more secular.

(4) *Knowledge of the world was limited.* Exploration, discovery, development of the natural sciences all flourished as European expansion entered previously unknown regions of the earth. This provided a flood of new knowledge about the world. It was an exciting time.

The Origins of Evolutionary Thought

Darwin's theory of evolution wasn't just his idea. He didn't just roll out of bed one day and proclaim it. For Darwin, it came only after years of agonizing thought on his own observations and the thinking of others. We owe much of the theory's origins to clergymen.

(1) *Archbishop Ussher of Ireland.* If the Earth had a Grand Designer, when did He create it? Based on careful calculation of the generations in the Bible, Ussher determined that the year of creation was 4004 B.C. Subsequently this date was inserted into the authorized versions of the Bible, and before long it acquired the infallibility of Scripture itself.

Barely had Ussher made this announcement, a critic came forward. Ussher was off by a few hours! Another cleric of that time, James Lightfoot of Cambridge University came up with the exact day and time: the moment of creation was 9:00 A.M. on October 23rd. Sceptics may scoff at this time and date, but an IDEA was born: a way to date the age of the earth.

(2) *The Great Chain of Being.* The 'great chain' was a concept dating from Aristotle which placed life in an ascending order with man as the highest of the animals, just below the gods. It assumed that all the possibilities in nature already did exist. This viewpoint-inspired searches for the 'missing links'. An inventory of God's creation was necessary and collectors provided an abundance for natural scientists to examine. The flood of new discoveries caused

problems One was--how to classify living things. The other was--what about those things we call fossils. How did they fit in?

(3) *Classification and its implications.* The concept of species was first clearly defined by John Ray, an ordained minister at Cambridge University. But it was the Swedish naturalist Linnaeus who established binomial nomenclature which we use today. The system brought order out of the chaos by classifying animals by their most basic characteristics.

Linnaeus took another bold step: he classified humans amongst the animals. This defied conventional thought that humans, made in the image of God, should be separate and distinct from the animals. Over his lifetime, the Linnaeus classification grew in succeeding editions from 142 pages to twenty-three hundred pages.

The Chain of Being assumed that species were fixed at did not change. Now late in his life, Linnaeus had doubts about the fixity of species. His system of classification implied that closely related species had a common descent. Evolutionary change could explain relatedness in his classification system. You think this way in everyday life. When you meet two persons who are very similar, you assume that they are siblings-and have the same parents. The evolutionary implications of systematics (classification) has the same implications.

In France, intellectual thought was changing. The universe was increasingly viewed as one of change... another step toward evolutionary thinking.

But how could it occur? The prolific Frenchman Comte de Buffon, who wrote a 44-volume natural history, provided two important clues. One was that he calculated the age of the earth at 70,000 years based on the time that it took for the earth to cool. That increased the possible time for species to change. He also suggested a mechanism for evolution: Environment was the external agent of change just as people were the agents of change in domesticated animals. Buffon did not come to a good end: he was forced to recant his heretical ideas. In the French revolution, his remains were exhumed and scattered; has son was guillotined. And a bad day for us is being caught in expressway traffic?

(4) *Geology and the antiquity of the earth.* We owe the concept of 'deep time', the realization of the true antiquity of our planet to the geologists. The testimony of the rocks, the various layers of different kinds of sediments--river gravels, sands. Marine limestones--that they encountered, one layer beneath another indicated that these layers, or strata, had been laid down over long periods of time.

James Hutton, trained as a physician, became the father of geology. A Scotsman and a rigorous thinker, he demanded logical explanations for natural phenomena. He originated the modern theory that the forces operating to change the surface of the earth had been operating in the same manner and at the same rate over a very long period of time. He perceived a world with 'no vestige of a beginning, no prospect of an end.' Geologic forces were gradual with the forces at work long ago that we see today: ceaseless uplifting and wearing down of the earth. Now Ussher's 6000 years and Buffon's 70,000 years has been extended to a vastly longer time, another idea to facilitate the possibility of species change and evolution.

(5) *Uniformitarianism and catastrophism.* One way to explain anomalies in the landscape was by dramatic events--by catastrophe. Sea bed fossils in mountains, large rocks in open plains, and caves were explained by the Great Flood. This thinking meshed with the Bible's account of Noah. If you think these ideas are from the dustbin of history, modern day 'creationists' firmly believe that the Grand Canyon was fashioned in a few weeks.

Hutton proposed uniformitarianism as a natural way for geological events to take place. What we see now taking place on the earth has always taken place. The processes are slow and our lives are short. The earth is indeed older than we think. Given enough time, a remote possibility can become near certainty.

(6) *Environment, species change, and the origin of life.* Expanding beyond Buffon who said that environment was the 'agent of change', Jean Baptiste Lamarck postulated that as environment changed, animal activity changed. Through use and disuse, body parts became altered. Part of this we do accept today and we know it as adaptation. Don't weight lifters employ this principle? Use a muscle and its gets bigger. Lamarck was the first to stress the importance of interactions between organisms and their environment in evolution. Lamarck also coined the term biology.

Lamarck went a step farther. He said that such changes are heritable. This theory is known as 'inheritance of ACQUIRED characteristics.' A giraffe stretching its neck and passing that greater length to offspring is a Lamarckian example. It is not accepted today. As a hypothesis, the hypothesis that animal features acquired during life can be passed on to offspring is well constructed. It can be tested, verified or refuted.

Has it been tested? Weismann cut off the tails of mice for 22 generations and kept getting tails. Jewish boys have been circumcised for thousands of years, but their male offspring keep getting foreskins. People keep having haircuts and have children who still need haircuts. This evidence refutes the hypothesis.

Later, with developments in microscopy and embryology, the germ plasm theory was articulated. It says that germ cells which we know as ova and spermatocytes are a distinct and separate cell line from somatic cells. They separate early on in embryogenesis. Their genetic content is passed on whether or not body parts are mutilated, exercised, or removed.

Another problem of the time was the origin of life. As you read this, you are thinking of origins deep in time billions of years ago. That is a recent idea: until the middle of the last century, it was a common belief that smaller organisms could originate spontaneously from mud or organic matter. One famous experiment was growing little 'beasties' from dirty underwear. Reproduction of large animals had been understood for a long time, but it remained for Pasteur and Tyndale to demonstrate that life arises from life. Consider the implication that anything alive had to come from something alive. A way to explain diversity was to accept 'deep time' and the great antiquity for origins of life on earth.

(7) *The fossil problem.* Early naturalists had found fossil sea shells in strata in mountains far above the sea while identical shells were found alive in contemporary seashores. For a time, Noah's flood seemed a satisfactory explanation. Fossil bones of creatures unlike any living were a further problem. Were they jokes of nature? Was God playing tricks on us?

A wealth of fossil bones uncovered in Paris inspired Georges Cuvier to reassemble the bones with startling realism. Mammoths, giant reptiles, and other large creatures with only a vague resemblance to modern forms went on display. People loved it.

Furthermore, they appeared in layers, suggesting that some layers were sea beds, that others recorded a time of dry land with freshwater lakes whose sediment retained the bones of land animals. Where one ended, the other began. Cuvier showed that extinction was an important contribution because it opened the way for fossils to be used as historical markers in the geological record.

These dramatic new ideas about life on Earth, its origin and development were crucial in Darwin's theory of evolution. He would live in a time when the earth was seen as millions of years old that fossils were accepted as reality, and the close similarities between different species would be noticed by embryologists and comparative anatomists. It was also understood that characteristics would be passed on by inheritance.

Mendel, unknown to Darwin, would unlock the puzzle of inheritance. Unlike Darwin, however, Mendel would remain in obscurity until our century when he was rediscovered. The stage was set for Darwin to make a crucial step: a mechanism for evolution, which was natural selection. In another twist of fate, that idea would come from a clergyman-turned economist. We will treat that story separately.

Dental Anthropology

What is Dental Anthropology?

Dental Anthropology is the stūdy of teeth in a perspective beyond clinical science. That perspective includes the study of dental growth, theories on dental origin, primate dentition, and population variation. The first comprehensive review of research on primate dentition was a 108-page treatise by Krogman in 1927. That document comprised an entire issue of the Journal of Dental Research and was the first step toward recognition of dental anthropology as a sub field within the discipline.

While preparing to revise this article for 1998, a colleague asked me; "just what is dental anthropology? What do dental anthropologists do? Here is a brief answer to that question.

(1) Genetically controlled variables such as tooth crown size and morphology are used to trace phylogenetic relationships and historic trends in size, shape, and number of teeth.

(2) Crown wear and dental pathology give clues to dietary and cultural behavior.

(3) Gross and microscopic defect analyses reflect disease and dietary stress.

(4) Intentional cultural modifications of teeth (dental scarification) reflect society and culture of people, both present and past.

(5) Bite marks, distinctive patterns of occlusion and wear, missing and filled teeth, and radiographic landmarks make teeth pivotal in many cases of forensic identification.

(6) The comparative anatomy of teeth provides crucial evidence for systematics (classification) and determining biological relatedness.

(7) There is sexual dimorphism in crown diameters. In modern humans, there is a 10% difference in standing height, a 20% difference in weight, and a 30% difference in weight. In most living populations, lower canines show the greatest dimorphism, up to 7.3%, followed by the upper canines.

The best understanding of dental anthropology's perspective is gained by tracing its historical background. Many of the core ideas in the field were developed by people you should know.

The Emergence of Descriptive Dental Science

The foundations of dental science in general can be traced to the seventeenth and eighteenth centuries when Pierre Fauchard and John Hunter made basic observations on the number of human teeth. This was an issue hotly debated at the time. Why such a seemingly silly debate? Aristotle had said that females supposedly had a greater number of teeth than males.

Also, there were studies of components of teeth, tooth eruption, terminology, and descriptive anatomy. In the nineteenth century development of microscopy and cell theory brought study of the micro structure of teeth. The names of some of these pioneers are known to every dental student: Retzius, Tomes, and Carabelli.

The rise of zoological systematics (Linnaeus in 1735) stimulated paleontologists and comparative anatomists to study teeth more closely. Until Darwin, evolution was not widely accepted and the notion those living humans came from 'lower life forms' was unknown. Tooth form and function in different species were seen as homology and analogy but without an evolutionary perspective.

From Darwin to Gregory: The Emergence of Evolutionary Theory

The emergence of evolutionary theory with its tenets of natural selection, common descent, importance of variation steered research into evolutionary studies of teeth. Comparative odontology (study of teeth) now examined tooth form among fossil and living vertebrates.

Workers paid more attention to variation in tooth size and morphology among sub fossil and living populations. By the turn of the century, articles appeared that dealt with racial variation in molar cusp number, supernumerary cusps, hypodontia, and hyperdontia.

Although most anthropological attention focused on tooth size and form, John Mummery studied caries (tooth decay) rates in prehistoric British populations. His landmark study was published in 1870. He reported that the increase in caries rates through time was attributable to an ever increasing reliance on softer, more highly processed foods. Late in the nineteenth century Henry Fairfield Osborn elaborated upon Edward Drinker Cope's ideas of mammalian teeth and proposed a 'theory of trituberculy' which sought to explain the evolution of multi cusped teeth in mammals from the simple conical teeth of reptiles. Osborn subsequently related the theory to the human dentition in 1907.

William King Gregory published his seminal work, The Origin and Evolution of the Human Dentition in 1922. This project represented the culmination of efforts in comparative odontology during that period. That work was first published as a series of articles in the Journal of Dental Research in 1921. His comparative studies of fossil hominoid and hominid dentitions were lasting contributions to the field.

In particular he noted certain dental morphology similarities, in particular the Dryopithecus (Y-5) pattern of the lower molars, indicated phylogenetic connections between the Miocene apes, living apes and humans.

He also characterized non-metric traits as low characters (primitive) or as high characters (modern). In this effort he anticipated contemporary methods of cladistics (the grouping of animals according to the derived traits they share). Primitive and derived traits are useful in disentangling evolutionary history.

Between the World Wars: 1920-1939

Ales Hrdlicka, known for many contributions to physical anthropology was a pioneer of dental anthropology. His now classic papers on shovel-shaped incisors described a characteristic of upper incisors that reminded him of a 'coal shovel.' Hrdlicka had access to the diverse collections of the National Museum of Natural History.

From his work with those specimens he reported the close similarity between Asians and American Indians and their decided difference from European and African populations in the frequency and degree of shoveling expression. Asians and American Indians had the shoveling trait; North American whites and blacks did not. This dental character was one of the earliest identified that clearly demonstrated the Asian origins of native Amerindians.

Hrdlicka also used tooth size of the first and second molars to assess the relationships of fossil and living apes, fossil hominids, and recent humans. As curator of physical anthropology at the National Museum of Natural History, Hrdlicka's strength was in his comparative studies of primate and human dentitions. (My note: Hrdlicka was quite an accomplished person. Trained as a physician, he became interested in anthropometry and rose to prominence in anthropology. He founded the Journal of Physical Anthropology in 1918.)

Thomas Draper Campbell published his Dentition and Palate of the Australian Aboriginal as a monograph based on his PhD thesis. It covered a wide array of dental topics, including observations of upper and lower molar cusp number, upper premolar and molar root number, and the Carabelli trait. He noted that shovel-shaped incisors were NOT a trait seen in Australian aborigines. Campbell, an Australian influenced another figure well known in orthodontics, P. R. Begg, noted for his studies of proximal wear and mesial migration of posterior teeth in the Australian Aborigine.

Wilton Marion Krogman (1927) published the first comprehensive review of research on primate dentition. It was obvious to Krogman that dental anthropology included the study of dental growth, theories on dental origin, primate dentition and population variation.

J.C.M. Shaw (1931), inspired by Campbell made observations of South African Bantu dental features. This work and that of Campbell were pioneer studies that provided a baseline for future comparative work in human dental anthropology, some of which we will cite shortly.

Articles in dental anthropology were scarce in the period from 1918 to 1940. The American Journal of Physical Anthropology published only about one article a year on teeth. (My note: by the mid-1990s, the AJPA was publishing an average of twenty papers a year on teeth.) A few other dental publications are worth noting here.

An important article during this period was by Rufus W. Leigh, an instructor at the Army Dental School. He demonstrated how societies which practiced different subsistence strategies varied in terms of crown wear, alveolar abscesses, and periodontal disease. A basic lesson of this paper published in 1925, was that adoption of an agricultural economy carries with it a major cost in terms of dental health.

These observations confirm and extend the findings of John Mummery mentioned earlier in this article. Similar observations have emerged from studies at the Dickson Indian Mounds in Illinois, where a transition from a food foraging life way to one based on maize (corn) resulted in increased dental caries and crowding of the lower anterior teeth. Weston Price, to be mentioned shortly, made similar observations across the globe.

In 1933 at the University of Chicago, Huggins and Dahlberg transplanted developing dog tooth germs to the abdominal wall and achieved new understanding of the interaction of developing tissues. The following year, Glasstone in England independently had success with transplants in tissue culture. Their work preceded Kolar and Baird's seminal work in epithelial-mesenchymal interactions developing dental tissues by thirty-five years.

Milo Hellman, a figure well-know in academic orthodontics for his application of anthropometry to craniofacial growth and development, published his classic paper on lower molar crown trait variation in 1928.

Weston Price, a dentist, traveled world wide to contrast the traditional diets and health of primitive tribes with those of contemporary peoples living on 'civilized' diets. He documented the contribution of modern diet to dental caries and malocclusion. His text Nutrition and Physical Degeneration published in 1939. It confirms and extends the work of Leigh. His extensive work is largely ignored today, dismissed as just anecdotal reporting. This is unfortunate. (My note: I've been in dentistry since beginning dental school in 1960. The only person I've ever met who was acquainted with Price was a naturopath whom I met in a Peruvian rainforest in 1995!) The disuse theory, implicit in Price's writings is skillfully developed in recent years by Corrucinni who has applied it to the study of malocclusion. Corrucinni reports numerous studies of diet in humans and laboratory animals. His work also hasn't received the attention that it deserves.

At the close of this period, the concept of morphogenetic fields was proposed by Butler in 1939. Known also as the field theory, it sought to explain heterodonty (regional specialization of teeth). In humans, the differences between the classes of teeth are sharp and distinct. In many species of animals, however, the class boundaries are not distinct. Incisiform canines, caniniform premolars and so on are seen as transitional forms at class borders.

Transition to the Modern Period: 1939-1963

Albert Dahlberg of the University of Chicago over a 35-year period in-depth study of Pima Indians in the American Southwest provided valuable comparative data for this group. In 1963 he released a series of dental plaques designed to serve as three-dimensional standards for making morphological observations of human teeth. Workers around the world now had a useful reference; others have since appeared.

Early on, Dahlberg applied Butler's field concept to the human dentition.

P. O. Pederson (1949) published his monograph The East Greenland Eskimo Dentition which soon became a primary reference for comparative data since its publication. C. F. A. Moorrees's The Aleut Dentition (1957) remains a classic today for studies of this genre. These followed in the tradition of Hrdlicka who also did work with Eskimo teeth earlier in this century.

The Modern Period, 1963 to Today

In 1963, the study of human dental variation received its most significant boost with the publication of Dental Anthropology, edited by D.R. Brothwell. It served to define the subject, including such topics as third molar agenesis, incisor shoveling variation, odontometrics, crown wear, and root morphology. Now, dental anthropology was 'on the map' as a distinct sub field of physical anthropology.

The first international symposium on dental morphology was held in Denmark in 1965, largely through the efforts of Dahlberg, Pederson, and Alexandersen. Similar symposia have since been held every three years. Proceedings of these symposia, published as edited volumes, include many valuable papers on human dental morphology. There is now an increasing interaction between dental anthropologists, oral biologists, paleontologists, and dentistry. This is especially well illustrated by the work of Kollar and Baird (1971) who demonstrated the crucial epithelial-mesenchymal interactions in chicken and mice embryos. This work confirmed and extended earlier experimental work in amphibians and reptiles that dates back to early in this century. Their work is now orthodox science appearing in dental textbooks and in dental anthropology literature.

The 'three-wave' model of Native American origins developed by Christy Turner II on the basis of tooth crown and root morphology has introduced the historical potential of teeth to linguists, archaeologists, and geneticists.

In 1986, the Dental Anthropology Association (DAA) was formally recognized by the American Association of Physical Anthropology. The DAA publishes the Dental Anthropology Newsletter on a regular basis.

Information on dental anthropology associations and literature in the field are easily accessible under that title on the Internet.

WHAT IS SCIENCE?

Science and Knowledge

Scientific knowledge may be thought of as a refinement and extension of common sense, perception, and practical knowledge. Science has a systematic character and rigorous standards of methods and results. It seeks to comprehend the laws of nature, confirmed by experimental evidence. The aim of science is material truth of the most general character.

The challenge is this: to come up with a testable hypothesis and then to verify it or disprove it. If I say to you 'cranial bone growth occurs at the sutures between cranial bones,' you can devise experiments to verify or refute this hypothesis with relative ease. Let us say instead that 'nasal cavity expansion is a necessary and obligatory response to its functional matrix.' Because of its wording, verification or refutation of this statement, is difficult.

Consider this outrageous hypothesis: 'Gravity is caused by a great big ugly green giant sucking air into the middle of the earth thereby pulling things down.' It is a reasonably good hypothesis.

Upon reading it, you can conjure up several ways to refute it. Here is a hypothesis that is less scientific in its design: 'The Almighty in his infinite wisdom made fossils during the Great Flood to confuse us.' You may agree with it on faith, but is it testable? Taken on its face, it isn't a scientific statement subject to verification or refutation. It may be profound religious truth for some people, but as it is stated, it is not a scientific hypothesis.

As we look at the development of evolutionary thought, pay attention to the reasoning involved as the idea came into being. The 'theory of evolution' is a refined, elegant theory that ties together existing evidence and suggests lots of ways to verify it--or refute it. As theories go, it is about as elegant as they can be in science.

What is a Good Hypothesis?

The word itself comes from Greek (hypo = under; tithenai = to place) which illustrates what a scientific hypothesis does: it provides an explanation which will have certain consequences subject to experimentation. What are some qualities of a well stated hypothesis?

(1) It should be testable.

(2) It should be the simplest explanation to explain, bring into order, and summarize a body of facts. This is the 'law of parsimony.' Later in this article we will meet 'Occam's Razor,' which equates simplicity with truth.

(3) It should be consistent with related principles and verified facts.

(4) It should have predictive power. The best hypothesis should predict discovery.

How is Knowledge Acquired?

Before the Enlightenment, the Church was the authority. It taught that the Earth was the center of the universe. One particular invention, the telescope, was a fateful turning point for science. The Polish astronomer Copernicus (1473-1543) came to a different conclusion by using observational evidence to show that the Earth orbited the Sun. In 1632, the Italian Galileo dared to agree with him. For that heresy, he was hauled up before the Inquisition and as placed under house arrest. Scientific discovery in Italy ceased for 100 years.

Earlier, the English philosopher Francis Bacon (1561-1626) argued for the use of experiment rather than deduction as a way to increase knowledge. It was an idea which changed the world. The use of observational evidence was taken up by Newton (1642-1727) and he made great advances in physics. Pay attention to the word deduction: it will become important shortly.

Deduction, Induction, and Science

This section is theoretical, but I have a practical goal in mind, so be patient.

Deduction is correct reasoning from a premise to a conclusion. If I say, all mammals are warm-blooded; you are a mammal. Therefore, you are warm-blooded. You would logically accept your warm-bloodedness. You have moved from the general to the particular. If the premise is true and the inference drawn properly, that inference is true.

Induction works the other way around. It moves from the particular to the general. It is both science's achievement and its Achilles heel. Let us use a classic from college logic to illustrate the thorny problem in science or moving from particulars to universals.

The expression "all swans are white" is true only if there aren't any black ones. The statement is true if you live in Britain and you only see white swans; however, the discovery of black swans in New Zealand at a later date would prove it false.

The philosopher Karl Popper has this cautionary note about sweeping general statements: induction cannot yield certainty until we can observe the universe in all times and all places.

Popper argues that science can approach truth, but we can never be sure of having the final explanation.

What practical suggestion does Karl Popper have for the scientist? The serious scientist should seek to falcify his hypotheses, not merely verify them. Science progresses when an accepted theory is shown to be wrong and a new theory is found that better explains the phenomenon.

Newton's laws of motion work at low velocities, but under extreme conditions those laws fail. Einstein's special theory of relativity reached into the larger universe to show relationships between time, matter, and space.

The American philosopher Thomas Kuhn has argued that scientific progress comes when anomalies refute an established paradigm and new ideas achieve acceptance.

Sense and Nonsense in Science

Originating a new hypothesis is a creative process. Innovation is the product of independent thinking. Sometimes there can be several hypotheses to explain something. In anthropology, some of them can be rather silly.

Archaeology in particular seems to attract the odd, the bizarre, and the occult. How can we discern between sense and nonsense?

One of the oldest and most practical rules is known variously as the Law of Parsimony or, as mentioned in the movie Contact, Occam's Razor. It says the following: the simplest of several proposed hypotheses is usually the best.

Let us cite an example. In southern Peru is a stark desert plateau of brown pebbles devoid of plant or animal life known as the Nazca Pampa. Large radial line patterns and designs of plants and animals were discovered by an aircraft survey in 1926. They have puzzled scientists and inspired science fiction writing ever since. What are some explanations to explain them?

(1) They are beacons for the gods.

(2) Space craft from another galaxy landed here, aliens mated with monkeys, and people today is their offspring.

(3) They were made to be seen from ancient paper hot air balloons.

(4) Ancient people made them by scuffing the surface of the ground with their feet.

Now, I concede that the first three sell books and might be a plot for a late-night movie. But consider, the last is the simplest and closest to ordinary life. Has the proposition (4) been tested? As it works out, yes. Large designs are easily made by scuffing aside the pebbles with one's foot to reveal the lighter soil underneath. In the arid environment, the designs seem able to last centuries.

One other comment: remember reductio ad absurdum from college logic? This ancient technique in debate refutes a proposition by demonstrating the absurd conclusions to which it would logically lead. This can also be used to repudiate fantasy and the fantastic.

Sample Size

The problem of sampling is central in the attempt to make valid inferences when moving from the particular to the general. Sampling is an especially vexing problem for the paleoanthropologist studying human fossils: there simply are not many of them and we have no ideas whatsoever if they are representative of the larger populations from whence they have come.

The ideal conditions for a representative sample of a population are that the materials in a sample fairly reflect the homogeneity of the entire population. Polls used to predict election results work out so well because their chosen sample reflects the views of the larger whole.

Paleoanthropologists aren't so lucky! Early hominid fossils are few, how the 'sample' was selected by the fortuitous events of fossilization and discoveries are not under anyone's control.

Problems Unique to the Problem of Human Origins

Human evolution is our evolution and everyone has an opinion about it. It is an emotionally charged issue for many people. The scientific community devoted to human origins has been plagued by jealousies (often called bone wars), outright fraud (Piltdown is a shameful example), and a lack of fossils. Other intellectual fields have their stormy debates also; the Dead Sea Scrolls are a good example.

Milford Wolpoff cites four factors that contribute to contentious debate in paleoanthropology.

(1) Public interest has put human origins in the spotlight. New finds often get reported before properly analyzed, dated, and subjected to peer review.

(2) Human evolution is about us and everyone has an idea about it. (My note: I am subjected to nutty ideas about human origins all the time!).

(3) We've already mentioned the third problem: a lack of data. There are a limited number of fossils, and access to them is sometimes restricted.

(4) Human frailty causes us sometimes to see things not as they are, but the way we are. Sometimes we are blind to the obvious.

In concluding this article, consider this thought about anthropology: the debate represents intellectual vigor, and as long as it is free and open, the discipline will continue to advance toward the truth.

RELIGION, SCIENCE, AND EVOLUTION

Science and Religion

Science and religious faith have no quarrel. Each discipline shares much in common. Both seek to understand the universe and our place in the universe. The conflict between the 'creationists' and advocates of evolutionary theory dates from the publication of Darwin's Origin of Species in 1859. That conflict flourishes today as 'creationists' seek to discredit science itself and prevent the teaching of evolution in public schools. The 'creationists' are a threat to our schools.

The most infamous event in that conflict was the famous 'monkey' trial of 1925 when a high-school teacher, John T. Scopes went on trial in Tennessee charged with violating state law by teaching the theory of evolution. He was convicted and fined $100. That state law was repealed in 1967.

'Creationism' is the term used in this article for the anti evolution backlash. That movement is known today also as 'creation science' or by other terms which intentionally obscure its real mission in opposing science.

What is Evolution?

In its loosest sense, it describes any change in anything. If a newspaper article appears entitled 'evolution of the automobile,' the reader would expect a historical account of automobiles, probably from Model T's to SUVs.

Here is a more specific definition applicable to biological evolution: 'the origin and development of life forms through time, of all species originating from pre-existing species. It is an ongoing process being the result of change produced by natural selection and genetic change.' Implicit in this is that humans are animals and are themselves a product of biological evolution. Accumulating evidence reveals that humans have an evolutionary origin that is extremely ancient, from life forms very unlike humans today.

The Nature of Science and the Scientific Attitude

Science requires a testable hypothesis that explains existing observations and predicts ways of gathering new observations to support or reject the hypothesis. One of the most important requirements of scientific method is that no hypothesis is ever beyond the reach of additional testing and the possibility of falsification.

In its most rigorous sense, the only scientific hypotheses are those that can be verified or falsified. This fundamental requirement separates science and religion. The critical thinker must determine what is, and what is not, a scientific statement. In one of the finest opening lines anywhere in religious literature, the Bible begins with: "In the beginning, God created heaven and earth." For many people, it is religious truth. The important distinction here is that "In the beginning... " isn't a scientific statement. The authors had other purposes which will be documented later in this article. In an egregious slight of hand, the 'creationists' have taken the opening lines of Genesis out of context.

A scientific statement by definition must be stated so that it can be verified or falcified. When a hypothesis has been broadly accepted by those most qualified to examine it, the idea is called a theory. Evolution enjoys such broad acceptance that it is called a theory.

The Scientific Frame of Mind

Science requires a distinctive intellectual attitude which has been well summarized by Karl Pearson: 'The classification of facts, the recognition of their sequence and relative significance is the function of science, and the habit of forming a judgement upon these facts, unbiased by personal feeling, is characteristic of what may be termed the scientific frame of mind.'

Do Biologists Believe in Evolution?

No. Is the theory of evolution central in their thinking? Yes. Is evolution a theory? Yes. It is supported by evidence and the theory suggests a vast number of ways to verify--or falcify it. Evolutionary theory makes much of the universe intelligible. The theory helps to explain a wide range of biological phenomena ranging from antibiotic resistance, the diversity of HIV viruses, to the origins of very different life forms--from bacteria to baboons.

For biologists, the evidence for evolution is so overwhelming, the theory of evolution is a certainty.

What Does the Bible Say, and How Does it Say It?

The eloquence of the Biblical authors in their opening statement strike the keynote of the whole Bible: "In the beginning God... " With that, the priestly authors dramatically unroll the process of Creation: of light, of heaven, of life upon the earth, the sun, moon and stars, and man himself. It is a masterpiece of religious literature.

However, something that strikes the thoughtful Bible reader right off is that there are two accounts (Genesis 1:1-2:3 and 2:4-26). In a formal theology these dual accounts (there are many in the Bible) are known as doublets. Why are they there?

In a formal theology, their presence is explained by the widely accepted documentary hypothesis. Early editors of the Bible drew upon several sources. Scholars today have identified them by the initials "J', "P," E" and more recently "D" (for the Deuteronomist). "P" describes priestly sources; "J" for the divinity Jehovah and "E" for the divinity Elohim.

Are the two accounts the same, or are they different? In some ways they duplicate each other, but in other significant ways there are contradictions.

The order or creation Genesis One is:

1. plants

2. animals
3. man and woman

The order of creation in Genesis Two is:

1. man
2. plants
3. animals
4. woman

What else is different in the accounts? Account one uses only the deity title God. Account two uses only the deity title Yahweh. (My note: you find doublets also in accounts of Noah and the Flood and elsewhere. What is said here is an orthodox theology, not opinion.) How shall we read these variously and at times conflicting accounts of Creation?

The 'Creationist' Dogma

'Creationists' rest their entire case on a strict, literal interpretation of the Biblical account of Creation (or Creations as we have seen) and the universal Flood (two accounts of Floods). The age of the earth is taken as 6,000 to 10,000 years based largely on Bishop Ussher's calculation in the year 1650. 'Creationists' say that women were cloned from man. Land plants came before fish. Birds came before reptiles. All animals were herbivores before the First Sin.

All of this contradicts the fossil record and mainstream science. Have the creationists read the Bible correctly? No, they have not. Taking Genesis 1:1-11:9 as a whole as the writers intended, the correct emphasis is: "In the Beginning, God... " Genesis was to be read as a whole, not in pieces taken out of context. This is explained fully in the next section.

The Position of Mainstream Religion

Mainstream religion made its accommodation with evolution decades ago. The most forthright position statement comes from the Roman Catholic Church.

In 1996, Pope John Paul II made headline news when he endorsed evolution. Italian tabloids screamed "Pope says we came from monkeys!" Is that what he said? No, it is not. Here is a direct quote from his written message to the Pontifical Academy of the Sciences. "It is indeed remarkable that this theory has progressively taken root in the minds of researchers following a series of discoveries made in different spheres of knowledge."

Earlier in 1981, Pope John Paul II, in an address to the same Pontifical Academy of Science, he said the following: "The Bible itself speaks to us of the origin of the universe and its make-up, not in order to provide us with a scientific treatise but in order to state the correct relationships of man with God and the Universe."

A later commentator has said the following: "... scripture... contains essential truths, which vastly transcend the literal text." Long ago, St. Augustine clearly rejected literalism in favor of the deeper spiritual truths in scripture. In fact, literal interpretation didn't even appear until after the industrial revolution!

Genesis 1:1 isn't a scientific statement because it isn't a testable hypothesis. It is there for spiritual meaning, not literal truth. The priestly writers never intended it as science.

'Creationists', Textbooks, and Equal Time

'Creationists' want to keep evolution out of textbooks and out of the teaching curriculum in sciences courses today. If evolution does appear, they want equal time--a chance to tell about 'creation science.' Should they have equal time?

Is 'creation science' science? To say it again, a plausible scientific statement must be subject to verification or falcification. They demand blind acceptance of a nonscientific story of creation taken out of context. 'Creationism' is not science. It is dogma with a hidden agenda. We discuss that issue shortly.

Should creationism have equal time for the sake of fairness? The problem is this: if science admits 'creationism' to the discussion, then it should--in fairness--accept other creation accounts as well. There were more than 500 North American Indian nations on this continent 500 years ago. Each had a creation story. Shouldn't they have a say? If this is done, the curriculum becomes comparative religion, not legitimate science.

'Creationism' fails on another basic requirement of science: peer review. In any rigorous discipline--including a theology--authors in journals must subject what they write to critical examination by their peers.. In this sense, 'creationism' is dogma, not science. If they are a science, shouldn't they meet this requirement? Science is what science does, and 'creationism' fails on all counts. This leads us to another issue--intellectual freedom.

Should the Teaching of Evolution be Suppressed?

In an open society, freedom of thought and expression are a given. When creationists seek to suppress or remove evolutionary science from our schools, it affects everyone's freedom. Most of all it impacts our children. Is it reasonable for religious pressure groups to suppress the rigorously reasoned, well established, widely accepted, easily verifiable scientific theory of evolution? In a free an open society, should they be allowed to suppress truth?

Is the case for biological evolution weakened if it is 'just a theory?' Being a theory is evolution's greatest strength. As such, it places itself beyond the dogma of misdirected 'creationist' zealots and is allowed to stand or fall based on the evidence. The strength of any idea must rest upon open discussion and critical thinking. We owe no less to ourselves and our children..

In contrast, 'creation science' is not science. It is religion in disguise. In 1981, Alabama passed a law requiring equal treatment of 'creation science' and evolution science. Out of this legislation arose a test case brought by the ACLU. Joining it as plaintiffs were several mainstream Christian and Jewish denominations.

The 'creation science' law was struck down and the plaintiffs were sustained on all counts. Most notable was the judge's ruling that 'creation science' was nothing more nor less than a particular religious doctrine. 'Creationists' lost their case against mainstream religion!

Why Can't they Reconcile their Differences?

One of the serious issues is the matter of limited time. How much time should scholars spend to oppose nonsense? Let us illustrate by example. Supposing you taught geology, but each year you had to argue with people who believe that the earth is flat. Each year they come to the school board, demand equal time only to recite the same foolishness over and over. There comes a time when enough is enough! People in science cannot waste productive careers dealing with 'creationist' nonsense.

A more insidious issue is unlawful behavior. Some anti evolution zealots now advocate vandalizing public libraries by removing references to evolution in books with the use of razor blades or glue. Such behavior is intolerable in a free society.

Concluding Remarks

In a final analysis the issue of teaching biological evolution gets down to intellectual freedom. If the 'creationists' prevail in keeping evolution out of the schools, the free exchange of ideas is diminished and ultimately the education of our children is impaired. 'Creationists' should be concerned about intellectual freedom. When freedom is restricted in a society, one of the first freedoms denied is religious choice.

2

History of Anthropology

This article mainly discusses 18th-and 19th-century precursors of modern anthropology. For more information on modern social and cultural anthropology as they have developed in Britain, France, and North America since approximately 1900, see the relevant sections under Anthropology.

OVERVIEW

The anthropologist Eric Wolf once characterized anthropology as "the most scientific of the humanities, and the most humanistic of the social sciences." Understanding how anthropology developed contributes to understanding how it fits into other academic disciplines.

Contemporary anthropologists claim a number of earlier thinkers as their forebears and the discipline itself has many sources. One view sees anthropology as an outgrowth of the Age of Enlightenment, when European thinkers began systematically examining human behaviour and institutions. In the 18th and 19th centuries, the fields of study that eventually gave rise most directly to modern anthropology attempted to deal with Europeans' (and their colonists') exanded awareness in three broad areas:1) a greater appreciation of their own past, new discoveries regarding Greek, Roman, Egyptian, and Near Eastern antiquities, and the social changes with the growth of cities and industry (Classics, Egyptology, folklore, etc.); 2) encounters with non-European peoples, whose customs, appearance, languages, religious beliefs, and social organization often differed strikingly from those of Europeans (ethnology, philology, etc.);

and 3) growing curiosity about the biological history of humanity, the historical relationships among existing populations, and the relatively new idea that human beings could be related to other primates (Natural history, Zoology, etc.),.

Scholarly traditions of jurisprudence, history, philology and sociology developed during this time and informed the development of the social sciences of which anthropology was a part. At the same time, the Romantic reaction to the Enlightenment produced thinkers such as Herder and later Wilhelm Dilthey whose work formed the basis for the culture concept which is central to the discipline.

These intellectual movements in part grappled with one of the greatest paradoxes of modernity: as the world is becoming smaller and more integrated, people's experience of the world is increasingly atomized and dispersed. As Karl Marx and Friedrich Engels observed in the 1840s:

All old-established national industries have been destroyed or are daily being destroyed. They are dislodged by new industries, whose introduction becomes a life and death question for all civilized nations, by industries that no longer work up indigenous raw material but raw material drawn from the remotest zones; industries whose products are consumed, not only at home, but in every quarter of the globe. In place of the old wants, satisfied by the production of the country, we find new wants, requiring for their satisfaction the products of distant lands and climes. In place of the old local and national seclusion and self-sufficiency, we have intercourse in every direction, universal interdependence of nations.

Ironically, this universal interdependence, rather than leading to greater human solidarity, has coincided with increasing racial, ethnic, religious, and class divisions, and new-and to some confusing or disturbing-cultural expressions. These are the conditions of life with which people today must contend, but they have their origins in processes that began in the 16th century and accelerated in the 19th century.

Institutionally anthropology emerged from natural history (expounded by authors such as Buffon). This was the study of human beings-typically people living in European colonies. Thus studying the language, culture, physiology, and artifacts of European colonies was more or less equivalent to studying the flora and fauna of those places. It was for this reason, for instance, that Lewis Henry Morgan could write monographs on both The League of the Iroquois and The American Beaver and His Works. This is also why the material culture of 'civilized' nations such as China have historically been displayed in fine arts museums alongside European art while artifacts from Africa or Native North American cultures were displayed in Natural History Museums with dinosaur bones and nature dioramas. This being said, curatorial practice has changed dramatically in recent years, and it would be wrong to see anthropology as merely an extension of colonial rule and European chauvinism, since its relationship to imperialism was and is complex.

ANTHROPOLOGY IN THE MUSLIM WORLD

Abu Rayhan al-Biruni (973-1048), a Muslim scholar who carried out extensive, personal investigations of the peoples, customs, and religions of the Indian subcontinent, has been described as "the first anthropologist." He wrote detailed comparative studies on the anthropology of religions and cultures in the Middle East, Mediterranean and South Asia. Biruni's anthropology of religion was only possible for a scholar deeply immersed in the lore of other nations. Al-Biruni and Ibn Khaldun have also been praised by several scholars for their anthropology of Islam.

Al-Biruni developed a sophisticated methodology for his anthropological studies. For example, he wrote the following in the opening passages of his Indica:

"No one will deny that in questions of historic authenticity hearsay does not equal eyewitness; for in the latter the eye of the observer apprehends the substance of that which is observed, both in the time when and in the place where it exists, whilst hearsay has its peculiar drawbacks."

He was also aware that there are limitations to eye-witness accounts: "The object of eye-witness can only be actual momentary existence, whilst hearsay comprehends alike the present, the past and the future"

19TH-CENTURY ANTECEDENTS: BRITAIN

Museums such as the British Museum weren't the only site of anthropological studies: with the New Imperialism period, starting in the 1870s, zoos became unattended "laboratories", especially the so-called "ethnological exhibitions" or "Negro villages". Thus, "savages" from the colonies were displayed, often nudes, in cages, in what has been called "human zoos". For example, in 1906, Congolese pygmy Ota Benga was put by anthropologist Madison Grant in a cage in the Bronx Zoo, labelled "the missing link" between an orangutan and the "white race"-Grant, a renowned eugenicist, was also the author of The Passing of the Great Race (1916). Such exhibitions were attempts to illustrate and prove in the same movement the validity of scientific racism, which first formulation may be found in Arthur de Gobineau's An Essay on the Inequality of Human Races (1853-55). In 1931, the Colonial Exhibition in Paris still displayed Kanaks from New Caledonia in the "indigenous village"; it received 24 million visitors in six months, thus demonstrating the popularity of such "human zoos".

Anthropology grew increasingly distinct from natural history and by the end of the nineteenth century the discipline began to crystallize into its modern form-by 1935, for example, it was possible for T.K. Penniman to write a history of the discipline entitled A Hundred Years of Anthropology. At the time, the field was dominated by 'the comparative method'. It was assumed that all societies passed through a single evolutionary process from the most primitive to most advanced. Non-European societies were thus seen as evolutionary 'living fossils' that could be studied in order to understand the European past. Scholars wrote histories of prehistoric migrations which were sometimes valuable but often also fanciful. It was during this time that Europeans first accurately traced Polynesian migrations across the Pacific Ocean for instance-although some of them believed it originated in Egypt. Finally, the concept of race was actively discussed as a way to classify-and rank-human beings based on inherent biological difference.

19TH-CENTURY ANTECEDENTS: UNITED STATES

Late eighteenth century ethnology established the scientific foundation for the field, which began to mature in the United

States during the presidency of Andrew Jackson (1829-1837). Jackson was responsible for implementing the Indian Removal Act, the coerced and forced removal of an estimated 100,000 American Indians during the 1830s to Indian Territory in present-day Oklahoma; for insuring that the franchise was extended to all white men, irrespective of financial means while denying virtually all black men the right to vote; and, for suppressing abolitionists' efforts to end slavery while vigorously defending that institution. Finally, he was responsible for appointing Chief Justice Roger B. Taney who would decide, in Scott v. Sandford (1857), that Negroes were "beings of an inferior order, and altogether unfit to associate with the white race... and so far inferior that they had no rights which the white man was bound to respect." As a result of this decision, black people, whether free or enslaved, could never become citizens of the United States.

It was in this context that the so-called American School of Anthropology thrived as the champion of polygenism or the doctrine of multiple origins-sparking a debate between those influenced by the Bible who believed in the unity of humanity and those who argued from a scientific standpoint for the plurality of origins and the antiquity of distinct types. Like the monogenists, these theories were not monolithic and often used words like races, species, hybrid, and mongrel interchangeably. A scientific consensus began to emerge during this period "that there exists a Genus Homo, embracing many primordial types of 'species'." Charles Caldwell, Samuel George Morton, Samuel A. Cartwright, George Gliddon, Josiah C. Nott, and Louis Agassiz, and even South Carolina Governor James Henry Hammond were all influential proponents of this school. While some were disinterested scientists, others were passionate advocates who used science to promote slavery in a period of increasing sectional strife. All were complicit in establishing the putative science that justified slavery, informed the Dred Scott decision, underpinned miscegenation laws, and eventually fueled Jim Crow. Samuel G. Morton, for example, claimed to be just a scientist but he did not hesitate to provide evidence of Negro inferiority to John C. Calhoun, the prominent pro-slavery Secretary of State to help him negotiate the annexation of Texas as a slave state.

The high-water mark of polygenic theories was Josiah Nott and Gliddon's voluminous eight-hundred page tome titled Types of Mankind, published in 1854. Reproducing the work of Louis Agassiz and Samuel Morton, the authors spread the virulent and explicitly racist views to a wider, more popular audience. The first printing sold out quickly and by the end of the century it had undergone nine editions. Although many Southerners felt that all the justification for slavery they needed was found in the Bible, others used the new science to defend slavery and the repression of American Indians. Abolitionists, however, felt they had to take this science on its own terms. And for the first time, African American intellectuals waded into the contentious debate. In the immediate wake of Types of Mankind and during the pitched political battles that led to Civil War, Frederick Douglass (1818-1895), the statesman and persuasive abolitionist, directly attacked the leading theorists of the American School of Anthropology. In an 1854 address, entitled "The Claims of the Negro Ethnologically Considered," Douglass argued that "by making the enslaved a character fit only for slavery, [slaveowners] excuse themselves for refusing to make the slave a freeman.... For let it be once granted that the human race are of multitudinous origin, naturally different in their moral, physical, and intellectual capacities... a chance is left for slavery, as a necessary institution.... There is no doubt that Messrs. Nott, Glidden, Morton, Smith and Agassiz were duly consulted by our slavery propagating statesmen."

20TH-CENTURY DEVELOPMENTS

Drawing on the methods of the natural sciences as well as developing new techniques involving not only structured interviews but unstructured "participant-observation"-and drawing on the new theory of evolution through natural selection, they proposed the scientific study of a new object: "humankind," conceived of as a whole. Crucial to this study is the concept "culture," which anthropologists defined both as a universal capacity and propensity for social learning, thinking, and acting (which they see as a product of human evolution and something that distinguishes Homo sapiens-and perhaps all species of genus Homo-from other species), and as a particular adaptation to local conditions that takes the form of highly variable beliefs and practices. Thus, "culture" not only transcends the opposition between nature and nurture; it transcends and absorbs the peculiarly European distinction between politics, religion, kinship, and the economy as autonomous domains. Anthropology thus transcends the divisions between the natural sciences, social sciences, and humanities to explore the biological, linguistic, material, and symbolic dimensions of humankind in all forms.

In the mid-20th century, American anthropology began to study its own history more systematically. In 1967 Marvin Harris published his The Rise of Anthropological Theory, presenting argumentative examinations of anthropology's historical developments, and George W. Stocking, Jr., established the historicist school, examining the historical contexts of anthropological movements.

ARCHAEOLOGICAL REPRESENTATIONS OF THE ECONOMY

Representations of the economy by archaeologists have widespread currency because of the popularity and frequency of stories about ancient civilizations and societies in the media. Their representations also figure prominently in K-12 courses that deal with ancient societies-such as Egypt, Greece, or Rome-as well as in the introductory chapters of college-level Western civilization or world history texts (Segal 1997). The influence of their accounts derives partly from the association of archaeologists with the idea of civilization and partly from their use of the concept. Civilization, as you know, is an idea rich in powerful, evocative imagery (Patterson 1997). Archaeologists, the media and textbooks tell us, not only find lost civilizations but also study their origin and development around the globe. Archaeologists tell us that they reconstruct the past and bring ancient societies and cultures back to life (Patterson 1993). This means that they have some understanding of what constitutes an economy as well as some insight into the economies of the ancient societies they study. Their representations of economy are complex. They are based partly on concepts and perspectives of economy and society shared with other practitioners of the historical and social sciences and partly on the interplay of these conceptual frameworks with empirical evidence.

Sociocultural evolution-the idea that society normally progresses over time through a succession of stages, each with distinctive economic or sociopolitical forms-is perhaps the core concept that many archaeologists share with colleagues in other disciplines. The idea came of age in the mid-eighteenth century in the works of French and Scottish social theorists-e.g., Anne-Robert-Jacques Turgot or Adam Smith-and was elaborated a century later by Herbert Spencer, Lewis Henry Morgan, and others. Archaeologists have debated the idea for the last century and a half. At some moments, it was wildly popular; at other moments, its existence was more muted as its utility was contested or denied. There was a resurgence of interest in sociocultural evolution among archaeologists in the wake of the Second World War; this renascence refracted the period of sustained economic growth experienced in the United States from the end of the war through the early 1970s. Names frequently associated with the rekindling of social evolutionary thought during this period were Australian archaeologist, V. Gordon Childe, and anthropologists, Julian Steward and Leslie White. A host of archaeologists built on their works.

What I propose to examine in this paper is the work of archaeologist Timothy Earle-who with some of his colleagues and former students, notably Elizabeth Brumfiel, Christine Hastorf, and Terence D'Altroy-has produced some of the discipline's more thoughtful analyses and representations of the economy in recent years. Since the late 1970s, Earle has systematically grounded his discussions of the economy in terms of a perspective that builds ultimately, I believe, on Spencer's concerns with the aggregation of population, the effects of population pressure on the evolution of sociopolitical complexity, and the emergence of increasingly differentiated regulative structures.

Earle (e.g. 1997:66) has written extensively about chiefdoms-which he sees as regional polities with institutionalized governance, some degree of social stratification, populations ranging from a few thousand to tens of thousands of people, and potentially different, historically contingent developmental trajectories. My analysis will draw mainly, though not exclusively, from his later writings.

Earle (2002) has recently charted the intellectual currents that influenced his work. He writes that he has drawn "rather eclectically" from five approaches: (1) the "evolutionary" accounts that Marx and Engels and Morgan proposed to account for changes in political economies; (2) Polanyi's (1957) "The Economy as Instituted Process," its precursors in the cultural relativism of Boasian anthropology and British structural-functionalism, and Sahlin's (1972) subsequent development of the concept of the domestic mode of production; (3) Steward's notions of the culture core as adaptation to particular environmental conditions and of levels of sociocultural integration; (4) Friedman and Rowlands's (1977) structural Marxist model of civilizational evolution that emphasizes the interrelations of initial conditions and different developmental trajectories, on the one hand, and the importance of the superstructure in relation to the economic base narrowly defined, on the other; and (5) the new institutional economics of North (1990) and others which provides opportunities to examine how political and social institutions regulate commodity flows in a region.

This map reflects a core set of ideas that have cohered in Earle's work since the late 1970s. These include commitments to (1) evolutionary accounts of the development of human society in general as well as of particular societies with the motor of development located in the interaction of population growth and technological change; (2) a base-superstructure model of society; (3) mediation of the metabolism between society and nature by the forces and relations of production at different stages of technological development; (4) the embeddedness of the economy in webs of social relations-initially domestic (family-level or local) and ultimately political-economic; and (5) domination or determination as historically contingent and largely superstructural-that is, there is no determination by the economy in the last instance. Let us consider in more detail how Earle conceptualizes these currents and how he sees them intersecting to form a coherent whole. It is important to keep in mind that he has honed and refined his theoretical perspective over time, and, consequently, that positions he held firmly at one moment may not be accorded the same degree of commitment at another.

These beliefs and commitments underpin his representation of traditional economies-that is, those minimally affected by merchant capital and by integration into an economic system dominated by industrial capitalist social relations.

He writes that Economies are open systems of production, distribution, and consumption of material things and social services. Economies involve resources extracted and goods manufactured, commodities and labor moved, and goods and services consumed in everyday life and in exceptional situations. From family meals to community religious ceremonies to imperial wars and affairs of state, economies provision and support human action. Economies vary greatly. ... (Earle 2002:8) Traditional economies contain two interrelated sectors: the subsistence economy and the political economy.

The subsistence economy involves the ways that households maintain themselves through everyday activities. ... In traditional economies, each household can produce much of what it wants, and this household self-sufficiency is the Domestic Mode of Production. Households do, however, exchange for some goods because of local resource deficiencies and local uncertainties at any time of need.

The political economy, in contrast, involves the ways that surpluses are mobilized and allocated to support political activities, lifestyles, and operations of social institutions and their leaders. The political economy is inherently competitive; since more is better (more resources = more power), the political economy is inherently growth oriented. Many are involved in ruling relationships, and the institutions of complex societies depend on finance to maintain their operations.

The mobilization of a surplus requires a productive economy and its practical control. That control derives from command over quite specific activities involving production, distribution, and even consumption.

By practical control, political economies are built on subsistence economies, and together they organize all production, distribution and consumption. The three factors of production are land, labor, and capital.

Earle proceeds to raise a series of questions about the first factor of production--land--which he discusses variously in terms of tenure, ownership, and property relations. He makes historical-developmental Boserup's (1965) largely spatial distinction between extensive and intensive land use and ties these to ownership. In family-level and local or tribal societies manifesting the communal mode of production, he argues that the use of land and resources is relatively open and non-exclusive; however, as land use becomes intensified, land ownership is more easily asserted and becomes vested progressively in fewer hands.

Ownership of resources creates relationships of power, allows control over the economy, and this partly determines the nature of stratification in society (Earle 2002:9).

This statement needs to be unpacked.

First, Earle is not arguing that property rights are vested solely in land or resources; earlier, he had pointed out that, in many instances, the rights to exclusive use are also vested, for example, in productive technology and moveable objects (Earle 2000:44).

Second, while he seems to give primacy to power relationships emerging in the economic base, he is not implying that property ownership is the only means of power, which he defines as the "capacity to control and manage the labor and activities of a group to gain access to the benefits of social action." Elsewhere, he and his associates adopt Mann's (1986) argument that power originates in the interaction of economic, ideological, political, and military relationships. The relative importance of one or another source of power varies from one society to another according to the different trajectories along which they are developing.

Third, because of his commitment to an evolutionary perspective, he argues that the different developmental stages of society--family-level, local group (tribes and bigman), and regional polity (chiefdoms and archaic states)--exhibit different forms of property.

Fourth, what does occur as a consequence of sociocultural evolution as a consequence of intensification--"the positive development between population growth and technological development"--is the development of increasingly exclusive or restricted property rights to things and their use.

"Labor (people working)" is Earle's (2002:10) second factor of production. In his view, it is the most significant factor of production in traditional economies. He writes that the simplest motivation for labor is immediate self-interest; people work to meet their own needs and desires. In traditional societies, the basic unit of labor organization is the household unit in which activities are divided by age and sex. Certain activities are male or female activities; old or young activities, but rarely is such a division of labor absolute; others help as asked or needed. For the DMP [domestic mode of production], the household is a microcosm of the broader society containing within it the basic categories of labor.

With the evolution of more complex institutions, the problem is always how to mobilize labor to perform activities required for the operation of these institutions. With the evolution of complex societies, tradition requires specific individuals to provide work for others (commoners work for chiefs to prepare for specific ceremonies). These labor contributions become formalized corvée obligations. ... Labor can be organized along a continuum from the generalized labor of the DMP (producing for household needs) to the highly specialized labor of markets (producing goods for exchange among specialists). The division of labor within a society is a fundamental description of its complexity.

In my view, Earle's definition and discussion of labor as a factor of production might profitably be elaborated in order to avoid the conflation of issues that need to be distinguished. First, labor involves the interaction between persons who toil purposively and with foresight to transform the raw materials provided by nature to produce use-values that satisfy culturally defined needs. Thus, the labor process involves not only the work itself, the objects on which this work is performed, and the instruments used but also the social relations that facilitate it. Second, while I agree with his characterization of the flexibility of labor organization in kin-communal (family-level or local) groups, it is necessary to distinguish age and gendered divisions of labor within local communities from those divisions of labor that may occur in labor processes that involve the cooperation of a number of individuals, each of whom performs a particular task in the production of a use-value. It is also necessary to keep in mind that households are never entirely self-sufficient units of production and reproduction, even when they may be the units of appropriation (e.g. Leacock 1982).

Third, both should be distinguished from social divisions of labor, in which the members of one group in a community or polity appropriate the labor time and/or goods of group whose members are engaged in direct production. This means that an explicit discussion of exploitation and the historic specificity of various forms of surplus appropriation, including the specificity of the conditions underwriting the emergence of industrial capitalism, might diminish the potential for misunderstanding and ultimately strengthen his discussion of the role of labor as a factor of production.

Earle (2002:10-11) conceptualizes capital, his third factor of production, as "technology and storable wealth." Thus, capital is a thing. It potentially produces income (profit-making), and it can be accumulated. It was also, he suggests, a less important factor of production in traditional societies than it is in modern societies dominated by mercantile and industrial capitalist economies. Earle's focus on capital as a thing rather than a social relationship between groups that appears as a thing puts his analyses clearly in the classical political economy school. It is not surprising, in this perspective, that he focuses on the circulation of goods and the development of exchange relations rather than on the relations of production and distribution; in other words, while Marx entered the sequence of production, circulation, distribution, and consumption at the point of production, Earle enters it at the moment of circulation or exchange which he conceptualized in evolutionary terms. For example, in his view, many archaic states (early civilizations) "were financed not primarily through markets but by mobilizing and distributing needed products to specialist personnel," and, further, "the development of markets in many states comes well after state formation and appears as part of a shift to wealth finance, using currency or other money-like commodities, which permit more central control and greater managerial flexibility" (Earle 1985:391). Thus, the issues were the processes by which chiefdoms and archaic states appropriated goods from local communities and then redistributed them.

Earle and Terence D'Altroy related the development of states to the growth of two distinct systems of finance that channeled resources from local production to the state. The first which they called staple finance "involves payment in kind to the state of subsistence goods;" these tribute exactions are "a share of commoner produce, as a specified levy, or as produce from land worked by corvee labor." They are appropriated by archaic states and distributed to state bureaucrats "who use them to meet basic household needs." These goods are typically bulky, costly to move over great distances; in Earle's view (1987), specialization in the production of staple goods does not play a significant role in the formation of states.

Earle and D'Altroy' called their second system of finance wealth finance. It did play a significant role in state formation, and involves the manufacture and procurement of special products (valuables, primitive money, and currency) that are used as a payment. These wealth items often have established values with respect to other goods of a similar nature but vary in their convertibility into staples. They may be amassed as direct payment from subservient populations, or they may be produced by craft specialists attached to local authorities. In the latter case, raw materials given as tribute are often used in the manufacture of these goods, and the craftsmen may be provided as part of a labor obligation from local communities. Wealth held by the state is used to pay officials and other personnel who work for the state. The obvious advantage of such financial units is their storability and transportability, which allow a more centralized control of finance that is possible with bulky staples.

Thus, both tribute exaction (goods and labor) and subsequently market relations built on a natural economy that was focused on the production of foodstuffs and other goods which satisfied needs in the local community; this natural economy was rooted in the domestic mode of production. The political economy, which is linked with the rise and development of chiefdoms and states, is an emergent configuration of institutions and practices concerned with exchange writ large-that is, where the circulation of goods is not conceptually distinguished from tribute exactions and exploitation. It is also the developmental stage that witnessed the elaboration of craft specialization and the support of these artisans by the political and religious institutions of the state (Earle 1987:75). This conceptualization of political-economic developments incorporates Julian Steward's notion of "levels of sociocultural integration," by which the latter meant that

> In the growth continuum of any culture, there is a succession of organizational types which are not only increasingly complex but which represent new emergent forms. ... In culture, simple forms, such as those represented by the family or band, do not wholly disappear when a more complex stage of development is reached, nor do they merely survive fossil-like. ... They gradually become modified as specialized, dependent parts of new kinds of total configurations.

If my analysis of Earle's conceptualization of the economy is correct, then it is possible to draw a number of tentative conclusions about his formulation and to point to potential lacunae in the logic of his representations. First, his representations of the economy are rooted ultimately in the market (exchange) rather than systemic social relations. Second, modern state-based societies differ from their predecessors; their distinctive features involve the increased importance of capital in its merchant, moneylending (finance), and industrial forms. Third, the state is distinct from the economy; the economy is primary; and the state is derivative. This implies that the economy is ultimately concerned with the wants and interests of family units and then of local communities. Chiefdoms and states emerge when wants cannot be satisfied within domestic and local units; in a sense, they stand above society and pursue interests and agendas concerning the allocation of values that are at least partly distinct and autonomous from those of their subjects.

Fourth, this is why Earle finds Mann's "four sources of power" so appealing; however, he has not fully examined the relationship between power and politics. As many have pointed out, power/domination does not necessarily involve politics except when the authoritative allocation of resources potentially makes it a central feature of politics. This raises questions about social relations, agency, and the voluntary nature of exchange. It suggests that, instead, that in class-stratified, state-based societies exchange (in the sense of distribution) is not voluntary and equal. Exchange, in these early civilizations, involves exploitative social relations that are reproduced over time. Fifth, in a parallel rather than lineal manner, why is there a tendency for technology to develop, for efficiency to increase with the passage of time? For example, Robert Brenner (1986) and Rodney Hilton (1973) have, in different ways, attempted to specify social relations that, under certain historically specific conditions, might promote the development of technology Acknowledgements. I am preparing this paper for the "Representations of the Economy" Conference organized by David Ruccio and Stephen Cullenberg that will be held at the University of California, Riverside on April 2-3, 2004.

3

Recent Trends in Anthropology

Anthropology (the science of man), denotes the natural history of mankind. In the general classification of knowledge it stands as the highest section of zoology or the science of animals, itself the highest section of biology or the science of living beings. To anthropology contribute various sciences, which hold their own independent places in the field of knowledge.

Thus anatomy and physiology display the structure and functions of the human body, while psychology investigates the operations of the human mind. Philology deals with the general principles of language, as well as with the relations between the languages of particular races and nations. Ethics or moral science treats of man's duty or rules or conduct toward his fellow men. Lastly, under the names of sociology and the science of culture, are considered the origin and development of arts and sciences, opinions, beliefs, customs, laws, institutions generally among mankind, their course in time being partly marked out by the direct record of history, while beyond the historical limit our information is continued by inferences from relics of early ages and remote districts, to interpret which is the task of prae-historic archaeology and geology.

Not only are these various sciences concerned largely with man, but several among them have in fact suffered by the almost entire exclusion of other animals from their scheme. It is undoubted that comparative anatomy and physiology, by treating the human species as one member of a long series of related organism, have gained a higher and more perfect understanding of man himself and his place in the universe than could have been gained by the narrower investigation of his species by and for itself. It is to be regretted that hitherto certain other sciences--psychology, ethics, and even philology and sociology-have so little followed so profitable an example. No doubt the phenomena of intellect appear in vastly higher and more complete organization in man than in beings below him in the scale of nature, that beasts and birds only attain to language in its lower rudiments, and that only the germs of moral tendency and social law are discernible among the lower animals.

Yet though the mental and moral interval between man and the nearest animals may be vast, the break is not absolute, and the investigation of the laws of reason and instinct throughout the zoological system, which is already casting some scattered rays of light on the study of man's highest organization, may be destined henceforth to throw brighter illumination into its very recesses.

Now this condition of things, as well as the accepted order in which the sciences have arranged themselves by their mode of growth, make it desirable that anthropology should not too ambitiously strive to include within itself the sciences which provide so much of its wealth, but that each science should pursue its own subject through the whole range of living beings, rendering to anthropology an account of so much of its results as concerns man. Such results it is he office of anthropology to collect and co-ordinance, so as to elaborate as completely as may be the synopsis of man's bodily and mental nature, and the theory of his whole course of life and action from his first appearance on earth. As will be seen from the following brief summary, the information to be thus brought together form contributing sciences is widely different both in accuracy and in soundness. While much of the descriptive detail is already clear and well filled in, the general principles of its order are still but vaguely to be discerned, and as our view quits the comparatively distinct region near ourselves the prospect fades more and more into the dimness of conjecture.

MAN'S PLACE IN NATURE

It is now more than thirty years since Dr. Prichard, who perhaps of all others merits Man to the title of founder of modern anthropology, stated in the following forcible passage, which opens his Natural History of Man, the closeness of man's physical relation to the lower animals:-

"The organized world presents no contrasts and resemblances more remarkable than those which we discover on comparing mankind with the inferior tribes. That creatures should exist so nearly approaching to each other in all particulars of their physical structure, and yet differing so immeasurably in their endowments and capabilities, would be a fact hard to believe, if it were not manifest to our observation. The differences are everywhere striking: the resemblances are less obvious in the fullness of their extent, and they are never contemplated without wonder by those who, in the study of anatomy and physiology, are first made aware how near is man in his physical constitution to the brutes. In all the principles of his internal structure, in the composition and functions of his parts, man is but an animal. The lord of the earth, who contemplates the eternal order of the universe, and aspires to communion with its invisible Maker, is a being composed of the same material, and framed on the same principles, as the creatures which he has tamed to be the servile instruments of his will, or slays for his daily food. The points of resemblance are innumerable; they extend to the most recondite arrangements of that mechanism which maintains instrumentally the physical life of the body, which brings forward its early development and admits, after a given period, its decay, and by means of which is prepared a succession of similar beings destined to perpetuate the race.

Referring the reader to the articles HISTOLOGY and PHYSIOLOGY for evidence of the similarity of minute organization both in structure and function, through the range of animal life upward to man, and to the article ANIMAL KINGDOM for the general classification of the series of invertebrate and vertebrate animals, we have here to-show in outline the relations between man and the species most closely approaching him. It is admitted that the higher apes come nearest to man in bodily formation, and that it is essential to determine their zoological resemblances and differences as a step toward ascertaining their absolute relation in nature. "At this point," writes Professor Owen in a paper on the "Osteology of the Apes," "every deviation from the human structure indicates with precision its real peculiarities, and we then possess the true means of appreciating those modifications by which a material organism is especially adapted to become the seat and instrument of a rational and responsible soul." Professor Huxley, in his Man's Place in Nature (London 1863), comparing man with order after order of the mammalia, decies "There would remain then but one order for comparison, that of the Apes (using that word in its broadest sense), and the question for discussion would narrow itself to this--is Man so different from any of these Apes that he must form an order by himself? Or does he differ less from them than they differ from one another, and hence must take his place in the same order with them?"

This anatomist states the anatomical relations between man and ape in untechnical terms suited to the present purpose, and which would be in great measure accepted by zoologists and anthropologists, whether agreeing or not with his ulterior views. The relations are most readily stated in comparison with the gorilla, as on the whole the most anthropomorphous ape. In the general proportions of the body and limbs there is a marked difference between the gorilla and man, which at once strikes the eye. The gorilla's brain-case is smaller, its trunk larger, its lower limbs shorter, its upper limbs longer in proportion than those of man. The differences between a gorilla's skull and a man's are truly immense. In the gorilla, the face formed largely by the massive jaw-bones, predominates over the brain-case or cranium; in the man these proportions are reversed. In man the occipital foramen, through which passes the spinal cord, is placed just behind the center of the base of the skull, which is thus evenly balanced in the erect posture, whereas the gorilla, which goes habitually on all fours, and whose skull is inclined forward, in accordance with this posture has the foramen further back. In man the surface of the skull is comparatively smooth, and the brow-ridges project but little, while in the gorilla these ridges overhang the cavernous orbits like penthouse roofs.

The absolute capacity of the cranium of the gorilla is far less than that of man; the smallest adult human cranium hardly measuring less than 63 cubic inches, while the largest gorilla cranium measured had a content of only 34 , cubic inches. The large proportional size of the facial bones, and the great projection of the jaws, confer on the gorilla's skull its small facial angle and brutal character, while its teeth differ from man's in relative size and number of fangs. Comparing the lengths of the extremities, it is seem that the gorilla's arm is of enormous length, in fact about one-sixth longer than the spine, whereas a man's arm is one-fifth shorter than the spine; both hand and foot are proportionally much longer in the gorilla than in man; the leg does not so much differ. The vertebral column of the gorilla differs from that of man in its curvature and other characters, as also does the conformation of its narrow pelvis. The hand of the gorilla corresponds essentially as to bones and muscles with that of man, but is clumsier and heavier, its thumb is "opposable" like a human thumb, that it, it can easily meet with its extremity the extremities of the other fingers, thus possessing a character which does much to make the human hand so admirable an instrument; but the gorilla's thumb is proportionately shorter than man's. The foot of the higher apes, though often spoken of as a hand, is anatomically not such, but a prehensile foot.

It is argued by Professor Owen and others that the position of the great toe converts the foot of the higher apes into a hand, an extremely important distinction from man; but against this Professor Huxley maintains that it has characteristic structure of a foot, with a very movable great toe. The external unlikeness of the apes to man depends much on their hairiness, but this and some other characteristics have no great zoological value. No doubt the difference between man and the apes depends, of all things, on the relative size and organization of the brain. While similar as to their general arrangement to the human brain, those of the higher apes, such as the chimpanzee, are much less complex in their convolutions, as well as much less both in absolute and relative weight-the weight of a gorilla's brain hardly exceeding 20 ounces, and a man's brain hardly weighing less than 32 ounces, although the gorilla is considerably the larger animal of the two.

These anatomical distinctions are undoubtedly of great moment, and it is an interesting question whether they suffice to place man in a zoological order by himself. It is plain that some eminent zoologists, regarding man as absolutely differing as to mind and spirit from any other animal, have had their discrimination of mere bodily differences unconsciously sharpened, and have been led.to give differences, such as in the brain or even the foot of the apes and man, somewhat more importance than if they had merely distinguished two species of apes. Among the present generation of naturalists, however, there is an evident tendency to fall in with the opinion, that the anatomical differences which separate the gorilla or chimpanzee from man are in some respects less than those which separate these man-like apes from apes lower in the scale. Yet naturalists agree to class both the higher and lower apes in the same order. This is Professor Huxley's argument, some prominent points of which are the following:-As regards the proportion of limbs, the hylobates of gibbon is as much longer in the arms than the gorilla as the gorilla is than the man, while on the other hand, it is as much longer in the legs than he man as the man is than the gorilla. As to the vertebral column and pelvis, the lower apes differ from the gorilla as much as, or more than, it differs from man.

As to the capacity of the cranium, men differ from one another so extremely that the largest known human skull holds nearly twice the measure of the smallest, a larger proportion than that in which man surpasses the gorilla; while, with proper allowance for difference of size of the various species, it appears that some of the lower apes fall nearly as much below the higher apes. The projection of the muzzle, which gives the character of brutality to the gorilla as distinguished from the man, is yet further exaggerated in the lemurs, as is also the backward position of the occipital foramen. In characters of such importance ads the structure of the hand and foot, the lower apes diverge extremely from the gorilla; thus the thumb ceases to be opposable in the American monkeys, and in the marmosets is directed forwards, and armed with a curved claw like the other digits, the great toe in these latter being insignificant in proportion.

The same argument can be extended to other points of anatomical structure, and, what is of more consequence, it appears true of the brain. A series of the apes, arranged from lower to higher orders, shows gradations from a brain little higher than that of a rat, to a brain like a small and imperfect imitation of a man's; and the greatest structural break in the series lies not between man and the man-like apes, but between the apes and monkeys on one side, and the lemurs on the other. On these grounds Professor Huxley, restoring in principle the Linnen classification, desires to include man in the order of Primates. This order he divides into seven families: first, the Anthropini consisting of man only; second, the Catarhini, or Old World apes; third, the Platyrhini, all New World apes, except the marmosets; fourth, the Arctopithecini, of marmosets; fifth, the Lemurini, or lemurs; sixth and seventh, the Cheiromyini and Galeopithecini. It seems likely that, so far as naturalists are disposed to class man with other animals on purely zoological grounds, some such classification as this may, in the present state of comparative anatomy, be generally adopted.

It is in assigning to man his place in nature on psychological grounds that the greater difficulty comes into view. The same naturalist, whose argument has just been summarized against an absolute structural line of demarcation between man and the creatures next in the scale, readily acknowledges an immeasurable and practically infinite divergence, ending in the present enormous gulf between the family of apes and the family of man. To account for this intellectual chasm as possibly due to some minor structural difference, is, however, a view strongly opposed to the prevailing judgment. The opinion is deeply rooted in modern as in ancient thought, that only a distinctively human element of the highest import can account for the severance between man and the highest animal below him. Differences in the mechanical organs, such as the perfection of the human hand as an instrument, or the adaptability of the human voice to the expression of human thought, are indeed of great value. But they have not of themselves such value, that to endow an ape with the hand and vocal organs of a man would be likely to raise it through any large part of the interval that now separates it from humanity. Much more is to be said for the view that man's larger and more highly organized brain accounts for those mental powers in which he so absolutely surpasses the brutes.

The distinction does not seem to lie principally in the range and delicacy of direct sensation, as may be judged from such well-known facts as man's inferiority to the eagle in sight, or to the dog in scent. At the same time, it seems that the human sensory organs may have in various respects acuteness beyond those of other creatures. But, beyond a doubt, man possesses, and in some way possesses by virtue of his superior brain, a power of coordinating the impressions of his senses, which enables him to understand the world he lives in, and by understanding to use, resist, and even in a measure rule it. No human art shows the nature of this human attribute more clearly than does language. Man shares with the mammalia and birds the direct expression of the feelings by emotional tones and interjectional cries; the parrot's power of articulate utterance almost equals his own; and, by association of ideas in some measure, some of the lower animals have even learnt to recognize words he utters.

But, to use words in themselves unmeaning, as symbols by which to conduct and convey the complex intellectual processes in which mental conception are suggested, compared, combined, and even analyzed, and new one created-this is a faculty which is scarcely to be traced in any lower animal. The view that this, with other mental processes, is a function of the brain, is remarkably corroborated by modern investigation of the disease of aphasia, where the power of thinking remains, but the power is lost of recalling the word corresponding to the thought, and this mental defect is found to accompany a diseased state of a particular locality of the brain. This may stand among the most perfect of the many evidences that, in Professor Bain's words, "the brain is the principal, though not the sole organ of mind." As the brains of vertebrate animals form an ascending scale, more and more approaching man's in their arrangement, the fact here finds its explanation, that lower animals perform mental processes corresponding in their nature to our own, though of generally less power and complexity.

The full evidence of this correspondence will be found in such works as Brehm's Thierleben; and some of the salient point are set forth by Mr. Darwin in the chapter on "Mental Powers," in his Descent of Man. Such are the similar effects of terror on man and the lower animals, causing the muscles to tremble, the heart to palpitate, the sphincters to be relaxed, and the hair to stand on end. The phenomena of memory, both as to persons and places, is strong in animals, as is manifest by their recognition of their masters, and their returning at once to habits disused for many years, but of which their brain has not lost the stored-up impressions. Such facts as that dogs "hunt in dreams," make it likely that their minds are not only sensible to actual events, present and past, but can, like our minds, combine revived sensations into ideal scenes in which they are actors,-that is to say, they have the faculty of imagination.

As for the reasoning powers in animals, the accounts of monkeys learning by experience to break eggs carefully, and pick off bits of shell, so as not to lose the contents, or of the way in which rats or martens after a while can no longer be caught by the same kind of trap, with innumerable similar facts, show in the plainest way that the reason of animals goes to far as to form by new experience a new hypothesis of cause and effect which will henceforth guide their actions. The employment of mechanical instruments, of which instances of monkeys using sticks and stones, and some other similar cases, furnish the only rudimentary traces among the lower animals, is one of the often quoted distinctive powers of man.

With this comes the whole vast and ever-widening range of inventive and adaptive art, where the uniform hereditary instinct of the cell-forming bee and the nest-building bird are supplanted by multiform processes and constructions, often at first rude and clumsy in comparison to those of the lower instinct, but carried on by the faculty of improvement and new invention into ever higher stages. "From the moment," writes Mr. Wallace, "when the first skin was used as a covering, when the first rude spear was formed to assist in the chase, when fire was first used to cook his food, when the first seed was sown or shoot planted, a grand revolution was effected in nature, a revolution which in all the previous ages of the earth's history had had no parallel; for a being had arisen who was no longer necessarily subject to change with the changing universe,-a being who was in some degree superior to nature, inasmuch as he knew how to control and regulate her action, and could keep himself in harmony with her, not by a change in body, but by an advance of mind."

As to the lower instincts tending directly to self-preservation, it is acknowledged on all hands that man has them in a less developed state than other animals; in fact, the natural defencelessness of the human being, and the long-continued care and teaching of the young by the elders, are among the commonest themes of moral discourse. Parental tenderness and care for the young are strongly marked among the lower animals, though so inferior in scope and duration to the human qualities; and the same may be said of the mutual forbearance and defence which bind together in a rudimentary social bond the families and herds of animals.

Philosophy seeking knowledge for its own sake; morality, manifested in the sense of truth, right, and virtue; and religion, the belief in and communion with superhuman powers ruling and pervading the universe, are human characters of which it is instructive to trace, if possible, the earliest symptoms in he lower animals, but which can there show at most only faint and rudimentary signs of their wondrous development in mankind. That the tracing of physical and even intellectual continuity between the lower animals and our own race, does not necessarily lead the anthropologist to lower the rank of man in the scale of nature, cannot be better shown than by citing one of the authors of the development theory, Mr. A.R. Wallace. Man, he considers is to be placed "apart, as not only the head and culminating point of the grand series of organic nature, but as in some degree a new and distinct order of being."

To regard the intellectual functions of the brain and nervous system as alone to be considered in the psychological comparison of man with the lower animal, is a view satisfactory to those thinkers who hold materialistic views. According to this school, man is a machine, no doubt the most complex and wonderful adapted of all known machines, but still neither more nor less than an instrument whose energy is provided by force from without, and which, when set in action, performs the various operations for which its structure fits it, namely, to live, move, feel, and think. This doctrine, which may be followed up from Descartes's theory of animal life into the systems of modern writers of the school of Moleschott and Buchner, underlies the Lectures on Man of Professor Carl Vogt, one of the ablest of modern anthropologists. Such views, however, always have been and are strongly opposed by those who accept on theological grounds a spiritualistic doctrine, or what is, perhaps, more usual, a theory which combines spiritualism and materialism in the doctrine of a composite nature in man animal as to the body and in some measure as to the mind, spiritual as to the soul. It may be useful, as an illustration of one opinion on this subject, to continue here from an earlier page the citation of Dr. Prichard's comparison between man and the lower animals:-

"If it be inquired in what the still more remarkable difference consists, it is by no means easy to reply. By some it will be said that man, while similar in the organization of his body to the lower tribes, is distinguished from them by the possession of an immaterial soul, a principle of conscious feeling, of intellect and thought. To many persons it will appear paradoxical to ascribe the endowment of a soul to the inferior tribes in the creation, yet it is difficult to discover a valid argument that limits the possession of an immaterial principle to man. The phenomena of feeling of desire and aversion, of love and hatred, of fear and revenge, and the perception of external relations manifested in the life of brutes, imply, not only through the analogy which they display to the human faculties, but likewise from all that we can learn or conjecture of their particular nature, the superadded existence of a principle distinct from the mere mechanism of material bodies.

That such a principle must exist in all beings capable of sensation, or of anything analogous to human passions and feelings, will hardly be denied by those who perceive the force of arguments which metaphysically demonstrate the immaterial nature of the mind. There may be no rational grounds for the ancient dogma that the souls of the lower animals were imperishable, like the soul of man; this is, however, a problem which we are not called upon to discuss; and we may venture to conjecture that there may be immaterial essences of divers kinds, and endowed with various attributes and capabilities. But the real nature of these unseen principles eludes our research: they are only known to us by their external manifestations. These manifestations are the various powers and capabilities, or rather the habitudes of action, which characterize the different orders of being, diversified according to their several destinations."

Dr. Prichard here puts forward distinctly the time-honoured doctrine which refers the mental faculties to the operation of the soul. The view maintained by a distinguished comparative anatomist, Professor Mivart, in his Genesis of Species, ch. Xii., may fairly follow. "Man, according to the old scholastic definition, is Îa rational animal' (animal rationale), and his animality is distinct in nature from his rationality, though inseparably joined, during life, in one common personality. Man's animal body must have had a different source from that of the spiritual soul which informs it, owing to the distinctness of the two orders to which those two existences severally belongs."

Not to pursue into its details a doctrine which has its place rather in a theological than an anthropological article, it remains to be remarked that the two extracts just given, however significant in themselves, fail to render an account of the view of the human constitution which would probably, among the theological and scholastic leaders of public opinion, count the largest weight of adherence. According to this view, not only life but thought are functions of the animal system, in which man excels all other animals as to height of organization; but beyond this, man embodies an immaterial and immortal spiritual principle which no lower creature possesses, and which makes the resemblance of the apes to him but a mocking simulance. To pronounce any absolute decision on these conflicting doctrines is foreign to our present purpose, which is to show that all of them count among their adherents men of high rank in science.

ORIGIN OF MAN

Available information on this great problem has been multiplied tenfold during the present generation, and the positive dicta of the older authorities are now more and more supplanted by hypotheses based on biological evidence. Opinions as to the genesis of man is divided between the theories of the two great schools of biology, that of creation and that of evolution. In both schools the ancient doctrine of the contemporaneous appearance on earth of all species of animals having been abandoned under the positive evidence of geology, it is admitted that the animal kingdom, past and present, includes a vast series of successive forms, whose appearances and disappearances have taken place at intervals during an immense lapse of ages.

The line of inquiry has thus been directed to ascertaining what formative relations subsists among these species and genera, the last link of the argument reaching to the relation between man and the lower creatures preceding him in time. Pn both the theories here concerned to would be admitted, in the words of Agassiz, that "there is a manifest progress in the succession of beings on the surface of the earth. This progress consists in an increasing similarity of the living fauna, and, among the vertebrates especially, in their increasing resemblance to man." Agassiz continues, however, in terms characteristic of the creationist school: "But this connection is not the consequence of a direct lineage between the faunas of different ages. There is nothing like parental descent connecting them.

The fishes of the Palaeozoic age are in no respect the ancestors of the reptiles of the Secondary age, nor does man descend from the mammals which preceded him in the Tertiary age. The link by which they are connected is of a higher and immaterial nature; and their connection is to be sought in the view of the Creator himself, whose aim in forming the earth, in allowing it to undergo the successive changes which geology has pointed out, and in creating successively all the different types of animals which have passed away, was to introduce man upon the surface of our globe. Man is the end towards which all the animal creation has tended from the first appearance of the first Palaeozoic fishes."

The evolutionist school, on the contrary, maintains that different successive species of animals are in fact connected by parental descent, having become modified in the course of successive generations. Mr. Darwin, with whose name and that of Mr. Wallace the modern development theory is especially associated in the preface to his Descent of Man (1871), gives precedence among naturalists to Lamark, as having long ago come to the conclusion "that man is the to descendant with other species of some ancient, lower, and extinct form." Professor Huxley, remarking on the crudeness and even absurdity of some of

Lamark's views, dates from Darwin the scientific existence of the development theory. The result of Darwin's application of this theory to man may be given in his own words:-

"The Catarhine and Platyrhine monkeys agree in a multitude of characters, as is shown by the unquestionably belonging to one and the same Order. The many characters which they possess in common can hardly have been independently acquired by so many distinct species; so that these characters must have been inherited. But an ancient form which possessed many characters common to the Catarhine and Platyrhine monkeys, and others in an intermediate condition, and some few perhaps distinct from those now present in either group, would undoubtedly have been ranked, if seen by a naturalist, as an ape or a monkey. And as man under a genealogical point of view belongs to the Catarhine or Old World stock, we must conclude, however much the conclusion may revolt our pride, that our early progenitors would have been properly thus designated. But we must not fall into the error of supposing that the early progenitor of the whole Simian stock, including man, was identical with, or even closely resembled, any existing ape or monkey."

The problem of the origin of man cannot be properly discussed apart from the full problem of the origin of species. The homologies between man and other animals which both schools try to account for; the explanation of the intervals, with apparent want of intermediate forms, which seem to the creationists so absolute a separation between species; the evidence of useless "rudimentary organs,: such as in man the external shell of the ear, and the muscle which enables some individuals to twitch their ears, which rudimentary parts the evolutionists claim to be only explicable as relics of an earlier specific condition,-these, which are the main points of the argument on the origin of man, belong to general biology. The philosophical principles which underlie the two theories stand for the most part in strong contrast, the theory of evolution tending toward the supposition of ordinary causes, such as "natural selection," producing modifications in species, whether by gradual accumulation or more sudden leaps, while the theory of creation is prone to have recourse to acts of supernatural intervention. A theory has been propounded by Mr.

Mivart of a natural evolution of man as to his body, combined with a supernatural creation as to his soul; but this attempt to meet the difficulties on both sides seems at present not to have satisfied either. Anthropology waits to see whether the discovery of intermediate forms, which has of late years reduced so many asserted species to mere varieties, will go on till it produces a disbelief in any real separation between neighbouring species, and especially whether geology can furnish traces of the hypothetical animal, man's near ancestor, but not as yet man. In the present state of the argument it may here suffice to have briefly indicated the positions held on either side.

RACES OF MANKIND

The classification of mankind into a number of permanent varieties or races, rests on grounds which are within limits not only obvious but definite. Whether from a popular or a scientific point of view, it would be admitted that a Negro, a Chinese, and an Australia, belong to three such permanent varieties of men, all plainly distinguishable from one another and from any European. Moreover, such a division takes for granted the idea which is involved in the word race, that each of these varieties is due to special ancestry, each race thus representing an ancient breed or stock, however these breeds or stocks may have had their origin. The anthropological classification of mankind is thus zoological in its nature, like that of the varieties or species of any other animal group, an the character on which it is based on in great measure physical, though intellectual and traditional peculiarities, such as moral habit and language, furnish important aid. Among the best-marked race-characters are the following:--

The colour of the skin has always been held as specially distinctive. The coloured race-portraits of ancient Egypt remain to prove the permanence of complexion during a lapse of a hundred generations, distinguishing coarsely but clearly the types of the red-brown Egyptian, the yellow-brown Canaanite, the comparatively fair Libyan, and the Negro. These broad distinctions have the same kind of value as the popular terms describing white, yellow, brown, and black races, which often occur in ancient writings, and are still used. But for scientific purposes greater accuracy is required, and this is now satisfactorily attained by the use of Dr. Broca's graduated series of colours as a standard. By this table the varieties of the human skin may be followed from the fairest hue of the Swede and the darker tint of the Provencal, to the withered-leaf brown of the Hottentot, the chocolate brown of the Mexican, and the brown-black of the West African. The colour of the eyes and hair is also to be defined accurately by Broca's table. This affords, however, less means of distinction, from the extent in which dark tints of hair and iris are common to races whose skins are more perceptibly different; yet some varieties are characteristic, such as the blue eyes and flaxen hair of that fair race of Northern Europe.

As to the hair, its structure and arrangement is a better indication of race than its tint. The fair differs in quantity between scantiness of the body of the Mongol and profusion on the body of the Aino; while as to the arrangement on the scalp, the tufts of the Bushman contrast with the more equal distribution on the European head. The straight hair of the North American or Malay is recognizable at once as different from the waving or curling hair of the European, and both from the naturally frizzed hair of the Negro. These marked differences are due to the structure of the hair, wick, examined in sections under the microscope, varies from the circular section proper to the straight-haired races, to the more or less symmetrically oval or reniform sections belonging to races with curled and twisted hair.

Stature is by no means a general criterion of race, and it would not, for instance, be difficult to choose groups of Englishmen, Kafirs, and North American Indians, whose mean height should hardly differ. Yet in many cases it is a valuable means of distinction, as between the tall Patagonians and the stunted Fuegians, and even as a help in minuter problems, such as separating the Teutonic and Keltic ancestry in the population of England. Proportions of the limbs, compared in length with the trunk, have been claimed as constituting peculiarities of African and American races; and other anatomical points, such as the conformation of the pelvis, have speciality. But inferences of this class have hardly attained to sufficient certainty and generality to be set down in the form of rules.

The conformation of the skull is second only to the colour of the skin as a criterion for the distinction of race. The principal modes of estimating the differences of skulls are the following:- The skull being seen from above, the proportions of the two diameters are estimated on the principle employed by Retzius: taking the longer diameter from front to back as 100, if the shorter or cross diameter falls below 80, the skull may be classed as long (dolichocephalic; while if it exceeds 80, the skull may be classed as broad (brachycephalic); or a third division may be introduced between these as intermediate (mesocephalic), comprehending skulls with a proportionate breadth of 75 to 80, or thereabout. The percentage of breadth to length measured in this manner is known as the cephalic index; thus, the cephalic index of a Negro or Australian may be as low as 72, and that of a Tatar as high as 88, while the majority of Europeans have an index not departing in either direction very far from 78.

The cephalic height is measured in the same way as a percentage of the length. The back view (norma occipitalis) of the skull is distinguished as rounded, pentagonic, etc., and the base view of the skull shows the position of the occipital foramen and the zygomatic arches. The position of the jaws is recognized as important, races being described as prognathous when the jaws project, far, as in the Asutralian or Negro, in contradistinction to the orthognathous type, which is that of the ordinary well-shaped European skull. On this distinction in great measure depends the celebrated "facial angle," measured by Camper as a test of low and high races; but this angle is objectionable as resulting partly from the development of the forehead and partly from the position of the jaws. The capacity of the cranium is estimated in cubic measure by filling it with sand, etc., with the general result that the civilized white man is found to have a larger brain than the barbarian or savage.

Classification of races on cranial measurements has long been attempted by eminent anatomists, such as Blumenbach and Retzius, while the later labours of Von Baer, Welcker, Davis, Broca, Busk, Lucae, and many others, have brought the distinctions to extreme minuteness. In certain cases great reliance may be placed on such measurements. Thus the skulls of an Asutralian and a Negro would be generally distinguished by their narrowness and the projection of the jaw from that of any Englishman; while, although both the Australian and Negro are thus dolichocephalic and prognathous, the first would usually differ perceptibly from the second in its upright sides and strong orbital ridges. The relation of height to breadth may furnish a valuable test; thus both the Hafir and the Bushman are dolichocephalic, with an index of about 72, but they differ in the index of height, which may be 73 and 71 respectively, in the one case more than the width and in the other less. It is, however, acknowledged by all experienced craniologists, that the shape of the skull may vary so much within the same tribe, and even the same family, that it must be used with extreme caution, and if possible only in conjunction with other criteria of race.

The general contour of the face, in part dependent on the form of the skull, varies much in different races, among whom it is loosely defined as oval, lozenge-shaped, pentagonal, etc. Of particular features, some of the most marked contrast to European types are seen in the oblique Chinese eyes, the broad-set Kamchadal cheeks, the pointed Arab chin, the snub Kirghis nose, the fleshy protuberant Negro lips, and the broad Kalmuk ear. Taken altogether, the features have a typical character which popular observation seizes with some degree of correctness, as in the recognition of the Jewish countenance in a European city.

The state of adaptation in which each people stands to its native climate forms a definite race-character. In its extreme form this is instanced in the harmful effect of the climate of India on children of European parents, and the corresponding danger in transporting natives of tropical climates to England. Typical instances of the relation of race-constitutions to particular diseases are seen in the liability of Europeans in the West Indies to yellow fever, from which Negroes are exempt, and in the habitation by tribes in India of so-called "unhealthy districts," whose climate is deadly to Europeans, and even to natives of neighboruing regions. Even the vermin infesting different races of men are classified by Mr. A. Murray as distinct.

The physical capabilities of different races are known to differ widely, but it is not easy to discriminate here between hereditary race-differences and those due to particular food and habit of life. A similar difficulty has hitherto stood in the way of any definite classification of the emotional, moral and intellectual characters of races. Some of the most confident judgment which have been delivered on this subject have been dictated by prejudice or willful slander, as in the many lamentable cases in which slave-holders and conquerors have excused their ill-treatment of subject and invaded races on the ground of their being creatures of bestial nature in mind and morals. Two of the best-marked contrasts of mental type recorded among races are Mr. A. R. Wallace's distinction between the sky, reserved, and impassive Malay and the sociable and demonstrative Papuan, and the very similar difference pointed out by Spix and Martius between the dull and morose natives of the Brazilian forests, an the lively sensuous African Negroes brought into contact with them. In general, however, descriptions of national or racial character are so vitiated by the confusion of peculiarity of natural character with stage of civilization, that they can only be made use of with the greatest reserve.

The relation of language to race is discussed below.

Were the race-character indicated in the foregoing paragraphs constant in degree or even in kind, the classification of races would be an easy task. In fact it is not so, for every division of mankind presents in every character wide deviations from a standard. Thus the Negro race, well marked as it may seem at the first glance, proves on closer examination to include several shades of complexion and features, in some districts varying far from the accepted Negro type; while the examination of a series of native American tribes shows that, notwithstanding their asserted uniformity of type, they differ in stature, colour, features, and proportions of skull.

Detailed anthropological research, indeed, more and more justifies Blumenbach's words, that "innumerable varieties of mankind run into one another by insensible degrees." This state of things, due partly to mixture and crossing of races, and partly to independent variation of types, makes the attempt to arrange the whole human species within exactly bounded divisions an apparently hopeless task. It does not follow, however, that the attempt to distinguish special races should be given up, for there at least exist several definable types, each of which so far prevails in a certain population as to be taken as its standard. M. Quetelet's plan of defining such types will probably meet with general acceptance as the scientific method proper to this branch of anthropology. It consists in the determination of the standard, or typical "mean man" (homme moyen) of a population, with reference to any particular quality, such as stature, weight, complexion, etc. In the case of statute, this would be done by measuring a sufficient number of men, and accounting how many of them belong to each height on the scale.

If it be thus ascertained, as it might be in an English district, that the 5 ft. 7 in. men form the most numerous group, while the 5 ft. 6 in. and 5 ft. 8 in. men are less in number, and the 5 ft. 5 in. and 5 ft. 9 in. still fewer, and so on until the extremely small number of extremely short or tall individuals of 5 ft. or 7 ft. is reached, it will thus be ascertained that the stature of the mean or typical man is to be taken as 5 ft. 7 in. The method is thus that of selecting as the standard the most numerous group, on both sides of which the groups decrease in number as they vary in type. Such classification may show the existence of two or more types in a community, as, for instance, the population of a Californian settlement made up of Whites and Chinese might show two predominant groups (one of 5 ft. 8 in., the other of 5 ft. 4 in) corresponding to these two racial types. It need hardly be said that this method of determining the mean type of a race, as being that of its really existing and mist numerous class, is altogether superior to the ere calculation of an average, which may actually be represented by comparatively few individuals, and those the exceptional ones. For instance, the average stature of the mixed European and Chinese population just referred to might be 5 ft. 6 in--a worthless and, indeed, misleading result. The measurement and description of the various races of men are now carried to great minuteness (the tables in Scherzer and Schwarz, Reise der Novara, and those of Fritsch Die Eingeborenen Sud-Afrika's, 1872, may be cited as examples of modern method), so that race classification is rapidly improving as to both scope and accuracy. Even where comparatively loose observations have been made, it is possible, by inspection of considerable number of individuals, to define the prevalent type of a race with tolerable approximation to the real mean or standard man. It is in this way that the subdivision of mankind into races, so far as it has been done to any purpose, has been carried out by anthropologists.

These classifications have been numerous, and though, regarded as system,s most of them are now seen at the first glance to be unsatisfactory, yet they have been of great value in systematizing knowledge, and are all more or less based on indisputable distinctions. Blumenbach's division, though published nearly a century ago (1781), has had the greatest influence. He reckon five races, viz., Caucasian, Mongolian, Ethiopian, American, Malay. The ill-chosen name of Caucasian, used by Blumenbach to denote what may be called white men, is still current; it brings into one race peoples such as the Arabs and Swedes, although these are scarcely less different than the Americans and Malays, who are set down as two distinct races. Again, two of the best-marked varieties of mankind are the Australians and the Bushmen, neither of whom, however, seem to have a natural place in Blumebach's series.

The yet simpler classification by Cuvier into Caucasian, Mongol, and Negro, corresponds in some measure with a division by mere complexion into white, yellow, and black races; but neither this threefold division, nor the ancient classification into Semitic, Hamitic, and Japhetic nations can be regarded as separating the human types either justly or sufficiently. Schemes which set up a larger number of distinct races, such as the eleven of Pickering, the fifteen of Bory de St Vincent, and the sixteen of Desmoulins, have the advantage of finding niches for most well-defined human varieties; but no modern naturalist would be likely to adopt any one of these as it stands. In criticism of Pickering's system, it is sufficient to point out that he divides the white nations into two races, entitled the Arab and the Abyssinian Agassiz, Nott, Crawfurd, and others who have assumed a much larger number of races or species of man, are not considered to have satisfactorily defined a corresponding number of distinguishable types. On the whole, Professor Huxley's recent scheme probably approaches more nearly than any other to such a tentative classification as may be accepted in definition of the principal varieties of mankind, regarded from a zoological point of view, though anthropologists may be disposed to erect into separate races several of his widely-differing sub-races. He ditinsguishes four principal types of mankind, the Australioid, Negroid, Mongoloid, and Xanthochoroic, adding a fifth variety, the Melanochroic.

The special points of the Australioid are a chocolate-brown skin, dark brown or black eyes, black hair (usually wavy), narrow (dolichocephalic) skull, brow-ridges strongly developed, projecting jaw, coarse lips, and broad nose. This type is best represented by the natives of Australia, and next to them, by the indigenous tribes of Southern India, the so-called coolies. The Egyptians to some degree approach this type; they are, however, held by good authorities to be a modified African race.

The Negroid type is primarily represented by the Negro of Africa, between the Sahara and the Cape district, including Madagascar. The skin varies from dark brown to brown-black, with eyes of similar dark hue, and hair usually black, and always crisp or woolly. The skull is narrow (dolichocephalic), with orbital ridges not prominent, prognathous, with depressed nasal, bones, causing the nose to be flat as well as broad; and the lips are coarse and projecting. Two important families are classed in this system as special modifications of the Negroid type. First, the Bushman of South Africa is diminutive in stature, and of yellowish-brown complexion; the Hottentot is supposed to be the result of crossing between the Bushman and ordinary Negroid. Second, the Negritos of the Andaman Islands, the peninsula of Malacca, the Philippines and other islands, to New Caledonia and Tasmania, are mostly dolichocephalic, with dark skins and woolly hair. In various districts they tend towards other types, and show traces of mixture.

The Mongoloid type prevails over the vast area lying east of a line drawn from Lapland to Siam. Its definition includes a short, squat build, a yellowish brown complexion, with black eyes and black straight hair, a broad (brachycephalic) skull, usually without prominent brow-ridges, flat small nose, and oblique eyes. The dolichocephalic Chinese and Japanese in other respect correspond. Various other important branches of the human species are brought into connection with the Mongoloid type, though on this view the differences they present raise difficult problems of gradual variations, as well as of mixture of race; these are the Dyak-Malays, the Polynesians, and the Americans.

The Xanthochroi, or fair whites-tall, with almost colourless skin, blue or grey eyes, hair from straw colour to chesnut, and skulls varying as to proportionate width-are the prevalent inhabitants of Northern Europe, and the type may be traced into North Africa, and eastward as far as Hindostan. On the south and west it mixes with that of the Melanochroi, or dark whites, and on the north and east with that of the Mongoloids.

The Melanochroi, or dark whites, differ from the fair whites in the darkening of the complexion to brownish and olive, and of the eyes and hair to black, while the stature is somewhat lower and the frame lighter. To this class belong a large part of those classed as Kelts, and of the populations of Southern Europe, such as Spaniards, Greeks, and Arabs, extending as far as India; while endless intermediate grades between the two white types testify to ages of intermingling. Professor Huxley is disposed to account for the Melanochroi as themselves the result of crossing between the Xanthochroi and the Australioids. Whatever ground there may be for his view, it is obviously desirable to place them in a class by themselves, distinguishing them by an appropriate name.

In determining whether the races of mankind are to be classed as varieties of one species, it is important to decide whether every two races can unite to produce fertile offspring. It is settled by experience that the most numerous and well-known crossed races, such as the Mulattos, descended from Europeans and Negroes-the Mestizos, from Europeans and American indigenes--the Zambos, from these American indigenes and Negroes, etc., are permanently fertile. They practically constitute sub-races, with a general blending of the characters of the two parents, and only differing from fully established races in more or less tendency to revert to one or other of the original types. It has been argued, on the other hand, that not all such mixed breeds are permanent, and especially that the cross between European and Australian indigenes is almost sterile; but this assertion, when examined with the care demanded by its bearing on the general question of hybridity, has distinctly broken down. On the whole, the general evidence favours the opinion that any two races may combine to produce a new sub-race, which again may combine with any other variety.

Thus, if the existence of a small number of distinct races of mankind be taken as a starting-point, it is obvious that their crossing would produce an indefinite number of secondary varieties, such as the population of the world actually presents. The working out in detail of the problem, how far the differences among complex, nations, such as those of Europe, may have been brought about by hybridity, is still, however, a task of almost hopeless intricacy. Among the boldest attempts to account for distinctly-marked population as resulting from the intermixture of two races, are Professor Huxley's view that the Hottentots are hybrid between the Bushmen and the Negroes, and his more important suggestion, that the Melnochroic peoples of Southern Europe are of mixed Xanthochoric and Australioid stock.

The problem of ascertaining how the small number of races, distinct enough to be called primary, can have assumed their different types, has been for years the most disputed field of anthropology, the battle-ground of the rival schools of monogenists and polygenists. The one has claimed all mankind to be descended from one original stock, and generally from a single pair; the other has contended for the several primary races being separate species of independent origin. It is not merely as a question of natural history that the matter has been argued. Biblical authority has been appealed to, mostly on the side of the monogenists, as recording the descent of mankind from a single pair.

On the other hand, however, the polygenists not less confidently claim passages from which they infer the existence of non-Adamite, as well as Adamite races of man. Nor have political considerations been without influence, as where, for instance, one American school of ethnologists have been thought to have formed, under the bias of a social system recognizing slavery, their opinion that the Negro and the white man are of different species. Of the older school of scientific monogenists, Blumenbach and Prichard are eminent representatives, as is Quatrefages of the more modern. The great problem of the monogenist theory is to explain by what course of variation the so different races of man have arisen from a single stock. In ancient times little difficulty was left in this, authorities such as Aristotle and Vitruvius seeing in climate and circumstance the natural cause of racial differences, the Ethiopian having been blackened by the tropical sun, etc.

Later and closer observations, however, have shown such influences to be, at any rate, far slighter in amount and slower in operation than was once supposed. M. de Quatrefages brings forward (Unite de l'Espece Humanine, Paris, 1861, ch. 13) his strongest arguments for the variability of races under change of climate, &c (action du milieu), instancing the asserted alteration in complexion, constitution, and character of Negroes in America, and Englishmen in America and Australia. But although the reality of some such modification is not disputed, especially as to stature and constitution, its amount is not enough to upset the counter-proposition of the remarkable permanence of type displayed by races ages after they have been transported to climates extremely different from that of their former home. Moreover, physically different races, such as the Bushmen and Negroids in Africa, show no signs of approximation under the influence of the same climate; while on the other hand, the coast tribes of Tierra del Fuego and forest tribes of tropical Brazil continue to resemble one another, in spite of extreme differences of climate and food. Mr. Darwin, than whom no naturalist could be more competent to appraise the variation of a species, is moderate in his estimation of the changes produced on races of man by climate and mode of life within the range of history. The slightness and slowness of variation in human races having become known, a great difficulty of the monogenist theory was seen to lie in the shortness of the chromology with which it was formerly associated. Inasmuch as several well-marked races of mankind, such as the Egyptian, Phoenician, Ethiopian, etc., were much the same three or four thousand years ago as now, their variation from a single stock in the course of any like period could hardly be accounted for without a miracle. This difficulty was escaped by the polygenist theory, which, till a few years since, was gaining ground.

Two modern views have, however, intervened which have tended to restore, though under a new aspect, the doctrine of a single human stock. One has been the recognition of man having existed during a vast period of time (see sec. IV., Antiquity of Man0, which made it more easy to assume to continuance of very slow natural variation as having differenced even the white man and the Negro among the descendants of a common progenitor. The other wise is that of the evolution or development of species, at the present day so strongly upheld among naturalists. It does not follow necessarily form a theory of evolution of species that mankind must have descended from a single stock, for the hypothesis of development admits of the arguments, that several simious species may have culminated in several races of man. The general tendency of the development theory, however, is against constituting separate species where the differences are moderate enough to be accounted for a due to variation from a single type. Mr. Darwin's summing up of the evidence as to unity of type throughout the races of mankind is as distinctly a monogenist argument as those of Blumenbach, Prichard or Quatrefages-

> *"Although the existing races of man differ in many respects, as in colour, hair, shape of skull, proportions of the body, etc., yet, if their whole organization be take into consideration, they are found to resemble each other closely in a multitude of points. Many of these points are of so unimportant, or of so singular a nature, that it is extremely improbable that they should have been independently acquired by aboriginally distinct species or races. The same remark holds good with equal or greater force with respect to the numerous points of mental similarity between the most distinct races of man... Now, when naturalists observe a close agreement in numerous small details of habits, tastes, and dispositions between two or more domestic races, or between nearly allied natural forms, they use this fact as an argument that all are descended from a common progenitor, who was thus endowed; and consequently, that all should be classed under the same species. The same argument may be applied with much force to the races of man."*

A suggestion by Mr. A.R. Wallace has great importance in the application of the development theory to the origin of the various races of man; it is aimed to meet the main difficulty of the monogenist school, how races which have remained comparatively fixed in type during the long period of history, such as the white man and the Negro, should have, in even a far longer period, passed by variation from a common original. Mr. Wallace's view is substantially that the remotely ancient representatives of the human species, being as yet animals too low in mind to have developed those arts of maintenance and social ordinances by which man holds his own against influences from climate and circumstance, were in their then wild state much more plastic than now to external nature; so that "natural selection" and other causes met with but feeble resistance in forming the permanent varieties or races of man, whose complexion and structure still remain fixed in their descendants. On the whole, it may be asserted that the doctrine of the unity of mankind now stands on a firmer basis than in previous ages. It would be premature to judge how far the problem of the origin of races may be capable of exact solution; but the experience of the last few years countenances Mr. Darwin's prophecy, that before long the dispute between the monogenists and the polygenists will die a silent and unobserved death.

ANTIQUITY OF MAN

It was until of late years commonly held among the educated classes, that man's first appearance on earth might be treated on a historical basis as matter of record. It is true that the schemes drawn up by chronologists differed widely, as was naturally the case, considering the variety and inconsistency of their documentary data. On the whole, the scheme of Archbishop Usher, who computed that the earth and man were created in 4004 B.C., was the most popular. It is no longer necessary, however, to discuss these chronologies, inasmuch as new evidence has so changed the aspect of the subject, that the quasi-historical schemes of the last century would now hardly be maintained by any competent authority any school. Geology, notwithstanding the imperfection of its results, has made it manifest that our earth must have been the seat of vegetable and animal life for an immense period of time; while the first appearance of man, though comparatively recent, is positively so remote, that an estimate between twenty and a hundred thousand years may fairly be taken as a minimum. This geological claim for a vast antiquity of the human race is supported by the similar claims of prehistoric archaeology and the science of culture, the evidence of all three departments of inquiry being intimately connected, and in perfect harmony.

During the last half century, the fact has been established that human bones and objects of human manufacture occur in such geological relation to the remains of fossil species of elephant, rhinoceros, hyaena, bear, etc., as to lead to the distinct inference that man already existed during the ancient period of these now extinct mammalia. The not quite conclusive researches of MM. Tournal and Christol in limestone caverns of the south of France date back to 1828. About the same time Dr. Schmerling of Liege was exploring the ossiferous caverns of the valley of the Meuse, and satisfied himself that the men who bones he found beneath the stalagmite floors, together with bones cut and flints shaped by human workmanship, had inhabited this Belgian district at the same time with the cave-bear and several other extinct animals whose bones were imbedded with them (Recherches sur les Ossements fossils decouverts dans les Cavernes de la Province de Liege, Liege, 1833-4.

This evidence, however, met with little acceptance among scientific men. Nor, at first, was more credit given to the discovery by M. Boucher de Perthes, about 1841, of rude flint hatchets in a sand-bed containing remains of mammoth and rhinoceros at Menchecourt near Abbeville, which first find was followed by othrs in the same district (see Boucher de Perthes, De l'Industrie Primitive, ou les Arts a leur; between 1850 and 1860 competent French and English geologists, among them Rigollot, Falconer, Prestwich, and Evans, were induced to examine into the facts, and found the evidence irresistible that man existed and used rude implements of chipped flint during the Quaternary or Drift period. Further investigations were now made, and overlooked results of older ones reviewed. In describing Kent's Hole, near torquay, Mr. Godwin-Austen had maintained, as early as 1840, that the human bones and worked flints had been deposited indiscriminately together with the remains of fossil elephant, rhinoceros, etc., a minute exploration of this cavern has since been carriedon under the superintendence of Messrs Vivian, Pengelly, and others, fully justifying Mr. Godwin-Austen's early remark, that "there is no a priori reason why man and the several animals whose remains occur in caves and in gravel should not have lived here at some remote time." Especially certain caves and rock-shelters in the province of Dordogne, in central France, were examined by a French and an English archaeologist, Mons. Edouard Lartet and Mr. Henry Christy, the remains discovered showing the former prevalence of the rein-deer in this region, at that time inhabited by savages, whose bone and stone implements indicate a habit of life similar to that of the Esquimaux. Moreover, the coexistence of man with a fauna now extinct or confined to other districts was brought to yet clearer demonstration, by the discovery in these caves of certain drawing and carvings of the animals done by the ancient inhabitants themselves, such as a group of rein-deer on a piece of rein-deer horn, and a sketch of a mammoth, showing this elephant's long hair, on a piece of a mammoth's tusk from La Madeleine. These are among the earliest and principal of a series of discoveries of human relics belonging to what may be termed geological antiquity, with which should be mentioned Mr. Boyd Dawkins' examination of the hyaena den of Wokey, Hole, Dr. Lund's researches in the caves of Brazil, those in the south of France by the Marquis de Vibraye and MM. Garrigou and Filhol, those in Sicily by Dr. Falconer, and Mr. Bruce Foote's discovery of rude quartzite implements in the lateite of India. Fuller details of the general subject will be found in Sir C. Lyell's Antiquity of Man, 4th ed., London, 1873; Sir John Lubbock's Prehistoric Times, 3d ed., London, 1873; Dr. H Falconer's Palaeontological Memoirs, London, 1868; the volumes of Procedings of the International Congress of Prehistoric Archaeology; and the periodical Materiaux pour l'Histoire Primitive et Naturelle de l'Homme, edited at first by de Mortillet, and since by Trutat and Cartailhac.

This evidence is now generally accepted by geological as carrying back the existence of man into the period of the post-glacial drift, in what is now called the Quaternary period. That this indicates an antiquity at least of tens of thousands of years may be judged in several ways. The very position in which these rude instruments were found showed that they belonged to a time quite separate from that of history. Thus, at St, Acheul flint hatchets occur in a gravel-bed immediately overlying the chalk, which bed is covered by some 12 feet of sand and marl, capped by a layer of soil, which is shown by graves of the Gallo-Roman period to have been hardly altered during the last 1500 years. This distinction between the drift deposits and those containing relics of historic ages is, as a general rule, evident at a glance. Next, the succession of ages to which different classes of remains belong is well marked; the drift implements belongs to the palaeolithic or old stone age, when as yet the implements were extremely rude, and not ground or polished; above these in deposit, and therefore later in time, come the artistically shaped and polished celts of the Neolithic or new stone age; above these, again, relics of the bronze and early iron ages, with which historical antiquity in Europe begins.

Again, the animals of the Quaternary period, whose bones are found with the rude stone implements, comprise several species of mammalia which have since become extinct, such as the mammoth, the hairy rhinoceros, and the Irish elk, while others, such as the rein-deer and musk-ox, now only inhabit remote districts. It is generally considered that such a fauna indicates, at any rate during part of the Quaternary period, a severer climate than now prevails in France and England. This difference from the present conditions seems to confirm the view, that the twenty centuries of French and English history form but a fraction of the time which has elapsed since the stone implements of prehistoric tribes were first buried under beds of gravel and sand by the rivers now represented by the Thames or the Somme.

Still vaster, however, is the idea of antiquity suggested by the geographical conformation of such valleys as those in which these rivers flow. The drift-beds lie on their sides often 100 to 200 feet, and even more, above the present flood levels. As such highest deposits seem to mark the time when the rivers flowed at heights so far above the present channels, it follows that the drift-beds, and the men whose works they enclose, must have existed during a great part of the time occupied by the rivers in excavating their valleys down to their present beds. Granting it as possible that the rivers by which this enormous operation was performed were of greater volume and proportionately still greater power in flood-time than the present streams, which seem so utterly inadequate to their valleys, and granting also, that under different conditions of climate the causing of debacles by ground-ice may have been a powerful excavating agent, nevertheless, with all such allowances the reckoning of ages seems vastly out of proportion to historical chronology.

It is not convenient to discuss here Mr. Prestwich's division of the drift gravels into high and low level beds, nor Mr. A Tylor's argument against this division, nor he latter's theory of a Pluvial period. The geology of the Quaternary or Post-tertiary gravels, on which the geological argument for the high antiquity of man mainly rests, has been especially treated by Prestwich in the Philos. Trans. 1860, p. 277, and 1864, p. 247; see also J. Evans, Ancients Stone Impts., ch. 25; references to the writings of other geologists will be found in the already mentioned works of Lyell and Lubbock.

Beside these arguments, which suggest high antiquity rather than offer means of calculation, certain inferences (accounts of which are also given in the last-named works) have been tentatively made from the depth of mud, earth, peat, etc. which has accumulated above relics of human art imbedded in ancient times. Among these is Mr. Horner's argument from the numerous borings made in the alluvium of the Nile valley to a depth of 60 feet, where down to the lowest level fragments of burnt brick and pottery were, always found, showing that people advanced enough in the arts to bake brick and pottery have inhabited the valley during the long period required for the Nile inundations to deposit 60 feet of mud, at a rate probably not averaging more than a few inches in a century. Another argument is that of Professor von Morlot, based on a railway section through a conical accumulation of gravel and alluvium, which the torrent of the Tiniere has gradually built up where it enters the Lake of Geneva near Villeneuve. Here three layers of vegetable soil appear, proved by the objects imbedded in them to have been the successive surface-soils in two prehistoric periods and in the Roman period, and which now lie 4, 10 and 19 feet underground; on this it is computed that if 4 feet of soil were formed in the 1500 years since the Roman period, we must go 5000 years farther back for the date of the earliest human inhabitants. Calculations of this kind, loose as they are, deserve attention.

The interval between the Quaternary or Drift period and the period of historical antiquity is to some extent bridged over by relics of various intermediate civilisations, mostly of the lower grades, and in some cases reaching back to remote dates. The lake dwellings of Switzerland are perhaps among the more recent of these. They were villages of huts on piles in the water at some distance from the shore, for security from attack-in fact, fortified water settlements of the same nature as those of Lake Prasias in the time of Herodotus, and as those still inhabited in New Guinea and West Africa.

The remains of these Swiss villages are found with the stumps of the piles still standing, often imbedded in an accumulation of mud or growth of pear which has preserved a kind of illustrative museum of the arts and habits of the lake men. From examination of the sites, it appears that the settlements are of various dates, from the Neolithic or polished stone period, when instruments of metal were still unknown, to the time when bronze was introduced, and beyond this into the later age marked by the use of iron. A few of the lake villages lasted on till the roman dominion, as is proved by the presence of Roman coins and pottery, but they were soon afterwards abandoned, so that their very existence was forgotten, and their rediscovery only dates from 1853, when the workmen excavating a bed of mud on the shore of the Lake of Zurich found themselves standing among the piles of a lake settlement. In Germany, Italy, and other countries, similar remains of a long pre-Roman civilization have been found.

Indications of man's antiquity, extending farther back into prehistoric times, are furnished by the Danish shell-heaps or "kjokkenmodding," which term, meaning "kitchen refuse-heap," has been anglicized in "kitchen midden." Along the shores of nearly all the Danish islands extensive beds or low mounds, like raised beaches may be seen, consisting chiefly of innumerable cast-away shells, intermingled with bones, etc. Such shell-heaps are found in all quarters of the globe by the sea-shore, and may be sometimes seen in process of formation, they are simply the accumulations of shells and refuse thrown away near the huts of rude tribes subsisting principally on shell-fish. The Danish kitchen middens, however, are proved to belong to a very ancient time, by the remains of the quadrupeds, birds, and fish, which served as the food of these rude hunters and fishers; among these are bones of the wild bull, beaver, seal, and great auk, all now extinct or rare in this region. Moreover, a striking proof of the antiquity of these shell-heaps is, that the shells of the common oyster are found of full size, whereas it cannot live at present in the brackish waters of the Baltic except near its entrance, so that it is inferred that the shores where the oyster at that time flourished were open to the salt sea.

Thus, also, the eatable cockle, mussel, and periwinkle abounding in the kitchen middens are of full ocean size, whereas those now living in the adjoining waters are dwarfed to a third of their natural size by the want of saltness. It thus appears that the connection between the ocean and the Baltic has notably changed since the time of these rude stone-age people. Various other evidence is adduced in this part of the argument, such as that from the Danish peat-mosses, which show the existence of man at a time when the Scotch fir was abundant; at a later period the firs were succeeded by oaks, which have again been almost superseded by beeches, a succession of changes which indicate a considerable lapse of time. For further references to special accounts, the reader may consult the already mentioned general works on the antiquity of prehistoric man.

Lastly, chronicles and documentary records, taken in connection with archaeological relics of the historical period, carry back into distant ages the starting-point of actual history, behind which lies the evidently vast period only known by inferences from the relations of languages and the stages of development of civilization. Thus, Egypt affords some basis for estimating a minimum date for its Ancient population. The hieroglyphic inscriptions, the most ancient written records of the world, preserve direct memorials of a time which can hardly be less, and may be much more, than 3000 years before the Christian era. With all the doubt which besets the attempt to extract a definite chronology from the Egyptian names of kings and lists of dynasties (see EGYPT), their salient points fit with the historical records of other nations. Thus, the great Ramesside dynasty, known among Egyptologists as the 19th dynasty, corresponds with the mention of the building of the city of Raamses in Exod. I. 11; Amenophis III., called by the Greeks Memnon, belongs to the previous 18th dynasty; while the three pyramid kings, whom Herodotus mentions as Cheops, Chephren, and Mykerinos, and whose actual Egyptian names are read in the hieroglyphic lists as Chufu, Chafra, and Menkaura, are set down in the 4th dynasty. Lepsius may not be over-estimating when he dates this dynasty back as far as 3124 B.C., and carries the more dubious previous dynasties back to 3892 B.C. before reaching what are known as the mythical dynasties, which probably have their bases rather in astronomical calculations than in history.

The Greeks of the classic period could discuss the Egyptian chronologies with priests and scribes who perpetuated the languages and records of their earliest dynasties; and as the Septuagint translation of the Bible was made at Alexandria, it is not impossible that its giving to man a considerably greater antiquity than that of the Hebrew text may have been due to the influence of the Egyptian chronology. Even if the lowest admissible calculations be taken, this will not invalidate the main fact, that above 4000 years ago the Egyptian nation already stood at a high level of industrial and social culture. The records of several other nations show that as early or not much later than this they had attained to a national civilization. The Bible, whose earliest books are among the earliest existing chronicles, shows an Israelite nation existing in a state of patriarchal civilization previous to the already mentioned time of contact with Egypt. In ancient Chaldaea, the inscribed bricks of Urukh's temples probably belong to a date beyond 2000 years B.C.

The Chinese dynasties, like those of Egypt, begin with an obviously mythical portion, and continue into actual history; the difficulty is to draw the line where genuine record begins. Those who reckon authentic history only from, the dynasty of Chow, beginning about 1100 B.C. during which Confucius lived, will at any rate hardly deny the existence of the earlier dynasty of Shang, previous to which the yet earlier dynasty of Hea is recorded; so that, though much that is related of these periods may be fabulous, it seems certain that there was a Chinese nation and a Chinese civilization reaching back beyond 2000 B.C.

Till of late it was a commonly received opinion that the early state of society was one of comparatively high culture, and those who held this opinion felt no difficulty in assigning the origin of man to a time but little beyond the range of historical records and monuments. At present, however, the view has become paramount that the civilization of the world has been gradually developed from an original stone-age culture, such as characterizes modern savage life. To hold this opinion necessitates the adding to the 4000 or 5000 years to which the ancient civilizations of Egypt, Babylon, and China date back, a probably much greater length of time, during which the knowledge, arts, and institutions of these countries attained to their remarkably high level.

The evidence of comparative philology corroborates this judgment. Thus, Hebrew and Arabic are closely related languages, neither of them the original of the other, but both sprung from some parent language more ancient than either. When, therefore, the Hebrew records have carried back to the most ancient admissible date the existence of the Hebrew language, this date must have been long preceded by that of the extinct parent language of the whole Semitic family; while this again was no doubt the descendant of languages slowly shaping themselves through ages into this peculiar type. Yet more striking is the evidence of the Aryan or Indo-European family of languages. The Hindus, Medes, Persians, Greeks, Romans, Germans, Kelts, and Slaves make their appearance at more or less remote dates as nations separate in language as in history.

Nevertheless, it is now acknowledged that at some far remoter time, before these nations were divided from the parent stock, and distributed over Asia and Europe by the Aryan dispersion, a single barbaric people stood as physical and political representative of the nascent Ayran race, speaking a now extinct Aryan language, from which, by a series of modifications not to be estimated as possible within many thousands of years, there arose languages which have been mutually unintelligible since the dawn of history, and between which it was only possible for an age of advanced philology to trace the fundamental relationship.

From the combination of these considerations, it will be seen that the farthest date to which documentary record extends, is now generally regarded by anthropologists as but the earliest distinctly visible point of the historic period, beyond which stretches back a vast indefinite series of prehistoric ages.

LANGUAGE

In examining how the science of language bears on the general problems of anthropology, it is not necessary to discuss at length the critical questions which arise, the principal of which are considered elsewhere. Philology is especially appealed to by anthropologists as contributing to the following lines of argument. A primary mental similarity of all branches of the human race is evidence by their common faculty of speech, while at the same time secondary diversities of race-character and history are marked by difference of grammatical structure and of vocabularies. The existence of groups or families of allied languages, each group being evidently descended from a single language, affords one of the principal aids in classifying nations and races. The adoption by one language of words originally belonging to another, proving as it does the fact of intercourse between two races, and even to some extent indicating the results of such intercourse, affords a valuable clue through obscure regions of the history of civilization.

Communication by gesture-signs, between persons unable to converse in vocal language, is an effective system of expression common to all mankind. Thus, the signs used to ask a deaf and dumb child about his meals and lessons, or to communicate with a savage met in the desert about game or enemies, belong to codes of gesture-signals identical in principle, and to a great extend independent both of nationality and education; there is even a natural syntax, or order of succession, in such gesture-signs. To these gestures let there be added the use of the interjectional cries, such as oh! Ugh! Hey! And imitative sounds to represent the cat's mew, the click of a trigger, the clap or thud of a blow, etc. The total result of this combination of gesture and significant sound will be a general system of expression, imperfect but serviceable, and naturally intelligible to all mankind without distinction of race.

Nor is such a system of communication only theoretically conceivable; it is, and always has been, in practical operation between people ignorant of one another's language, and as such is largely used in the intercourse of savage tribes. It is true that to some extent these means of utterance are common to the lower animals, the power of expressing emotion by cries and tones extending far down in the scale of animal life, while rudimentary gesture-signs are made by various mammals and birds. Still, the lower animals make no approach to the human system of natural utterance by gesture-signs and emotional imitative sounds, while the practical identity of this human system among races physically so unlike as the Englishman and the native of the Australian bush, indicates extreme closeness of mental similarity throughout the human species.

When, however, the Englishman and the Australian speak each in his native tongue, only such words as belong to the interjectional and imitative classes will be naturally intelligible, and as it were instinctive to both. Thus the savage, uttering the sound waow! As an explanation of surprise and warning, might be answered by the white man with the not less evidently significant sh! Of silence, and the two speakers would be on common ground when the native indicated by the name bwirri his cudgel, flung whirring through the air at a flock of birds, or when the native described as a jackal-yakkal the bird called by the foreigner a cockatoo.

With these, and other very limited classes of natural words, however, resemblance in vocabulary practically ceases. The Australian and English languages each consist mainly of a series of words having no apparent connection with the ideas they signify, and differing utterly; of course, accidental coincidence and borrowed words must be excluded from such comparisons. It would be easy to enumerate other languages of the world, such as Basque, Turkish, Hebrew, Malay, Mexican, all devoid of traceable resemblance to Australian and English, and to one another. There is, moreover, extreme difference in the grammatical structure both of words and sentences in various languages. The question then arises, how far the employment of different vocabularies, and that to a great extent on different grammatical principles, is compatible with similarity of the speaker's minds, or how far does diversity of speech indicate diversity of mental nature? The obvious answer is, that the power of using words as signs to express thoughts with which their sound does not directly connect them, in fact as arbitrary symbols, is the highest grade of the special human faculty in language, the presence of which binds together all races of mankind in substantial mental unity. The measure of this unity is, that any child of any race can be brought up to speak the language of any other race.

To ascertain the causes to which languages owe their unlikeness in material and structure, how far to essential differences of mental type among the races of mankind, and how far to minor causes of variation, which may be called secondary, is a problem of extreme difficulty, towards the precise solution of which little has yet been done. One of the most remarkable of linguistic differences is the tendency of some languages to isolate their words, and of others to form elaborate inflexions. The extremes may be seen, on the one hand, in an ordinary Chinese sentence of isolated monosyllables, such as "yutsze nien chiu, tsin, tung chu," etc., i.e. "in this year autumn ended, winter begun," etc.; and, on the other hand, in one of the monstrous polysyllables into which the Greenlanders will agglutinate a whole phrase, inilertorniarpathlasargqorpa, i.e. "he will probably try too much to get it done soon." Among languages which form grammatical combinations or inflexions, the modes of so doing are as various as possible.

Thus, in Africa, the Hottentot noun forms its plural by a suffix, as khoi, "man;" khoin, "men;" while the Zulu employs prefixes to distinguish its numbers, as umu-ntu, " a man;" aba-ntu, "men." The Dinka may supply examples of forming the plural by internal change, ran, "man;" ror, "men." Nor are the differences of syntax in different tongues less absolute. In non-inflecting languages one of the most vital points is the relative position of two nouns, of which the one stands as substantive, and the other as defining it by an attribute. This may be illustrated by English compounds, such as work-house and house-work. Here our rule is to place the attribute-noun first, while, of two neighbouring language of Asia, the Burmese and the Siamese, the one settles this question in our way, the other in exactly the opposite. The Siamese expression for sailors, luk rua, means "sons of the ship," just as the Burmese expression for villagers, rwa tha, means "children of the village;" but in the first case the construction is "sons ship," whereas in the second it is "village children." Again, for reasons not yet fully explained, some languages place the adjective before the substantive, as Chinese pe ma, "white horse;" while other languages reserve this construction, as Maori, rakau roa, "tree long" (i.e., tall tree). These are but examples of possible divergences in linguistic structure, and no prudent ethnologist would assert that racial peculiarities have nothing to do with such various tendencies.

At the same time, there is no proof but that they may have resulted from historical circumstances more or less independently of race. Our own Aryan family of nations and languages affords what must always be prominent evidence in this argument. It is acknowledged that Sanskrit, Russian, Greek, Latin, Welsh, English, etc., are, philological speaking, dialects of a single Aryan speech, which no doubt at some ancient period was spoken by a single tribe or nation. Yet the languages sprung from this original Aryan tongue, by various courses of development and accretion, are mutually unintelligible. If a Greek sentence be taken at random, such as this, and it be translated even too verbally into English. "A counsel-bearing man ought not to sleep all night," the traces of linguistic connection between the Greek and English words (phoros, bear; nux, night) are hardly perceptible except to philologists.

Even the essential character of the two languages is seen to be different, for the construction of the Greek sentence depends mainly on the inflexions of the words, while in English such inflexions are almost discarded, and their effect is produced by the syntax an the auxiliary particles. Moreover, as to some most important points of syntax, Aryan languages differ widely from one another thus, to use a familiar instance, French and English take contradictory lines as to the relative position of the adjective and substantive, as also of the object-pronoun and verb,-"c'est un cheval blanc, je le vois," "it is a white horse, I see him." So Hindustani and English, though both Aryan tongues, reverse the positions of the verb and object, as "ghora lao" ("horse bring"), i.e. "bring the horse!" Thus on the whole, the endless variety in vocabulary and structure among the languages of the world affords important evidence as to the mental diversities of the nations speaking those languages. But the unity of the faculty of speech in man stands as the primary fact, while the character of the grammar and dictionary belonging to any one nation represents only a secondary fact, such as might be fairly set down as resulting from their particular stage and circumstances of linguistic development.

The principles of the development of a family of languages from a single parent tongue are laid down elsewhere. It has here to be noticed that the evidence on which such linguistic groups may be treated as allied by descent is of various degrees of fullness and strength. The most perfect available case is that of the Romance languages, comprising Italian, Spanish, French etc., inasmuch as not only does the classic Latin remain substantially the representative of their common original, but the very stages of their development from it are preserved in documents of successive ages. Thus, in comparing the vocabularies of Italian and French, it is, in the first place, seen that they to a great extent correspond,- this corresponding extending to words which one language is least likely to borrow from another, viz., pronouns, the lower numerals, and names of the most universal and familiar objects.

It is only, however, by etymological analysis that their depth of correspondence comes fully into view, it being seen that the ultimate elements or roots are largely common to the two languages, as are also the grammatical affixes by which words are formed from these roots, while general similarity of linguistic structure pervades both tongues. Such intimate correspondence could only result from derivation from a common parent language, which in this case exists in Latin. In other groups of languages the existence of the common parent may be inferred from correspondence of this highest order. Thus there must have existed, at some period, what may be called the parent Slavonic, whence descend the Russian, Polish, Bohemian, etc.,; and the parent Keltic, whence descend Welsh, Gaelic, Breton, etc., while behind the various branches of the whole Aryan family are dimly to be discerned the outlines of a primitive Aryan speech. In like manner, a comparison of the Arabic, Hebrew, Syriac, etc., shows that these must be all derived from a primitive Semitic speech, containing many of the simple root forms, which still exist in its modern descendants, and being already characterized by the principle of internal inflexion.

Beyond the limits of these two, the most important linguistic families, various others have been satisfactorily made out, though hardly with the same completeness of proof. In the Turanian or Tatar family are included the Turkish, Mongo, Hungarian, Finnish, Ostyak, etc.; the Dravidian family takes in the Tamil, Telugu, and various other South Indian dialects; the Polynesian family comprises the languages of the higher race of the South Sea Islands; the Negro-Kafir family consists of the prefixing languages spoken by most African tribes from the equatorial regions southward; the Guareni family in South America, the Algonquin and Athapascan families in North America, and the Australia family, each includes a number of tribes ranging over a vast extent of territory, and so on. As to smaller divisions, it is common for languages to occur in groups of several connected dialects, though not forming part of one of the wider linguistic families; thus the Aztec and Nicaraguan are closely related dialects, as are the Quichua and Aymara, while what philologists describe as isolated languages, as the Basque appears to be, are rather isolated groups of dialects, with no known analogues beyond a limited district.

If the present state of the philological classification of mankind be compared with that of half a century ago, it will be seen that much progress has been made in referring groups of language each to a common ancestral tongue. At the same time, greater cogency of proof is now demanded in such classification. The method of comparing a short vocabulary of twenty words or so in two languages is now abandoned, for where an extensive connection really exists, this is much better proved by a systematic comparison, while a few imperfect resemblances in the two lists might be due to accident, or the adoption of words. Nothing short of a similarity in the roots or elements of two languages, as well as in their grammatical structure, too strong to be explained by any independent causes, is now admitted as valid proof of common descent. This limitation, however, by no means amounts to a denial of the possibility of such descent. Thus it is often argued, on the strength of some similarities between Hebrew and Indo-

European roots, that the two so distinct Semitic and Aryan families of language are themselves sprung from some yet some remotely ancient tongue. Thus also it has been attempted to connect the Malay and Tatar groups of languages. Either or both of these opinions may be true; but the general verdict of philologists is, that they are not satisfactorily made out, and therefore cannot be recognized.

Under the present standard of evidence in comparing languages and tracing allied groups to a common origin, the crude speculations as to a single primeval language of mankind, which formerly occupied so much attention, are acknowledged to be worthless. Increased knowledge and accuracy of method have as yet only left the way open to the most widely divergent suppositions. For all that known dialects prove to the contrary, on the other hand, there may have been one primitive language, from which the descendant languages have varied so widely, that neither their words nor their formation now indicate their unity in long past ages, while, on the other hand, the primitive tongues of mankind may have been numerous, and the extreme unlikeness of such languages as Basque, Chinese, Peruvian, Hottentot, and Sanskrit, may arise from absolute independence of origin.

The language spoken by any tribe or nation is not of itself absolute evidence as to its race-affinities. This is clearly shown in extreme cases. Thus the Jews in Europe have almost lost the use of Hebrew, but speak as their vernacular the language of their adopted nation, whatever it may be; even the Jewish-German dialect, though consisting so largely of Hebrew words, is philologically German, as any sentence shows: "Ich hab noch hojom lo geachelt," " I have not yet eaten to-day." The mixture of the Israelities in European by marriage with other nations is probably much greater than is acknowledged by them; yet, on the whole, the race has been preserved with extraordinary strictness, as its physical characteristics sufficiently show. Language thus here fails conspicuously as a test of race, and even of national history.

Not much less conclusive is the case of the predominantly Negro populations of the West India Islands, who, nevertheless, speak a their native tongues dialects of English or French, in which the number of intermingled native African words is very scanty: "Dem hitti netti na ini watra bikasi dem de fisiman," "They cast a net into the water, because they were fishermen." "Bef pas ca jamain lasce poter cones li;" "Le boeuf n'est jamais las de porter ses cornes." If it be objected that the linguistic conditions of these two races are more artificial than has been usual in the history of the world, less extreme cases may be seen in countries where the ordinary results of conquest-colonisations have taken place. The Mestizos, who from so large a fraction of the population of modern Mexico, numbering several millions, afford a convenient test in this respect, inasmuch as their intermediate complexion separates them from both their ancestral races, the Spaniard, and the chocolate-brown indigenous Aztec, or other Mexican.

The mother-tongue of this mixed race is Spanish, with an infusion of Mexican words; and a large proportion cannot speak any native dialect. In most or all nations of mankind, crossing or intermarriage of races has thus taken place between the conquering invader and the conquered native, so that the language spoken by the nation may represent the results of conquest as much or more than of ancestry. The supersession of the Keltic Cornish by English, and of the Slavonic Old-Prussian by German, are but examples of a process which has for untold ages been supplanting native dialects, whose very names have mostly disappeared. On the other hand, the language of the warlike invader or peaceful immigrant may yield, in a few generation, to the tongue of the mass of the population, as the Northman's was replaced by French, and modern German gives way to English in the United States. Judging, then, by the extirpation and adoption of languages within the range of history, it is obvious that to classify mankind into races, Aryan, Semitic, Turanian, Polynesian, Kafir, etc., on the mere evidence of language, is an intrinsically unsound method. From the earliest times in which nations have been classified by languages, its unrestricted use has vitiated sound ethnology.

Nevertheless, under proper restrictions, speech affords information as to the affinities of races only second in value to the derived from physical characteristics. As a rule, language at least proves some proportion of ancestry. It could hardly happen that one people should come into so close a relation to another as to supplant its language, without strong intermixture of race in the next generation. This is true in the extreme case of the West Indian coloured population, among whom the majority are now crossed with European blood, so that in each succeeding generation the proportion of absolutely pure Negro families becomes less. Still more fully is it true of coloured races in Mexico or Brazil, whose Spanish or Portuguese language represents at least a large European element pf ancestry.

Thus in India many millions of people, whose blood is predominantly that of the darker indigenous race, nevertheless speak dialects of the languages of the fairer Aryans; but then they are for the most part distinctly mixed races of partly Aryan ancestry. With these facts before us, it is not difficult to determine the principles on which the ethnologist may use language as partial evidence of race. In the first place, it strengthens the evidence of bodily characters. Thus in South Africa the Zulu seems by colour, features, shape of skull, etc., to be, if not an absolute Negro, of a mixed and modified Negro type. This view of his origin is strengthened by the fact that the Zulu language belongs to the peculiar prefixing family which extends so widely among the Negro nations farther north. So the Hottentot language, in its evident connection with that of the Bushmen, adds its weight to the physical argument, that these two are descendants more or less mixed and varied from a single race, small, yellow, crisp-haired, and speaking an inflectional monosyllabic language, articulated with clicks. In the second place, language may prove race-connection where bodily characteristics, though they do not contradict, do not suffice.

Thus, comparing the dark Andalusian with the fair Swede, we ask the question, whether there is distinguishable common parentage between these two varieties of the white man? The anatomist might hesitate here. Nor, indeed, is the physical problem nearly solved, but at least a partial solution is involved in the philologist's proof that the two peoples speak languages inherited at some remote period from a common Aryan tongue, and must therefore have had a common element in their ancestry of at least sufficient strength to carry language with it. Thus each linguistic family affords at least partial evidence of race, proving, for instance, the existence of a common ancestry of the Irishman and the Russian, of the Jew and the Maltese, of the Tahitian and the Malagasy, though in such pairs of races the actual amount of common ancestry may be less than that of the different race-elements with which it has combined.

As regarded political nationality and the history of civilization, the evidence of speech is of still greater weight. In many cases of the mixture of nations the language of the dominant civilization prevails, as where Latin dialects superseded the native tongues in Western Europe, and Germanic languages encroached on Turanian in Finland, on Slavonic in Russia, and on Keltic in the Scotch Highlands. In other cases, where one nation has received elements of civilization from another, language is apt to keep record of the process by adopting foreign words and ideas together. Thus the language of the barbarian Turks has absorbed masses of Arabic, which itself had in like manner absorbed Persian, when Persia was the fountain-head of early Moslem culture.

In the same manner Dravidian languages of South India have been saturated with words and phrases from Sanskrit and its related dialects, so that a page of Tamil literature is of itself the proof of a non-Aryan race having received from an Aryan race a whole system of religion, philosophy, and social order. The most extreme cases of such verbal indication of foreign influence are to be found in languages of low races of America and the Pacific, which have adopted from European languages not only terms for imported arts and ideas, but names of such numerals 6 and 7, previously expressed by more clumsy native combinations. Thus the language of any people, though less effective than was once believed as a means of determining its place in the classified order of mankind, does, to some extent, indicate its physical, and, to a still greater extent, its intellectual ancestry.

DEVELOPMENT OF CIVILIZATION

The conditions of man at the lowest and highest known levels of culture are separated by a vast interval; but this interval is so nearly filled by known intermediate stages, that the line of continuity between the lowest savagery and the highest civilization is unbroken at any critical point. The Australians and forest Indians of Brazil may be taken as the lowest modern savages whose thought and life have been investigated with any thoroughness; while other less accurately-studied tribes are in some respects inferior even to these.

An examination of the details of savage life shows not only that there is an immeasurable difference between the rudest man and the highest lowest animal, but also that the least cultured savages have themselves advanced far beyond the lowest intellectual and moral state at which human tribes can be conceived as capable of existing, when placed under favourable circumstances of warm climate, abundant food, and security from too severe destructive influences. In fact, the Australian or Brazilian savage has already attained to rudimentary stages in many of the characteristic functions of civilized life. His language, expressing thoughts by conventional articulate sounds, is the same in essential principle as the most cultivated philosophic dialect, only less exact and copious. His weapons, tools, and other appliances, such as the hammer, hatchet, spear, knife, awl, thread, net, canoe, etc., are the evident rudimentary analogues of what still remains in use among Europeans. His structure, such as the hut, fence, stockade, earthwork, etc., may be poor and clumsy, but they are of the same nature as our own. In the simple arts of broiling and roasting meat, the use of hides and furs for covering, the plaiting of mats and baskets, the devices of hunting, trapping, and fishing, the pleasure taken in personal ornament, the touches of artistic decoration on objects of daily use, the savage differs in degree but not in kind from the civilized man.

The domestic and social affections, the kindly care of the young and the old, some acknowledgement of martial and parental obligation, the duty of mutual defence in the tribe, the authority of the elders, and general respect to traditional custom as the regulator of life and duty, are more or less well marked in every savage tribe which is not disorganized and falling to pieces. Lastly, there is usually to be discerned amongst such lower races a belief in unseen powers pervading the universe, this belief shaping itself into an animistic or spiritualistic theology, mostly resulting in some kind of worship. If, again, high savage or low barbaric types be selected, as among the North American Indians, Polynesians, and Kafirs of South Africa, the same elements of culture appear, but at a more advanced stage, namely, a more full and accurate language, more knowledge of the laws of nature, more serviceable implements, more perfect industrial processes, more definite and fixed social order and frame of government, more systematic and philosophic schemes of religion, and a more elaborated and ceremonial worship. At intervals new arts and ideas appear, such as agriculture and pasturage, the manufacture of pottery, the use of metal implements, and the device of record and communication by picture writing. Along such stages of improvement and invention the bridge is fairly made between savage and barbaric culture; and this once attained to, the remainder of the series of stages of civilization lies within the range of common knowledge.

The teaching of history, during the three to four thousand years of which contemporary chronicles have been preserved, is that civilization is gradually developed in the course of ages by enlargement and increased precision of knowledge, invention and improvement of arts, and the progression of social and political habits and institutions towards general well-being. The conditions of such races ads the older Jews, Greeks, and Germans, are known to us by ancient chronicles, and by poetry and myth even more valuable than chronicle in the details they unconsciously preserve of the state of society at the time whence they have been handed down. Starting from the recorded condition of such barbaric nations, and following the general course of culture into the modern world, all the great processes of mental an social development may be seen at work. Falling back or decay also takes place, but only to a limited extent destroys the results of growth in culture.

It is thus matter of actual record, that the ancestors of civilized nations were barbaric tribes, and the inference seems reasonable that the same process of development had gone on during previous ages outside the domain of direct history, so that barbaric culture itself arose out of an earlier and ruder condition of primitive culture, more or less corresponding with the state of modern savage tribes. The failure of direct record of this passage from savagery upward to barbarism was to be expected from the circumstances of the case. No people civilized enough to preserve history could have watched the age-long process of a savage tribe developing its culture; indeed, experience shows that independent progress could hardly have taken place among an uncivilized in contact with a civilized race.

Nor could a barbaric nation, though it had really and independent risen from savagery within some few thousand years, give any valid account of this gradual advancement, for the very reason of its having taken place while the nation was yet in, or but little removed from, the savage state, one part of the very definition of which is that it has no trustworthy means of preserving the history of events even for a single century, much less for the long period required for so vast a development. This view of the low origin and progressive development of civilization was already held in ancient times, as in the well-known speculations of the Epicurean school on the condition of the earliest men, who roved like wild animals, seeking their food from the uncultured earth, till arts and social laws arose among them; or where the like idea has taken in China the form of ancient legend, recording the time when their nation was taught to use skins for clothing, to make fire and to dwell in houses (Pauthier, Livres Sacres de.

In opposition to such views of primeval rudeness, traditions of a pristine state of human excellence have long been cherished, such as the "golden age." Till of late wide acceptance has been given to arguments, partly based on theological and partly on anthropological grounds, as to man's incapability of rising from a savage state, and the consequent necessity of a supernatural bestowal of culture on the first men, from whose high level savages are supposed by advocates of this theory to have degenerated. The anthropological evidence adduced in support of this doctrine is, however, too weak for citation, and even obviously erroneous arguments have been relied on. It has been especially the evidence of prehistoric archaeology which, within the last few years, has given to the natural development-theory of civilization a predominance hardly disputed on anthropological grounds. The stone implements, which form the staple proof of man's existence at the period of the river-drift, are of extreme rudeness as compared even with ordinary savage types, so that it is obvious that the most ancient known tribes were, as to be industrial arts, at a low savage level.

The remains in the caverns justify this opinion, especially where in central France more precision is given to the idea of prehistoric life by the discovery of bone weapons for hunting and fishing, which suggest a rude condition resembling that of the Esquimaux. The finding of ancient stone implements buried in the ground in almost every habitable district of the world, including the seats of the great ancient civilizations, such as Egypt, Assyria, India, China, Greece, etc., may be adduced to show that the inhabitants of these regions had at some time belonged to the stone age. This argument goes far to prove that the ancestors of all nations, high and low, were once in that uncultured condition as to knowledge, arts, and manners generally, which within our experience accompanies the use of stone implements and the want of metals. No valid refutation of this reasoning has been offered, and it is corroborated by arguments to be drawn from study of the facts of civilization, of which some will be here mentioned for their bearing on the theory of development.

History shows how development of the arts takes place by efforts of skill and insight, as where Phidias rose above the clumsier sculptors of the time before him, or where the earliest gnomon-a mere staff set up in order to have its shadow measured-passed into the graduated sun-dial; or adaptations of old contrivances produce new results, as when the ancient Pan's pipes, blown by a bellows, became the organ, when the earlier block-printing led up to the use of movable types, and when the magnetic-needle was taken out of the mariner's compass to find a new office on the telegraph-dial; or lastly, more absolutely original inventions arise, the triumphs of the scientific imagination, such as the pendulum and the steam-engine. In the evolution of science the new knowledge ever starts from the old, whether its results to be improve, to shift, 0r to supersede it.

The history of astronomy extends far enough back to show its barbaric stages, when the earth was regarded as a flat surface, over-arched by a solid dome or firmament; and when not only was the sun considered to move round the earth, but its motions, as well as the moons, were referred to the guidance and even the impulse of personal deities. Beginning with this first stage of the science, there lies before us the whole record of the exacter observation and closer reasoning which have gradually replaced these childlike savage conceptions by the most perfect of physical theories.

Thus, again, the history of medicine shows improvement after improvement on the rude surgical appliances and the meager list of efficient drugs which the barbaric leech had at his disposal, while its theory has changed even more absolutely than its practice; for medical history begins with the ancient world holding fast to the savage doctrine that madness, epilepsy, fever, and other diseases, are caused by demons possessing the patient--a belief which is still that of half the human race, but which it has been the slow but successful ask of scientific pathology to supersede in the civilized world.

In like manner, the history of judicial and administrative institutions may be appealed to for illustrations of the modes in which old social formations are reshaped to meet new requirements, new regulations are made, and new officers are constituted to perform the more complex duties of modern society, while from time to time institutions of past ages, which have lost their original purpose, and become obsolete and hurtful, are swept away.

--That processes of development similar to these had already been effective to raise culture from the savage to the barbaric level, two considerations especially tend to prove. First, there are numerous points in the culture even of rude races which are not explicable otherwise than on the theory of development. Thus, though difficult or superfluous arts may easily be lost, it is hard to imagine the abandonment of contrivances of practical daily utility, where little skill is required, and materials are easily accessible. Had the Australians or New Zealanders, for instance, ever possessed the potter's art, they could hardly have forgotten it.

The inference that these tribes represent the stage of culture before the invention of pottery is confirmed by the absence of buried fragments of pottery in the districts they inhabit. The same races who were found making thread by the laborious process of twisting with the hand, would hardly have disused, if they had ever possesses it, so simple a labour-saving device as the spindle, which consists merely of a small stick weighted at one end; the spindle may, accordingly, be regarded as an instrument invented somewhere between the lowest and highest savage levels.

Again, many devices of civilization bear unmistakable marks of derivation from a lower source; thus the ancient Egyptian and Assyrian harps, which differ from ours in having no front pillar, appear certainly to owe this remarkable defect to having grown up through intermediate forms from the simple strung bow, the still used type of the most primitive stringed instrument. In this way the history of numeral words furnishes actual proof of that independent intellectual progress among savage tribes which some writer shave rashly denied.

Such words as hand, hands, foot, man, etc., are used as numerals signifying 5, 10, 15 20, etc., among many savage and barbaric peoples; thus Polyesian lima, i.e. "hand," mean 6; Greenlandish, arfersanek-pingasut, i.e. "on the other foot three," means 18; Tamanc, tevin itoto, i.e., "one man," means 20 etc., etc. The existence of such expressions demonstrates that the people who use them had originally no spoken names for these numbers, but one merely counted them by gesture on their fingers and toes in low savage fashion, till they obtained higher numerals by the inventive process of describing in words these counting-gestures.

Second, the process of "survival in culture" has caused the preservation in each stage of society of phenomena belonging to an earlier period, but kept up by force of custom into the later, thus supplying evidence of the modern condition being derived from the ancient.

Thus the mitre over a English bishop's coat-of-arms is a survival which indicates him as the successor of bishops who actually wore mitres, while armorial bearings themselves, and the whole craft of heraldry, are survival bearing record of a state of warfare and social order whence our present state was by vast modification evolved. Evidence of this class, proving the derivation of modern civilization, not only from ancient barbarism, but beyond this, from primeval savagery, is immensely plentiful, especially in rites and ceremonies, where the survival of ancient habits is peculiarly favoured.

Thus the modern Hindu though using civilized means for lighting his household fire, retains the savage "fire-drill" for obtaining fire by friction of wood when what he considers pure or sacred fire has to be produced for sacrificial purposes; while in Europe into modern times the same primitive process has been kept up in producing the sacred and magical "need-fire," which was lighted to deliver cattle from a murrain. Again, the funeral offerings of food, clothing, weapons, etc., to the dead are absolutely intelligible and purposeful among savage races, who believe that the souls of the departed are ethereal beings, capable of consuming food, and of receiving and using the souls or phantoms of any objects sacrificed for their use.

The primitive philosophy to which these conceptions belong has to a great degree been discredited by modern science; yet the clear survivals of such ancient and savage rites may still be seen in Europe, where the Bretons leave the remains of the All Souls' supper on the table for the ghosts of the dead kinsfolk to partake of, and Russian peasants set out cakes for the ancestral manes on the ledge which supports the holy pictures, and make dough ladders to assist the ghosts of the dead to ascend out of their graves and start on their journey for the future world; while other provision for the same spiritual journey is made when the coin is still put in the hand of the corpse at an Irish wake. In like manner magic still exists in the civilized world as a survival from the savage and barbaric times to which it originally belongs, and in which is found the natural source and proper home of utterly savage practices still carried on by ignorant peasants in our own country, such as taking omens from the cries of animals, or bewitching an enemy by sticking full of pins and hanging up to shrivel in the smoke an image or other object, that similar destruction may fall on the hated person represented by the symbol.

To conclude, the comparative science of civilization thus not only generalizes the data of history, but supplements its information by laying down the lines of development along which the lowest prehistoric culture has gradually risen to the highest modern level. Among the most clearly marked of these lines is that which follows the succession of the stone, bronze, and iron ages. The stone age represents the early condition of mankind in general, and has remained in savage districts up to modern times, while the introduction of metals need not at once supersede the use of the old stone hatchets and arrows, which have often long continued in dwindling survival by the side of the new bronze and even iron ones.

The bronze age had its most important place among ancient nations of Asia and Europe, and among them was only succeeded after many centuries by the iron age; while in other districts, such as Polynesia and Central and south Africa, and America (except Mexico and Peru), the native tribes were moved directly from the stone to the iron age without passing through the bronze age at all. although the three divisions of savage, barbaric, and civilized man do not correspond at all perfectly with the stone, bronze, and iron ages, the classification of civilization thus introduced by Nilsson and Thomsen has proved a guide of extraordinary value in arranging in their proper order of culture the nations of the Old World. Another great line f progress has been followed by tribes passing from the primitive state of the wild hunter, fisher, and fruit gatherer to that of the settled tiller of the soil, for to this change of habit may be plainly in great part traced the expansion of industrial arts and the creation of higher social and political institutions.

These, again, have followed their proper lines along the course of time. Among such are the immense legal development by which the primitive law of personal vengeance passed gradually away, leaving but a few surviving relics in the modern civilized world, and being replaced by the higher doctrine that crime is an offence against society, to be repressed for the public good. Another vast social change has been that from the patriarchal condition, in which the unit is the family under the despotic rule of its head, to the systems in which individuals make up a society whose government is centralized in a chief or king. In the growth of systematic civilization, the art of writing has had an influence so intense, that of all tests to distinguish the barbaric from the civilized state, none is so generally effective as this, whether they have but the failing link with the past which mere memory furnishes, or can have recourse to written records of past history and written constitutions of present order.

Lastly, still following the main lines of human culture, the primitive germs of religious institutions have to be traced in the childish faith and rude rites of savage life, and thence followed in their expansion into the vast systems administered by patriarchs and priests, henceforth taking under their charge the precepts of morality, and enforcing them under divine sanction, while also exercising in political life an authority beside or above the civil law. These illustrations may suffice to make it clear that although the science of culture is still but rudimentary and imperfect, it indicates the one sound and indispensable method for the study of human arts and institutions, that of placing each at its proper stage in a line of evolution, and explaining it by the action of new conditions upon the previous stage whence it was derived.

4

Self-Interpretation, Agency, and the Objects of Anthropology: Reflections on a Genealogy

If there is anything that exemplifies a certain common style in ethnographical-ly-oriented approaches to culture and society today, and sets them apart from other kinds of social science, it is the habit, irritating to colleagues in some oth-er disciplines, frustrating to students, deemed perverse by potential funders, and bewildering to the public, of responding to explanations with the remark, "We need to complicate the story." The words "reductionist" and "essentializing" are brandished with scorn. One important perspective is expressed by this remark by Jean and John Comaroff, two influential anthropologists with solid roots in longterm fieldwork, the sobriety of British social anthropology, and the tough-minded realism of the Marxist tradition: ethnography "refuses to put its trust in techniques that give more scientific methods their illusory objectivity: their commitment to standardized, a priori units of analysis, for example, or their re-liance on a depersonalizing gaze that separates subject from object."

These words, offered almost in passing, take a host of important arguments as settled. One is that it is no longer in much dispute that cultural anthropology is not merely at an "immature" stage, en route to something more akin to natural science. Most significant, perhaps, is the assumption that the separation of sub-ject from object can be understood only in negative terms, that to say that a field of knowledge "depersonalizes" is ipso facto to discredit it. Yet in their own ethnographic and historical work the Comaroffs take their empirical materials very seriously and do not wholly reject the separation of subject from object-how could they? What is at issue, rather, is what kinds of "objects" and "subjects," and what categories of analysis and comparison, are epistemologically appropriate and ethically legitimate for the study of social actions and self-un-derstandings.

The ultimate aim of this essay is to propose that we rethink the problem of "objectification" in the study of culture and society. A productive understand-ing of objectification should go beyond the commonplace critiques of scientism or ideological reification. It would take seriously the materiality of signifying practices and the ubiquity and necessity of conceptual objectification as a component of human action and interaction. But first I want to step back for a look at the way in which this point has come to be obscured for us. I begin by re-visiting some old arguments about the nature of culture, meaning, and social science that have become a relatively taken-for-granted background shared by opponents in more recent debates about power, identities, and the observer.

If, as I suggest, ethnographic knowledge has always been marked by a tension be-tween epistemologies of estrangement and of intimacy, the latter has increas-ingly claimed the epistemological and moral high ground in much cultural anthropology, especially in America. The result is a number of familiar dilemmas about incommensurability, comparison, translation, and the possibilities for understanding. Now, simply to dismiss these (perhaps attributing them to sup-posedly occult forces like "postmodernism") and call for a return to earlier dis-ciplinary verities is hardly a solution. This article focuses on the themes of antideterminism, meaning, agency, and particularism as they have marked American cultural anthropology in contrast to more scientistic disciplines. I want to suggest that there is more underlying unity across at least some of the battle-lines than is commonly recognized, as fractured, factionalized, and fraught as anthropology presently is.

But this unity is obscured not least be-cause its roots in certain intuitions about freedom and agency are so little ex-amined. Although the current emphasis on intimacy and engagement, and the suspicion of objectification, are associated with post-colonial critique, practice theory, deconstruction, power/knowledge, and identity politics, I argue that its roots are deeper. To the extent that certain well-trod paths in anthropology con-verge with other anti-foundationalist disciplines in an intellectual world in-formed more, say, by Nietzsche than by Comte, by the later Wittgenstein than Chomsky, they do so from a distinctive angle.

The first part of this essay sketches out some of the ways in which the reflections on a genealogy Boasian, Weberian, and Durkheimian understandings of the objects and cate-gories of socio-cultural knowledge were transformed by the interpretive and symbolic turns in cultural anthropology in the 1960s and 1970s. It then looks at two exemplary contemporary critiques of the culture concept, by Lila Abu-Lughod, and by James Ferguson and Akhil Gupta. Although both critiques are animated by problems of power, knowledge, and agency, they work toward op-posite ends of the spectrum of intimacy and estrangement. Yet they share cer-tain assumptions about meaning and determinism not only with each other, but with those whom they attack. These assumptions are shaped by an underlying, often unspoken, ethic that stresses the value of human self-determination and opposes it both to reductionism, and to mere contingency.

This essay does not pretend to be a history nor does it claim to be inclusive. Rather, it is an interested reading, which tries to draw out certain themes that run through the effort to place people's self-interpretations at the center of study, and the privileging of intimacy over estrangement as a source of legitimate understanding. By retracing the logic of some of the earlier arguments about objectivism and "the particular," I hope to clarify their contribution to the present moment. If the central part of this paper focuses on the so-called sym-bolic and interpretive turns in America, it is because their enormous impact, in light of the dominance of scientism, positivism, and functionalisms elsewhere in the social sciences, is what most needs to be understood. It does, however, begin with the intuition that many of the contemporary debates can take place, their terms of relevance making sense to the participants, only to the extent that they are predicated on certain shared assumptions and even ethical motives ev-ident in those earlier generations. If anthropology is to make a difference at the convergence among disciplines like history, cultural criticism, sociology, and others, it must understand the genealogical peculiarities it brings into the mix. By reflecting on them, anthropological work may better take responsibility not only for its ethics but also its concepts.

ANTHROPOLOGY AND THE PARTICULARS

For proponents of nomothetic models of explanation, much of cultural anthro-pology is vitiated by excessive particularity. Almost forty years ago, Marvin Harris, who advocated a positivistic science of cultural evolution, complained that "there emerged a view of culture that exaggerated all the quixotic, irra-tional, and inscrutable ingredients in human life. Delighting in diversity of pat-tern, anthropologists sought out divergent and incomparable events.... By em-phasizing inscrutable values, vain prestige, irrational motives, they discredited the economic interpretation of history. Anthropology came increasingly to con-cern itself with idiographic phenomena, that is, with the study of the unique and the nonrepetitive aspects of history."

Although the complaint concerns the American scene of an earlier genera-tion, a similar objection has been expressed by scholars of very different perspectives and generations, from contemporary France (Sperber 1996) to the En-gland of the 1950s, when the structuralist Edmund Leach remarked that "Most of my colleagues are giving up the attempt to make comparative generaliza-tions; instead they have begun to write impeccably detailed historical ethno-graphies of particular peoples" (1959:1). If anthropology can look too particu-laristic from various points of view, it also seems to persist in whatever it is doing that provokes these complaints.

Some, of course, simply take this condition to be a symptom of confusion, incoherence, or worse. But I think we need to take it seriously as an approach to knowledge. There is something about what anthropology has been doing that, for all the shifts of paradigm and the fires of internal critique, continues to pro-duce both the particularistic symptom and the theorizing complaint. If this is a dialectic, it is recurrently threatened with collapse when either side-what might be called the epistemologies of estrangement, and of intimacy-is fa-vored at the expense of the other. Although the American academy has most elaborated the side of intimacy, the basic problems are of more general relevance.

The authority of ethnographic particularity for contemporary anthropologists is famously exemplified by Clifford Geertz, who asserted a generation ago that what anthropologists do is ethnography (rather than, say, theory-building), which is "microscopic," and that "the important thing about anthropology's findings" (and not just its methods or data) "is their complex specificness, their circumstantiality" (1973a:21-23; see also Ortner 1995). But the epistemolog-ical and ethical claims of concrete particularity were already laid out with re-markable vividness in 1887 by Franz Boas, before he became one of the found-ing figures of anthropology in the United States.

Like the historian, and in contrast to the natural scientist, Boas states, the geographer does not seek general laws, but rather "the thorough understanding of the phenomena" (1940:641) as singular facts. Not only is this interest in what actually exists for its own sake a legitimate alternative to the formulation of laws, the two are even antithetical: it is precisely because "he" takes an interest in them that the his-torian "is unwilling to consider" peoples and nations "as subject to stringent laws" (1940:642). Boas here makes two distinct points at once. First, he poses as alternatives the taking of the singular as evidence for a law and the singular as worthy of attention for its own sake. Second, these are not merely perspec-tives but are in conflict, for only when peoples are taken for their own sake can they be seen as agents and thus not subject to laws.

Thus Boas can be read either to emphasize historical contingency, or human agency-and, I will sug-gest, it is the latter that has tended to prevail.

But Boas makes two further, mutually implicated claims as well. In contrast to the physicist, who analytically resolves the phenomenon into its elements, the geographer takes "The whole phenomenon, and not its elements" as the ob-ject of study. Yet the geographer's phenomena have no objective unity at all, but form "an incidental conglomerate" (geology, meteorology, and so forth);

"Their connection seems to be subjective, originating in the mind of the ob-server" (1940:642). By contrast, the physicist, in comparing elements taken out of context, "loses sight altogether of the spot from which he started" (1940:646).

Our interest is a matter of contingency: the motive of cosmography is "love for the country we inhabit" (1940:647) in contrast to the natural-ist who views the whole world disinterestedly. The Grand Canyon is interest-ing because it is exists for me, as part of my world. And its weather, color, age, and size-each of which could be analytically distinguished for purposes of comparison to those of other physical entities-form an object only insofar as they are unified within my experience. That is, the very unity of the geograph-er's object of study is conditional on the situated character of human experi-ence, which is what motivates the interest in the object in the first place. This is a very peculiar kind of knowledge, and, as I will suggest below, it en-counters serious dilemmas that are both epistemological (what kind of starting point can something as problematic as "experience" possibly offer?) and ethi-cal (whose "country" is this anyway?). But I want to propose that in this foundational moment Boas named something distinctive about a kind of knowing that might be sought by a human science which survived the demise of his own school, and that pre-disposed it toward the anti-foundationalist thought of the twentieth century. First, however, I turn to the symbolic and interpretive turns of the 1960s and 1970s.

CULTURE, CONTEXT, AND THE ENDS OF ACTION

From the 1960s onwards, an anti-reductionist reaction increasingly set the an-thropological agenda in America. Here I want to trace just a few themes through certain texts, with particular attention to the unlikely convergence among struc-turalism, Boasian culturalism, symbolic anthropology, and the interpretive turn, which developed Boas'interest in freedom at the expense of contingency.

Marshall Sahlins is an exemplary figure with whom to start because he himself made the transition from a nomothetic model of science, and because he offered a rebuttal of positivism and functionalism that did not require one to abandon an idea of objective knowledge. Moreover, his appropriation of structuralism manifests the sea-change undergone by French thought in the American con-text, as its positivistic potential was muted in favor of the symbolic turn. The study of linguistic sound systems by Boas (1910) and Edward Sapir (1925), and Ferdinand de Saussure's structuralism as elaborated by Claude Lévi-Strauss (1962), showed that entities which, in strictly empirical terms, seem to be the identical, may in fact have quite different functions when analyzed in the context of different sound systems.

It follows that no sound can even be identified independently of the linguistic system that specifies its rele-vant features. Taking this as foundational, Sahlins offers a critical difference from his teachers and contemporaries such as Marvin Harris (1968), Julian Steward (1949), or Leslie White (1949), who were trying to create a scientific anthropology. The difference does not concern the nature of the material world, causality, or the hope for objectivity. Rather, it lies in the conditions for estab-lishing identity among observed entities. The argument from language forms a direct challenge to the possibility of specifying social or cultural units across the board. This kind of analysis depends on a concept of context that presumes three things, namely, that languages are best understood as total systems, that they are clearly bounded from one another, and that the units (being only "ar-bitrarily" connected to the object world) have no functionality apart from that of the overall system of which they are a part.

Much of Sahlins'writing is a defense and elaboration of these points.

Now, since it is common for critics to label him a "cultural determinist," he would seem to present an especially hard case for my claim that human self-determination has been a core value in American cultural anthropology. It is not my purpose to rehash the many debates about his work, but simply to point out the extent to which it offers a series of arguments against any purported "ex-ternal" determinations of cultural form such as biology, ecology, or economics. Even before his full turn to structuralism, he was already arguing (1968) that some societies have opted out of the maximization of material gain in favor of greater leisure time, and therefore cultures are not adaptive according to a single standard of utility or rational choice. Culture is thus in essence excessive (it goes beyond the demands of reproduction) and irrational (since it defines the terms by which things are valued as ends, it cannot be explained in terms of mean-ends rationality).

It manifests human self-creation at the level of com-munities. If this point has become difficult to see, it is in part because the very idea of collectivities has been put in question in contemporary America. Sahlins' attack on determinism is linked to a second, logically independent, assertion, that cultures can be understood as ethical or aesthetic unities. Sahlins himself attributes his view of culture as a unified ethos to Alfred Kroeber's (1917) "superorganic," that which is distinctively human by virtue of not hav-ing "organic" or biological determinants. It is thus ironic, in view of later at-tacks on cultural holism in the name of agency, that it is precisely this unity which was supposed to provide humans with their independence from external determination. It is in the nature of moral or aesthetic ends that they impose a unity on the diverse activities to which they provide guidance.

In Sahlins' work, holism helps explain culture's non-utilitarian character. Culture cannot be a thing of "shreds and patches" (Lowie 1920:441), because those could never provide a context that would give coherence to ultimate ends. The underlying assumption is the relative underdetermination of significance. And this in turn is associated with an ontological distinction between material and conceptual that is already evident, for example, both in Kroeber and in Saussure's doctrine of the arbitrariness of the sign. That interpretation of mate-rial reality is mediated conceptually had become a commonplace.

But the sym-bolic does not simply mediate reference to the things that exist in the world (a system of categories that tells us this is blue, that green, or this a wink, that a twitch). More than that, it facilitates questions of ends and their value. Sahlins' "culture," taken as existential stances toward life, seeks to provide an account of ends. It is meant to show, for instance, that economic maximization is a choice (one rejected by his "original affluent society" [1968]), not a given, something the West is driven toward not by the facts-of-the-matter, but by an underlying vision of humans as "imperfect creature[s] of need and desire."

CULTURE IN ITS OWN TERMS

The symbolic and interpretive turns are perhaps most commonly identified with Victor Turner (1967), Mary Douglas (1966), and Clifford Geertz (1973a; 1973b), and arguments for irreducible cultural specificity are found well be-yond them (e.g. Louis Dumont 1966). I draw here on David Schneider because of the polemical sharpness and explicitness with which he articulated some of the more radical criticisms of comparison, and displayed the conceptual links among particularism, totality, and cultural value.

Schneider's attack on structural-functionalism involves five logical steps.

First is an attack on superficial empiricism and the production of simplistic models.

Second, he challenged the idea that societies lend themselves to scien-tific comparison because they fall into objectively given types.

Third, if societies are not natural things, then the categories by which they had heretofore been compared must be ethnocentric.

Fourth, if the categories are not universal, then any analysis that uses them is taking its data out of context, and instead (fifth), the appropriate context within which to make sense of cultural categories is "the cultural system." None of these steps logically requires the subsequent one.

For instance, the first criticism alone could simply have led to a call for better cate-gories and more complex models. The third could have led him to construct We-berian ideal types for analytic purposes. Instead, Schneider ends up discrediting categories, models, generalities, and comparison altogether.

The reasons for this can be seen by considering the second step, exemplified in the statement "It is too late in the history of the social sciences to think we can go out among societies and, by keeping our eyes open, sort them out into their natural classes" (1965:78). Where neo-positivism would jettison the socio-cultural level of explanation in the name of sound methods, Schneider sought to preserve the level of explanation by abandoning an inappropriate method. Indeed, he writes as if this were a foregone conclusion. The attack on empiricism as ethnocentric and thus unrealistic (that is, not true to ethnograph-ic particulars) became an attack on sociological comparison.

Instead, Schneider maintained that anthropology's purpose is the study of cultures, as "different conceptual schemes of what life is and how it should be lived" (1972:44). Notice here the implicit role of the normative: cultures are concerned with how life should be lived. Such a definition seems to express an underlying commitment to the empirical study of self-determination, insofar as cultures manifest a generic capacity to decide how to live. But in this view, the normative is above all conceptual in status-indeed, Schneider eventually took a strong position against any cultural determination of action (1976:202-3).

Formed, like Geertz, in Talcott Parsons'milieu, Schneider presumed a clear dis-tinction between social and cultural systems and insisted that culture was dis-tinct from actual behavior.

In the struggle to distinguish social from natural science, and to escape functionalism and determinism, the value-orientation I have noted was often neglected in favor of concepts. What is important about culture, here, is that it imposes meaningful (and, by implication, arbitrary) cat-egories on an otherwise meaningless and unorganized world. This is one rea-son why culture came to be identified, for some, with structure and in sharp opposition to agency. As Geertz quoted W. H. Auden, to exemplify his anti-functionalist view of culture: "Poetry makes nothing happen" (1973b:443).

With the destruction of the cross-cultural category "kinship," Schneider (1972) produced one template for post-modern particularisms within anthro-pology. Cultural categories for Schneider could only be understood in the con-text of the entire "cultural system." Though he was no structuralist, the logic is close to that of the arbitrary sign. Thus kinship or gender categories, for in-stance, cannot be compared across cultures because the apparent biological ref-erents do not reflect their articulation with other components of a given culture. It is at this juncture, in justifying the autonomy, relatively undetermined char-acter, and holism of cultures, that the potentially opposed forces of symbolic anthropology and structuralism made common cause. Schneider and Sahlins differed on much, but they shared an underlying vision that human projects are more than aleatory only to the extent that they are identified with a cultural, and thus collective, enterprise.

As I will suggest below, subsequent critics of the concept of culture attacked its totalizing character, but they commonly did so on the anti-empiricist and anti-determinist grounds that were established by these earlier arguments. And herein lies one basis for the more radical conclu-sion that cultural meanings are irreducible, and therefore potentially incom-mensurable and untranslatable. metalanguages of agency What kind of knowledge ought we to hope for from this? Perhaps the most con-ventional answer was a richer access to "meanings." One of the founding state-ments for this approach is Geertz's appropriation of Gilbert Ryles' "thick de-scription" (1973a) for anthropology and his image of the anthropologist reading a cultural text over the native's shoulder (1973b; see also Ricoeur 1971). The debates about this are well known. But I want here to draw out an aspect of these "meanings" that is sometimes neglected, their implicit relationship to ac-tion.

The philosopher Charles Taylor, in his contribution to Rabinow and Sul-livan's seminal volume, Interpretive Social Science (1987, originally 1979), gives an especially clear account of what that "text" is doing for the person's capacity to be an agent. I want to suggest that a critical reading of this account can usefully be brought to bear on subsequent critiques, especially on the as-sumptions they make about the necessarily malign effects of "objectification."

If the interpretive turn was attacked from one side for lacking the rigor of nat-ural science, it has increasingly been attacked from another side for objectify-ing and essentializing culture. But what Taylor's account should make clear, whatever its shortcomings, is that we can understand the object of interpreta-tion to be not categories and meanings per se but rather the very capacity for agency that they mediate. By extension, we can see one opening to other social dimensions of power.

Taylor defines a text as a metalanguage, an expression that captures the same meaning as some original "text analogue."

This meaning is not simply semantic or expressive, and Geertz's portrayal of culture as something like a Shakespearian drama read over the native's shoulder turns out to be a poor il-lustration, as do many efforts in more recent cultural studies to link cultural forms directly to political positions. Rather, Taylor's account of "the meaning of a situation for an agent" (1987:42) centers on the purposiveness and the self-consciousness (and implicit bracketing of contingency) that distinguish action from mere behavior, and hearkens back to Max Weber's (1968) definition of the proper object of interpretive social science as meaningful action.

What kind of object of knowledge is this? For Taylor, "descriptions [of ac-tion] are not all on the same footing" (1985:259): "As I type, I am also dis-placing air, raising the noise level in the house, wearing out typewriter ribbons, increasing the custom of our local typing supplies shop, and so on. But what I'm doing is writing a paper... " Some obvious objections: Why, after all, stop with "writing a paper"? What of seeking fame, or a promotion, or to best an op-ponent, or to make mother proud, or to avoid facing a troubled domestic life? What of expressing a bourgeois world-view or a male subject position? What of a habitus for which the writing of papers is a naturalized mode of action re-gardless of individual intentions, like, say, a ritual?

Taylor claims that ordinary language serves as a metalanguage (reflexive lan-guage about action) that both defines actions for the actor and makes them available for the interpreting outsider. Its role in defining the boundaries of ac-tion explains why interpretation is not unbounded. We need to be specific about what this metalanguage does and does not offer us. Taylor is arguing against the objectivist metalanguages of positivist social science. Therefore the crucial point is to show that actions depend on self-interpretation. In this respect, the outsider's metalanguages of class or gender, unconscious desires, and so forth are not immediately pertinent. The crucial metalanguage is that which guides the actor herself with a description of what is going on. But intuitive intro-spection is not sufficient, for that description must be drawn from a vocabulary of actions shared with others, and it comes into play when one is accounting for one's own actions to them. Shared language provides a "public space, or com-mon vantage point" (1985:273; cf. 1987:59-61) that persons can share and know that they share. The alternative descriptions I have just offered may count as descriptions of someone else but they are not likely to function either in the agent's own self-accounting or in her sense of being with others.

A generation later, however, those who take the question of objectivism as settled may ask different questions of this account. First, who owes an account to whom? The existence of a shared moral domain, Taylor's "public," and the conditions that call for an accounting have become unobvious. If accounting to others is interaction, it is likely to occur between people with unequal capaci-ties and claims on one another, their very status as "insiders" to the same com-munity potentially subject to question. Second, the existence of a moral domain does not guarantee shared descriptions of action. The husband who insists on his conjugal rights confronts the wife who fears domestic rape, the joker's "fun" is the victim's "ethnic slur."

Third, as the development of the category "do-mestic rape" suggests, the contest of interpretations involves a historical dy-namic, in which, for example, emergent descriptions will have "looping ef-fects" (Hacking 1994) as they provide actors with new kinds of action. Finally, "culture's" relation to "society" is altered from the sharp distinction maintained by Parsonians if, as Taylor implies, it is not just sharing a culture but awareness of sharing it that forms a pragmatic condition for having a community (Urban 2001) or a public (Appadurai 1996) in the first place.

The actions that most concern Taylor are those that require terminology like "shame" and thus "a certain language of mutual action and communication by which we blame, exhort, admire, esteem each other" (1987:43). By acting we make ourselves available to evaluations by others. Hence cultural interpreta-tion is possible because the interpreter, theoretically, has available the very same interpretive possibilities that the insider has (1987:46). They cannot, at least in principle, be radically "other" to one another-at least as long as the interpreter situates herself within the moral sphere defining the actor's "public."

At this point Taylor's account captures some essential strengths and weak-nesses of the interpretive turn in its heyday. By showing that the local relevant terms for self-interpretation are necessary conditions for action, he helps fill out the argument for the particular. Local metalanguages demand an epistemology of intimacy. Indeed, they demand more, for it is not just a question of "per-spective." For if metalanguages of action mediate people's moral engagement with one another, what of the anthropologist's traditional license to enter and leave communities with ease, exempt from the give and take of claims-making? Certain Native American groups, for instance, have come simply to deny it al-together.

But an epistemology of intimacy, if necessary, is not sufficient. First, to the extent that metalanguages are not merely neutral guides to action but part of the discourse of self-justification, they offer poor purchase for certain kinds of crit-ical insight, help in sorting through the unequal relations among counter-claims, or understanding which of them wins out. And so the lineage I have sketched here has been confronted by-and often grafted to-critical theory, post-colonialism, Marxism, and feminism. Second, intimacy alone does not help us understand in semiotic, pragmatic, or cognitive terms what metalan-guages are possible or likely, what forms they may take and how those forms have consequences. Interpretation too often moved directly to "meaning" with-out, for example, analyzing the how those meanings are objectified and circu-late in public. Both of these points suggest that an epistemology of estrange-ment is crucial.

What does turning text analogues into texts do? As Taylor remarks, once in-terpretation is internalized, it changes the actor (1987:46-47). Consider Taylor's example of religious beliefs learned in a colonial missionary school. They are held only by individual subjects, in contrast to the circumstances of "the same" beliefs within the missionary's own society, where, being part of the background domain of "common meanings," they are known by all members of that society to be meanings they share (1987:58). They are still part of the common meanings of the home society even for atheists who have rejected them (what might today be called "contestation"), in contrast to the mission-ized subject who accepts them, but in the context of a different set of common meanings.

The distinction introduces one critical difference between the do-main of actions and the metalanguages that might interpret them. Today's an-thropologists might find it not coincidental that this distinction occurs precise-ly across the non-reciprocal space between colonizer and colonized. In addition, the beliefs taught in the missionary school are introduced in an explicit form. They are, that is, doctrines to which one could give or withhold one's adherence (Asad 1993). Their epistemic and practical status is quite dis-tinct from, say, Bourdieu's "habitus," Foucault's "discipline," or "iterable" sign forms to which no particular belief can be securely attached (Derrida 1972). To the extent that what Taylor calls common meanings are objectified as cultural metalanguages, they have a distinct status from the domain of unself-conscious practices-the stuff of culture in the Boasian tradition, or of everyday frames for action (Bateson 1955; Goffman 1974). They are forms that exist apart from actors and face them as texts to be read from outside.

Where is one standing when one stands outside that text? To privilege the agent's own description of the action, especially as it is linked to intentionali-ty, commonly presupposes a sovereign self-consciousness, a figure whose in-creasingly spectral character for psychological, psychoanalytic, and political thought I need not rehearse here. But explicit descriptions of action raise other questions as well. As Gilbert Ryle (1946) long ago pointed out, to transform "knowing-how" into the object of "knowing-that" is to change its very na-ture. Because Taylor's main concern is to argue against efforts to determine interpretation-free objects of social science on the model of natural science, he leaves this question largely unexamined. Nor is the distinction merely episte-mological or cognitive (though it is those too, Chaiklin and Lave 1993). Bour-dieu (1972), for instance, argues that "officializing" and "synoptic" discourses manifest a distance from practical activity that only the privileged can enjoy. But, lest we conclude that none but the powerful have access to the self-consciousness afforded by metalanguages, we must allow for a much wider range of modes of self-objectification. These may derive from everything from ritual distantiation (Keane 1995) to the alienation of the oppressed (J. C. Scott 1990).

And these are insights the epistemology of intimacy cannot offer by itself. The lack of further inquiry into the character of meta-languages, and their role in the processes of objectification and the transformations of social self-consciousness, has remained a persistent weakness both in the interpretive ap-proach as well as for many of its critics.

What I want to stress here is the centrality of agency to the subject implied by certain features of the interpretive turn. Moreover, Taylor's rejection of pos-itivism implies that positivism necessarily eliminates agency for both the ob-ject of knowledge and the knowing subject, and thus, their capacity to forge, out of the contest among competing interpretations, new, more insightful, meta-languages together.

THE CALL FOR MORE PARTICULARITY

In the previous section, I characterized certain themes at the heart of American anthropology's interpretive turn during the 1960s and 1970s. I suggested that a rejection of comparative categories in favor of particularism and an epistem-ology of intimacy, and an underlying anti-determinism, became part of the taken-for-granted across much of cultural anthropology. But by the end of the next decade, the discipline seemed increasingly riven with hotly contested di-visions and sometimes acidic self-critique.

There are many reasons for this, in-cluding the post-independence transformations of formerly colonial fieldsites, challenges to the Euro-American dominance of representations, the politics of identities, and legitimation crisis in the academy. In theoretical terms, these forces commonly added vigor to post-structuralist challenges to coherent and totalizing models, a revival of more culturally-inflected Marxism and critical theory, and the Foucauldian development of the Nietzschean thesis that the cri-tique of knowledge must go beyond disowning claims to "objectivity" and re-veal its inseparability from the power that produces it.

Nonetheless, I suggest that some aspects of these critiques were animated by the same general assumptions and values as their targets. Indeed, certain de-bates could only transpire to the extent that the participants agreed on what was most important (thus their greater impact in anthropology than, say, sociology [see Steinmetz n.d.]).

For all their differences, many protagonists in the debates can be understood as competing over whose approach better recognizes human agency and self-determination. To exemplify this I turn to Lila Abu-Lughod's "Writing against Culture" (1991) and Akhil Gupta and James Ferguson's "Be-yond 'Culture': Space, Identity, and the Politics of Difference" (1992).

Although these essays are over a decade old, they remain exemplary of two prominent, if distinct, directions for contemporary internal critiques of anthro-pology. Both raise important questions about the identity, coherence, and pow-er relations of the "we" that has been tacitly presupposed by anthropological discourse.

Both respond to changing status of particularism when ethnograph-ic attention shifts to colonialism and globalization. Both are concerned with the politics and ethics of representing "otherness" and take as a touchstone Marcus and Clifford's Writing Culture (1986), which is both apotheosis and immanent critique of the textualism of the interpretive turn.

In their efforts to provide an alternative to "culture," however, they would push the anthropologist to op-posed ends of the anthropological dialectic, Abu-Lughod inwards, toward in-dividual subjectivities, Gupta and Ferguson outwards, toward global political-economic forces. And yet, I argue, they remain within the parameters developed in the genealogy I am tracing, sharing the high value it places on agency and a tendency to associate agency with self-interpretation.

Lila Abu-Lughod has been an especially eloquent exponent of anthropolo-gy's responsibilities to multiple constituencies. And, certainly since September 2001, her call to humanize the Muslim world for Euro-Americans remains ur-gent. My concern here is her assertion that the culture concept is inherently a vehicle of unequal power between knower and known because it does violence to the actualities of lived experience. To be sure, her portrayal is a straw man, since few anthropologists have ever seen people as "robots programmed with 'cultural' rules" (1991:158), and traditional fieldwork would be impossible if they really thought there was "a fundamental distinction between self and oth-er" (1991:137).

But this is the stuff of polemics, and we might charitably re-frame her question: the Boasian geographer can treat Grand Canyon as a unity because it can be taken as a given that the canyon is in "his own" world. But who am "I" and what is "my" world such that "Bedouin culture" is "in" it? The question has become unavoidable (see Appadurai 1986; Asad 1973; Coronil 1996; Dirks 1992; Fabian 1983; Ortner 1995; Said 1978; Trouillot 1991).

There have been two common strategies for responding to the problem by restaging anthropology's claims to an epistemology of intimacy. One is to pre-sent oneself as a mere reporter of others'stories. Yet, of course, stories are not transparent-indeed, even simple transcription already implies theoretical choices (Ochs 1979), to say nothing of the pragmatics of interaction (Briggs 1984) and the politics of choosing among the stories that result (Myers 1988).

Speaking in a singular or monologic "voice"-and thus, with a singular social identity relative to a clear and distinct project-is the highly marked outcome of political effort rather than a natural or neutral condition.

The second strategy is to claim some identity with the people being repre-sented. But on what grounds? For clearly there are innumerable dimensions along which pre-existing identification can be asserted, denied, or confused (Alcoff 1991; Bhabha 1994; Butler 1997; Caton 1999), and the resulting reifi-cation itself can be dangerous (Said 1993).

Indeed, it is not only outsiders who betray intimacies (Herzfeld 1997). Moreover, as Susan Harding (1991) has ob-served, strategies that link insight directly to political identification with those one studies also fare poorly in the case of "the repugnant other," in her case, the radical Christian right, with whom one does not sympathize. How one defines the communities within which one has moral commitments cannot be given en-tirely in advance.

If, as I have suggested, the models of culture that were dominant by the 1970s were motivated in part by the effort to demonstrate a locus of autonomy for hu-man enterprises, they share with Abu-Lughod's "humanism" an underlying anti-determinism.

To be sure, they seek that autonomy at very distinct planes. For the former, self-determination is collective, for the latter, individual. But both take as their starting place an ethical commitment to an object of study that is not reduced to external determinants, and both seek its confirmation in peo-ple's self-interpretations, linked to an ideology of the particular.

Consider Abu-Lughod's proposal that anthropologists write "'ethnographies of the particular'as instruments of tactical humanism," stressing specificity and internal complexity over generality and simplicity (1991:145).

Only by view-ing individuals, she asserts, can one restore to people their actuality as doers. We must shift away from the metalanguages that they share with one another, which Taylor sees as the very condition for the possibility of agency. Rather, Abu-Lughod seems to imply that what is shared with others functions only as a constraint. Throughout, her focus is on conscious experience, taken as a foun-dation for intimate knowledge.

There is a paradox here. It arises, in part, from conflating the metalanguages that mediate actions and those an outsider to the action might construct about them. By trying to reject the latter, Abu-Lughod ends up treating the former as transparent-and, in effect, she silently smuggles in her own metalanguages to replace them.

Consider her interest in how people go "through their life agonizing over decisions, making mistakes, trying to make ourselves look good, enduring tragedies and personal losses, enjoying others, and finding moments of happiness" (1991:158). Can we understand why people can anticipate and make sense of what happens now, what happened before, what might happen, what could never happen, what had better not happen simply by appealing to "how life is lived"? Yet even such apparently natural and intuitively obvious concepts are not immediately present to the senses but depend on some mode of self-interpretation, and thus some potential for self-objectification.

Abu-Lughod's specific example of what a humanistic ethnography of the particular would consist of (1991:154-56) requires both author and reader to accept as transparent certain categories such as piety, immorality, the unthink-able, nostalgia, honor, reputation, authority, and prayer. This is what lends her humanism its sense of intimacy and familiarity.

For this view of humanism as-sumes there is nothing problematic about ordinary language, as if we had full mastery of it and as if it did not bring all sorts of things into our lives including both tacit values and modes of self-deception and domination. To point this out, I think, does not mean that "others" are not like "us." Rather, the point is that even "we" (whoever that problematic category might be) are not fully transparent to ourselves.

By favoring the epistemology of intimacy, Abu-Lughod pushes anthropology toward the concreteness of fieldwork and virtually elim-inates, or renders covert, the analytical distance that follows it. Note the irony: whereas the "individual" in a Boasian life history is supposed to be "typical" of a status, role, or community, Abu-Lughod's "particulars" offer us individu-als who, in the final instance, seem to be typical at the greatest level of social generality altogether, of "humanity" writ large.

THE CALL FOR GREATER SCOPE

Akhil Gupta and James Ferguson (1992), although oriented by similar political concerns about power and identity, exemplify the important-indeed, many would argue, crucial-effort to push anthropology in the opposite direction, broadening in spatial and temporal terms what counts as the relevant context.

Abu-Lughod dispenses with the question of "larger forces" by asserting that "because these 'forces' are only embodied in the actions of individuals living in time and place, ethnographies of the particular capture them best" (1992: 156). In contrast, Gupta and Ferguson follow the lead of earlier writers such as E. E. Evans-Pritchard (1961) and Bernard Cohn (1980), who argued for greater historical awareness in anthropology on the grounds that too close a focus-a perspective restricted only to what one can see in fieldwork-tends to conceal the workings of such larger forces.

Because it is easy to read Gupta and Ferguson as part of a turn to political economy, I want to draw attention to the other term in their discussion. "Cul-ture" plays several conflicting roles in their writing.

First, it refers to discrete public categories of identity. For example, they quote a man from Birmingham, England, discussing the mix of ethnicities in his neighborhood (1992:38, from Hebdige 1979). As their use of the tag "young white reggae fan" suggests (his own description being "I'm just a broad person"), this man's identity lies in his own hands, an active mode of self-construction. It is largely a matter of alle-giances, manifested in choices among co-existing options for expression and consumption.

Although this view of culture shares a great deal with the externally imposed reifications Abu-Lughod criticizes, here, by contrast, it implies conscious self-possession, in contrast to the unconscious habits of Boasian culture.

But as a bounded whole, culture denies self-creation, involving "supposed-ly natural connections between peoples and places". Yet this naturalization in turn stands opposed to "cultural con-struction" (1992:36), a mode of self-creation which it suppresses. The latter in-cludes "conceptual processes of place making" by which "space is made mean-ingful" (1992:39-40). As they note, this emphasis on imagination and mean-ing has been well established within anthropology since Durkheim and Mauss (1903), and their use of the modifier "cultural" seems to point to how humans impose meaning on an otherwise meaningless world. It poses, and valorizes, what humans create, over against mere givens, non-human determinants. One might recall here Boas'geographer, for whom the unity of "Grand Canyon" ex-ists not in nature but by virtue of his relationship to it.

Where Gupta and Ferguson see themselves differing from earlier anthropol-ogists is in asking "Who has the power to make places of spaces? Who contests this?" Now, one might ask cui bono even of agentless structures. But Gupta and Ferguson seek an agent.

At this point, they face a dilemma. For they seem to reproduce an earlier dichotomy between the meaningful and material, locating agency in the former, but subjecting it to power derived from "political-economic determinations that have a logic of their own" (1992:40). To analyze power therefore ultimately requires one to turn away from self-interpretation and toward the entities, forces, and causalities captured by an observer's inde-pendent categories of analysis.

If Abu-Lughod pushes anthropology toward particularities at the expense of any capacity to make a comparative claim, Gupta and Ferguson seem, at mo-ments, on the verge of heading in the opposite direction, toward a general po-litical economy whose workings transcend particulars-not just physical lo-calities-to provide an ultimate foundation for explanation. At the far end of that trajectory, perhaps, the concept of power threatens to become less a way of identifying the effects of actions and circumstances than of postulating their au-tonomous cause.

And now we might find ourselves back at Abu-Lughod's side to ask: can this perspective give an account not only of "who contests" but to what ends, in light of what values and desires, and guided by what imaginable possibilities or presumed constraints? To the extent that such an approach pre-supposes an opposition between "cultural" processes and "political-economic de-terminations," it is in danger of reproducing the separation of meaning and val-ues from causality and action, granting, perhaps, too much to both sides of the opposition. At that point, the relative "freedom" of self-interpretation becomes a function of its distance from "power."

THE "SELF " AND THE "INTERPRETATION" IN SELF-INTERPRETATION

My discussion of Taylor above should suggest, first, that to understand even "personal experience" requires a capacity to shift between epistemologies of intimacy and of estrangement. Second, this very capacity for shifting is already inherent to experience, action, and self-understanding. But does not estrange-ment lead to betrayal or reification, as Abu-Lughod claims? I want to suggest that, real as these dangers are, they do not inhere in either objectification or metalanguages per se. And clarifying the distinctions among kinds of objecti-fication and their roles in social action may help us reconfigure what a kinds of knowledge the human sciences might claim. To ask "what are you doing?"

seeks your language of self-description. To answer it requires both close un-derstanding and its externalization. But the question, even if asked of oneself, sees actions as a problem in search of a response, a stance that opens out to-ward estrangement, and the possibility of reformulation, of new answers. This becomes apparent when the question provokes reflection on what is otherwise tacit. As E. Valentine Daniel (1996) puts it, anthropological dialogue is like the disruption of habit that can produce objectification. And, one might add, no one ever lives by unreflecting habit alone.

Disruption and objectification are already innate possibilities, since meta-languages of action are not simply for "me," private and conceptual-they are for "you."

They are thus subject to objectification and circulation in semiotic form. As semiotic forms, they circulate publicly and are realized materially. Metalanguages are therefore not simply more or less arbitrary interpretations of a world. Rather, they are causally linked to material processes along sever-al dimensions, and in multiple directions.

As Charles Sanders Peirce (1955) ar-gued, semiotic forms are not arbitrary (in the Saussurean sense), and do not merely exist in a separate, disembodied world of ideas. If, for example, they purport to resemble their object, they depend on the specific qualities of things.

If they are indexical, such as knowledge, skills, habits, distinctive possessions, class and regional accents, they are subject to scarcity and causality, and thus exist in dynamic articulation with political economy and social institutions. This should figure into any analysis of power's authority, with-out collapsing authority into power.

And conversely, objectifications are subject to recontextualization embed-ded in actions. In contrast to the romantic critique of objectification as, say, in-herently alienating or a violation of self-presence, whether objectification is negative or not is a function of who I am for you and what epistemic status I accord that moment of objectification. Actions and tacit knowledge, for instance, are neither encompassed by, nor ultimate foundations for, explicit self-interpretation or even further metalanguages, since all enter into ongoing transformations of one another.

This is one reason why it is a mis-take to align "meaning" with the conceptual in a domain of freedom, over against materiality in a domain of determinism. Objectification puts actions and actors at risk by giving them semiotic (thus public) form and changing their epistemic and pragmatic status. But, far from being only a disease of social science, this is the very politics of everyday awareness and interaction.

"Local" metalanguages, however, cannot in themselves provide a sufficient account of action. Even as guides to "self-understanding," they cannot simply replace tacit know-how or intuitions of value.

They must be understood for what they are, potentially explicit objectifications that mediate but do not fully ground the actions within which they are situated. Narrative, for instance, has long been posed as an alternative to totalizing and distancing formulations. But narratives are not simply waiting for listeners to come along, they are crystallized contextual moments of explicitness, discursive actions that turn other actions-other contexts-into texts recognizable within genres.

Contrary to Abu-Lughod's assumption, "ordinary" discourses and "distancing" discourses do not exist in isolation from one another. As Bakhtin pointed out, the languages of officials, "experts," journalists, and so forth saturate so-called everyday speech with varying degrees and kinds of authority.

And local metalanguages are not exhaustive-they neither can nor aim to specify everything socially or conceptually relevant about an action or its context, but only those that are selected by the publicly available terms for the self-awareness of actors. These remarks about meta-languages of action constrain and contextualize (but do not eliminate) the importance that interpretive and symbolic anthro-pology accorded "the actors' own" categories. It should become apparent that the capacity to reflect on, criticize, and, especially, show the links among local meta-languages depends on the availability of some further meta-level.

To un-derstand the non-explicit features of action, the habitual or the covert, requires an epistemology of intimacy-but to take them as anything other than obvious, natural, self-contained, and unshakeable requires an epistemology of estrange-ment. This further level need not derive from something "external" to a community, since it builds on pervasive capacities for self-reflection, inherent to the semiotic mediation of action.

It is when we imagine that agency is naturally located within pre-existing individuals, rather than, say, forged among them, that other formations such as families, institutions, societies, and so forth seem most determinist. This parochial perspective is not only theoretically problematic, it is ill-equipped to deal empirically with people who would deny that they themselves are or would want to be humanist or liberal subjects, even in "the West" insofar as it contains such powerful alternatives as, say, technoscience and Christian fundamentalism.

Indeed, the critique of anthropology should not stop at its understanding of so-called "others," but should help show how, in any given instance, even "we" (however defined) are not who we think we are. It should insist on sustaining the project of anthropology as an episte-mological critique of received categories, of their givens, and accept that this project involves the anthropologist in commonplace strategies of (partial and situated) estrangement and self-estrangement, objectification and self-objectification. If this observation is not entirely new, it does seem to demand re-legitimation.

AN ETHIC AND ITS OBJECTS

I have suggested that certain core themes in the Boasian vision of "geography" run through a wide range of subsequent and sometimes antagonistic visions of human science. The impulse toward comparison and theorization has always encountered a deep countervailing insistence on ethnographic particularity, its most sweeping claims always threatened by the pointed exception.

At either end of anthropology's historical vagrancies, Boas' geographer joins forces with post-modernism in insisting on the historical situatedness and moral commit-ments that bind the observer and the observed. I want to close, however, by re-asserting the other side of that dialectic, anthropology's engagement with the ambitions of social theory.

The privileging of the particular has come to be intertwined with the concept of self-interpretation. This is not an inherent or necessary relationship but a ge-nealogical one. It is at least conceivable that the terms for self-interpretation will turn out to have universal underpinnings, that the categories of actions and actors are, underneath it all, natural kinds. Or that they are ultimately produced by "external" powers, or remain irreducibly contingent. But the genealogy de-lineated here has led elsewhere. The insistence that cultural things make com-parative metalanguages suspect has become for many anthropologists mere common sense.

But the results can verge on the incommunicable. And this can invite, by way of reaction, the return of a potentially imperial common sense-the notion, for instance, that "globalization" means that observers need no longer doubt their categories.

What has given these intertwined themes their persistence, their urgency, and perhaps even their sense of obviousness, I suggest, is in part the underlying eth-ic of demonstrating some locus of human self-creation not reducible to exter-nal determinations.

To be sure, few would eliminate determinations altogeth-er-debates over structure and agency, the historical turn, and so forth being efforts to reconcile this project with a sober appreciation of power effects. But the epistemic and even ethical project seems recurrently to circle back to the particularity and treacherously obvious grounds of experience.

These grounds are where people interact with one another, where deci-sions are-or seem to be-made, actors identified, responsibilities allocated, actions justified, moral claims asserted, and possible futures imagined.

Where the contending versions of anthropology that I have sketched differ is in situating the locus of self-creation and of that which lies "outside" it. It is perhaps the implicit values underwriting their shared interest in agency that will later, after this set of factions has been reconfigured, seem most distinctive about the study of culture at the beginning of the twenty-first century.

But more than its parochialism should make us question this ethic. Seeking to overcome determinism, it tends toward an equally problematic notion of freedom. Pitted against a hypostasized notion of science, it risks reifying humanism's subject. Identifying freedom with the domain of ideas, it risks opposing them to a domain of material determinants. And when linked to the epistemol-ogy of intimacy, it can encourage disingenuous claims to be eschewing analytic categories. In short, this ethic is in perpetual danger of reproducing the original terms of the opposition.

To this there seem to be three broad avenues of response. First, the anthro-pologist might decide openly to claim the project of demonstrating human self-determination, even if that means, say, to insist on the local genealogy of lib-eralism as part of her inescapable positionality, or in the name of an overriding set of moral and political commitments-to make its normativity explicit.

But to do so requires (at least) a certain disciplinary modesty in the face of potentially irreconcilable ethical stances and reality claims. Second, the anthropologist might reject the terms of the anti-deterministic project.

And indeed, alongside the genealogy traced out here, there has always been a parallel effort to seek some ultimate determination that will finally settle matters, with, perhaps, a wearied sigh of relief. We can see this today in the growing popularity in many fields of evolutionary and genetic models that would explain human behavior. It may be that a revived economism will pro-duce a similar return to foundations. Nor would it be adequate simply to counter them by saying that they deny human agency. After all, they could reply that the prevailing visions of agency are psychological or ideological illusions, that we must face up to how things actually are.

But even this response cannot tell us why these are their objects, why their explanations matter, and for whom. But there is a third possibility, that of keeping in sight the problematic ground of the ethnographic particular neither as a privileged foundation for knowledge nor as a locus of self-determination. Rather, this ground characterizes the space of encounter in which people seek or deny one another's recognition.

The di-alectic between estrangement and intimacy continually passes through-but should not simply rest at-these encounters. On the one hand, our analyses must take us away from them, and demand some portable objectifications. On the other hand, to the extent that our most distinctive questions begin with the fact that both we and our interlocutors act, think, hope, remember, foresee, and form judgments amidst a world of other people, our engagements should return us to them again. This, at least, would acknowledge that the instigation for so-cial knowledge arises from within sociality.

5

Cognitive Anthropology

Cognitive anthropology assumes that each culture orders events, material life and ideas, to its own particular criteria. The fundamental aim is to reliably represent the logical systems of thought of other people according to criteria which can be discovered and replicated through analysis. Its methodology and theoretical basis stem from the fields of both psychology and anthropology. The field can be divided into three phases: (1) ethnoscience, an early formative period in the 1950's; (2) the middle period during the 1960's and 1970's, commonly identified with the study of folk models; and (3) the growth of schema theory and the development of consensus theory in the 1980's and 1990's.

Many advances have been made in a relatively short period of time in understanding the human mind and in understanding people's world views through cognitive anthropology. It has something to offer each of anthropology's four fields: archaeology, biological anthropology, linguistics, and cultural anthropology. Moreover, it has significantly changed the face of cultural anthropology, particularly with respect to its methodological development.

INTRODUCTION

Cognitive anthropology is an extremely broad field of study. It is closely aligned with psychology, and has adopted theoretical elements and methodological techniques from structuralism and linguistics. In researching this paper, the divisions amongst the various subfields of anthropology became glaringly obvious. Theoretical approaches are well documented in the fields of linguistics and social/cultural anthropology, however, even though similar methods are employed in the fields of physical anthropology, primatology and archaeology, the theories employed are not treated as being equivalent. Thus, while it should be noted that Ian Hodder (1999), Colin Renfrew and Ezra Zubrow (1994) have employed cognitive methods in archaeological interpretation, and most theories of human evolution and primate behaviour rely heavily upon cognitive theories (Tattersal and Schwartz 2000; Boyd and Silk 1997), this paper will concentrate upon the specific field of cognitive anthropology.

Cognitive anthropologists view anthropology as a formal science. They maintain that culture is composed of logical rules that are based on ideas that can be accessed in the mind. There are four basic categories in cognitive anthropology: semantics, knowledge structures, models and systems, and discourse analysis. Semantic studies of terminology systems formed the basis of early cognitive anthropology. The analytical and ethnographic methods developed in these studies provided the foundation for ethnoscience (also called the new ethnography). In contrast with some earlier anthropological approaches to culture, cultures were not regarded as material phenomena, but rather as cognitive organizations of material phenomena.

Cognitive anthropology not only focuses on discovering how different peoples organize culture but also how they utilize culture. It does not claim to predict human behaviour but attempts to describe what is socially and culturally expected or appropriate in given situations, circumstances and contexts. However, it is not concerned with describing events in order to explain or discover processes of change. Furthermore, this approach declares that every every culture embodies its own unique organizational system for understanding things, events and behaviour. Thus, cognitive anthropology has produced both descriptive accounts of cultural categories and generative models.

To the core of ethnographic semantics and ethnoscience practiced in the 1950's and 1960's, decision models and narrative grammars were added to the agenda of cognitive anthropology in the 1970's. D'Andrade states that the linguistic preoccupation in cognitive anthropology has given away to more psychological approaches. This shift began in the late 1970's and became more prominent in the 1980's with interest in 'connectionist networks'.

Connectionist networks " put together schematic cluster of features into complex objects without any necessary linguistic base." Discourse semantics, consensus mapping and applications of artificial intelligence were incorporated in the 1980's. Throughout the 1990's, cognitive theories of emotions, interests in health and well being, religious symbolism and computer aided discourse analysis were all explored.

HISTORY

Cognitive anthropology is a recent subfield of anthropology. In 1950's, cognitive anthropology came to be regarded as a distinct theoretical and methodological approach within anthropology. However, its intellectual roots can be traced back much further in time. Tarnas (1991:333) and Sperber (1985:2) identify Enlightenment thinkers, such as Rousseau, Hobbes and Locke, with the contention that this interaction was of utmost importance for the understanding of society.

Rousseau postulated that humans were essentially good, but were detrimentally influenced by civilization and society. Hobbes maintained that humans' are by nature brutish and selfish, therefore it was the role of society and government to control and curb basic human nature. Locke rejected the Cartesian theory of innate ideas and presumed that humans are at birth 'blank slates.' Locke believed that knowledge of the world had its roots in sensory experience. While Kantian rationalism holds that human cognitive capacities already have categories and principles that structure human knowledge and limit variability. However, while Rationalist thinkers contended that the mind alone could achieve knowledge, the Enlightenment thinkers maintained that reason depended on sensory experience to know anything about the world, "excluding the minds own concoctions". Science was regarded as a mechanism for discovering the truths of human existence, not as a device for attaining absolute knowledge of general, universal truths.

Although operating form various theoretical assumptions, early intellectuals concentrated on the relationship between the mind and society but emphasized the impact of society on the mind. In 1750, Turgot wrote The Historical Progress of the Human Mind, which suggested that humanity passed through three stages of increasingly complexity: hunting, pastoralism and farming.

Condorcet's, The Outline of Progress of the Human Mind (1795), divided history into ten stages, cumulating with the French Revolution. In the early nineteenth century, Auguste Comte developed a philosophy which became known as positivism. He proposed that earlier modes of thought were imperfect and that knowledge should be gained by empirical observation. He reasoned that intellectual complexity evolved, just as societies become more complex over time.

One concept which is central to cultural and cognitive anthropology, is the psychic unity of mankind. This concept was developed by Adolf Bastian around the end of the nineteenth century. After observing similarities in customs throughout the world, Bastian concluded that all humans must have the same basic psychic or mental processes, and thus this unity produced similar responses to similar stimuli.

Cognitive studies in modern anthropology can be traced back to Franz Boas. Boasian anthropology incorporated interests in mental and cognitive concerns, while promoting the study of ideas, beliefs, values and cosmologies. Anthropologists involved in culture and personality studies, specifically Ruth Benedict and Margaret Mead, have been claimed as forerunners of cognitive anthropology. Boas realized that different peoples had different conceptions of the world around them. He devoted much of his work on understanding the relation between the human mind and the environment. Boas encouraged investigations of tribal categories of sense and perception, such as colour. These topics would be critical to the later development of cognitive anthropology.

Cognitive anthropology arose as much of the interest in "classical" culture and personality was waning. As such, it can be seen as a reaction against the traditional methods of ethnology practiced prior to the late 1950's. These ethnographies were strongly influenced by the works of Malinowski and Boas. Traditional ethnography stressed the "technology and techniques for providing material needs, village or local group composition, family and extended group composition and the roles of various members, political organization and the nature of magic, religion, witchcraft and other forms of native beliefs."

As more scholars entered the field, it was found that the ethnographies of places revisited did not always match the ethnographies of the previous generation. Ethnographic validity became a critical issue in cultural anthropology with the Redfield-Lewis controversy in the early 1950's.

Redfield had worked in the Mexican village of Tepoztlan in the late 1920's. In the late 1940's, Oscar Lewis and a team of ethnographers revisited the site. Although some of the differences in Lewis' findings could be attributed to culture change, the degree of differences caused the anthropological community to generally question the accuracy and reliability of ethnographic research methods.

Early practitioners of cognitive anthropology attempted to increase the validity of ethnography by using "interview techniques and analytical processes to bring out native categories of thought instead of imposing the analyst's own cultural system on the data."

One of its early goals was the construction of frameworks for cross-cultural comparisons of human behaviour. Additionally, linguistic anthropologists such as Kroeber, Whorf and Sapir, and the works of Saussure, Chomsky and Bloomfield, all exerted direct influence on the earliest cognitive anthropologists.

Ethnographic studies were often equated with laboratory experiments of the natural sciences and other social sciences, and thus crucial to anthropology's claims to scientific authority. The discovery of the phoneme, the smallest unit of meaningful sound, gave anthropologists the opportunity to understand and record cultures in the native language.

This method was thought to be a way of getting around the analyst's imposition of his own cultural bias on a society. These frameworks were rooted in an analogy which "linked the linguistic distinction between phonetics and phonemics to the anthropological distinction between etics and emics." It became a recognizable field of study within anthropology in the mid-1950's with ethnoscience studies at Yale University.

Much of the development of cognitive anthropology has been credited to Floyd Lounsbury and Ward Goodenough. Goodenough laid out the basic premises for the "new ethnography," as ethnoscience was sometimes known. A simple description of what was observed by the ethnographer was no longer sufficient. The new aim was to find the underlying structure behind a peoples' conception of the world around them.

The primary theoretical underpinning of the ethnoscientific approach was that culture exists only in people's minds. The methodology of ethnoscience attempted to remove the ethnographer's categories from the research process. The principal research goal identified by cognitive anthropologists was to determine the content and organization of culture as knowledge. From the late 1950s to the 1970s, research was strongly oriented towards method, formalization, and quantification.

The attraction for many was that the field was using methods developed in the study of semantics, and served as an access to the mind. Much of this early work centered on taxonomies and domains such as kinship, plants, animals, and colors. While the methodology was productive in reducing the anthropologist's bias, ethnoscience was subject to several criticisms, most focused on the limited nature and number of domains. Some critics charged that it appeared that some cognitive anthropologists valued the "eliciting technique more than the actual data produced from the procedures." Moreover, the data often did not lead to explanations of the respondents' world view.

Other critics noted that "the ethnoscientific approach to culture implied extreme cultural relativism." Since ethnoscience stressed the individuality of each culture, it made cross-cultural and comparisons very difficult. Practitioners claimed they were trying to capture the indigenous, not the anthropologist's, view of culture. However, these native views of culture depended on who the anthropologist chose to interview (e.g. male or female, young or old, high or low status).

During the 1960s and 1970s, a theoretical and methodological shift occurred within cognitive anthropology. While linguistic analyses continued to provide methods for understanding and accessing the cognitive categories of indigenous people, the focus was no longer restricted to items and relationships within indigenous categories.

Instead, the focus was upon analyzing categories in terms of mental processes. It was assumed that there were mental processes based on the structure of the mind which was common to all humans. This approach extended its scope to study "not only components of abstract systems of thought but also to examine how mental processes relate to symbols and ideas."

For example, Bruner, Goodnow, and Austin proposed that there are two primary mechanisms for reducing the strain on short-term memory: attribute reduction and configurational recoding. Attribute reduction was defined as the tendency to contract the number of criterial features of an object down to a very small number.

Configurational recoding was based upon the grouping or 'chunking' together of several features to form a single characteristic. Chunking was defined as a mental process where the short-term memory segments information by grouping items together. The reliance upon meaning, along with the broader goal of attempting to establish cross-cultural frameworks for comparison, soon came under fire from symbolic anthropologists who called for the (re)injection of "richer", "more true-to-life" meaning into ethnographic accounts.

By the early 1980s, schema theory had become the primary means of understanding the psychological aspect of culture. Schemas are entirely abstract entities which are unconsciously enacted by individuals. They are models of the world that organize the experiences and understandings shared by members of a group or society. Schemata, in conjunction with connectionist networks, provided even more abstract psychological theory about the nature of mental representations.

Schema theory created a new class of mental entities. Prior to schema theory, the major pieces of culture were thought be either material or symbolic in nature. Culture, as conceptualized by cognitive anthropologists, was now thought of in terms of parts instead of as a whole. Contemporary questions within cognitive anthropology include the following (ibid.):

(1) are cultural ideologies shared;

(2) if they are shared, to what extent;

(3) how are these units distributed across persons; and

(4) which distribution of units are internalized.

These issues have in fact taken cognitive studies away from the mainstream of anthropology and moved it closer to psychology.

Cognitive structure is being related to the physical structure of artifacts and the behavioral structure of groups. The future path of cognitive anthropology seems to be heading toward the study of how cultural schemas are related to action. Issues of emotion, motivation, and how individuals during socialization internalize culture have now become defined areas of research.

METHODOLOGIES

Cognitive anthropology is driven by methodology. Emphasis is given to systematic data collection in an effort to attain reliable and valid results.

The ultimate aim is the discovery and representation of mental processes. However, many anthropologists are using cognitive techniques for the purpose of "eliciting information to facilitate ethnographic description." In general, the focus is upon the intellectual and rational aspects of culture, particularly through studies of language use. This is reflected in its origins as an attempt to fit formal linguistic methods into linguistic and social anthropology.

Cognitive anthropology has experienced two major and linked shifts over its first half century. The first shift was theoretical. This was a move from a focus on rules, to a focus on schemas as means of characterizing cognition. The second was empirical. This was a change in the focus solely on language as the denotative meaning of terms, to a much broader definition of language, as well as "nonlinguistically coded understandings as the sources of data for characterizing cognition."

The field can be divided into three phases:

(1) ethnoscience, an early formative period in the 1950's;

(2) the middle period during the 1960's and 1970's, commonly identified with the study of folk models; and

(3) the growth of schema theory and the development of consensus theory in the 1980's and 1990's.

There are seven principle concepts within cognitive anthropology: the cultural or folk model, domain, the mazeway, mental scripts, prototype theory, schemata and semantic theory.

ETHNOSCIENCE

Cognitive anthropology has ties to linguistic and psychological anthropology, linguistics, cognitive linguistics, psycholinguistics, cognitive psychology and other cognitive sciences. One important linguistic methodology employed during this period was componential analysis.

Initially inspired by the work of Saussure, componential analysis, sought to analyze domains of meaning with structural linguistics as a model. Componential analysis sought to reveal the simple rules which underlie the "overtly complex distinctions made by members of a cultural group."

The other important methodology of this period was the cultural or folk model. The cultural model "served as a catchall phrase for many different kinds of cultural knowledge." In other words, the unconscious set of assumptions and understandings members of a society or group share. These were believed to greatly affect people's understanding of the world and of human behavior. Cultural models are assumed to be malleable structures which are effected by experience. As an experience is ascribed meaning, it can reinforce models. However, specific experiences can also challenge and change models, if the experiences are considered distinct. In general, cultural models are believed to be connected to the emotional responses of particular experiences, so that "people regard their assumptions about the world as natural."

Ethnoscientists tended to study such things as color categories and folk taxonomies, without being able to clarify their relevance to understanding culture as a whole. They attempted to discern how people construe their world from the way they label and talk about it. However, this study of elements rather than relational systems "failed to reveal a generative cultural grammar for any culture, and while generating elaborate taxonomies, failed to discover any internal cultural workings that could be compared internally or externally."

THE MIDDLE PERIOD

In the 1960s and through much of the 1970s, a great deal of work was done to "evoke native domains structured as taxonomies and paradigms." These methodologies attempted to formulate models which explained how different peoples organized their mental and social worlds.

To this end, the following methodologies were employed: taxonomies, paradigms, feature models,prototypes, domains, and the mazeway. Within cognitive anthropology, taxonomies were defined as beginning with a general concept, which was then divided into more precise categories and terms. This process was then repeated until no further subdivisions were possible. Paradigms were thought of in terms of a matrix structure. The fundamental difference between a paradigm and taxonomy was the way in which distinctions were structured.

Folk taxonomies are classes of phenomena arranged by criteria which show the relationship between kinds of things. The first level is the all-inclusive general category. Succeeding distinctions are then made by the classification of similarity and dissimilarity of items. With each separation the levels become more explicit, and the differences between groups of items more miniscule.

Several early methodologies used by cognitive anthropologists were embedded in the theory of the feature model. Feature models refer to a broad analytic concept that developed in the 1950's and 1960's, primarily within kinship studies. Its general methodological approach assumed that sets of terms can be contrasted to discover the fundamental attributes of each set. Feature models were not only concerned with how people organize information, but what that organization meant in terms of mental information processing.

Another important concept during this period was the domain. A domain was defined as being comprised of a set of related ideas or items which form a larger category. The individual items within a domain partially achieve their meaning from their relationship to other items in a "mutually interdependent system, reflecting the way in which a given language or culture classified the relevant conceptual sphere."

Some cognitive anthropologists attempted to formulate methodologies which expanded beyond merely classifying terminology employed by different societies. To that end, the concepts of the mazeway and mental scripts were employed. The mazeway was defined as "the mental image of society and culture."

The maze is comprised of perceptions of material objects. The methodology studies how people manipulate the maze to reduce stress, both individually and within their society. Similarly, mental scripts are a set of certain actions one performs in a given situation. Existing scripts do not guide every daily action, rather, they are set schemes or recipes for action in a given social situation.

SCHEMA THEORY

Schemata has been one of the most important and powerful concepts for cognitive anthropology in the past twenty years. A schema is defined as "an active organization of past reactions, or of past experiences, which must always be supposed to be operational in any well adapted organic response."

Cognitive anthropologists look for commonalities that can provide keys to the mental structures behind cultural ideologies. These notions are not necessarily culturally universal. Therefore, schemas are culturally specific, and the need for "an emic view is still a primary force in any ethnographic research."

Semantic theory is a recent development. It was built upon an approach that developed with kin terminologies and then extended to other domains. It assumes that there are core meanings and extensional meanings. Core meanings vary less among informants than the extensional meanings. Connectionist theory, on the other hand, allows for multiple flows of information processed "along axes learned and defined probabilistically." These theoretical approaches draw heavily from the fields of artificial intelligence and computer science. Hence they are attempt to look for simple, rigid, defined rules for cognitive functions within a society.

However, there are psychobiological constraints placed upon the human mind's capacity for organizing materials and phenomena. To be able to function, the mind must manufacture discriminations of attributes so it can process information without responding to information as if it were new each time it occurs. For example, in a cross-cultural study of kinship terminologies Wallace noted that despite the social and technological complexity of societies, the size of kinship terminologies generally remain constant. These finding helped to create a cognitive model of the mind that combine both cultural and biological aspects of human life.

In contemporary cognitive anthropology methods themselves no longer continue to be the overriding focus, but instead are used to produce ethnographic data in aid of advancing theoretical knowledge of how the mind operates.

This transformation has substantially altered the variety of work produced by cognitive anthropologists. Cognitive anthropologists stress systematic data collection and analysis to address issues of reliability and validity. Consequently, they rely heavily on structured interviewing and statistical analyses.

These techniques can be divided into three groups that produce different sorts of data: similarity techniques, ordering techniques, and test performance techniques. Similarity methods call for respondents to judge the likeness of particular items. Ordered methods require the ranking of items along a conceptual scale. Test performance methods regard respondents as "correct" or "incorrect" depending on how they execute a specified task.

Specific methods used by cognitive anthropologists include "free listing, frame elicitation, triad tests, pile sorts, paired comparisons, rank order, true and false tests, and cultural consensus tasks." The triad method involves either similarity or ordered data. Items are arranged into sets of three. Unlike a pile sort, the triad method is not dependent on the literacy of informants. Triad sorts have been used in studies of kinship terminologies, animal terms, occupations and disease terms.

Consensus theory directly addresses issues of reliability in data collection not of the information collected but rather of the people interviewed. Data is determined to be correct or incorrect by the respondents. Consensus theory requires response data rather than performance data, in which respondents themselves are coded as being correct or incorrect. This measures how much a respondent knows, and seeks to aggregate the answers of several respondents to achieve a synthesized representation of their knowledge. The goal of consensus theory is to use the pattern of agreement among respondents to make inferences about their knowledge.

While the cognitive anthropologists of the last two decades have attempted to address the methodological limitations of the past, there are still some areas of concern. One of the most glaring problems is that almost all investigators do the majority of their research in English. In addition, when studying something as fluid as human societies, it is difficult to account for variation by using standard methodologies. Cognitive anthropologists are now attempting to explore the emotional characteristics of culture, identified half a century ago by Benedict and Mead. However, as always, there is much more research to be completed before any consensus will be reached.

CONCLUSION

Cognitive anthropology has helped to provide a bridge between culture and the functioning of the mind. It has helped reveal some of the inner workings of the human mind, and given us a greater understanding of how people order and perceive the world around them. Cognitive anthropology has something to offer each of anthropology's four fields: archaeology, biological anthropology, linguistics, and cultural anthropology.

Cognitive anthropology deals with abstract theories regarding the nature of the mind. While there have been countless methods for accessing culture contained in the mind, questions remain about whether results in fact reflect how individuals organize and perceive society, or whether they are merely manufactured by investigators, having no foundation in their subjects' reality.

Moreover, it has significantly changed the face of cultural anthropology, particularly with respect to its methodological development. Cognitive methods are used in a variety of anthropological contexts and applied to a variety of subjects. While cognitive anthropology has relied on a strong tradition of linguistic and cultural approaches, perhaps its greatest challenge lay in demonstrating its applicability to the biological and archaeological subfields. In short, cognitive anthropology holds much promise for the future of cultural analysis.

6

Fishermen, Developmentalists and Conservationists on Lake Malawi

INTRODUCTION

Fish from Lake Malawi are a major source of animal protein for large numbers of people in Malawi and Mozambique, two of Sub-Saharan Africa's poorest countries. It is estimated that fish, supplied by a dynamic and diverse small-scale African fishing industry, contribute seventy percent of animal by Malawians per year.

PROTEIN CONSUMED

In this paper we briefly discuss the scale and social organization of fishing and what we have learned about use rights in the southern and central portions of Lake Malawi. We propose that the open access fishing which exists in these areas has not significantly harmed fish stocks to date, although problems may be emerging.

An equal, if not greater, threatjto the fish, fishing and the ecology of Lake Malawi than that posed by open access small-scale fishing originates from developmentalists-internal and external actors advocating large-scale, capital intensive exploitation of the fish and the development of an international tourism industry. We also suggest that conservationists will remain outside of the major debates about the lake so long as they concentrate on cichlid species diversity and natural beauty and neglect the lake's importance as a source of livelihood and protein. These combined forqes jeopardize the lake and its people.

We report on a three year study of fishing communities on Lake Malawi which is just getting underway.

Our findings are based on research conducted between July and September, 1990, in six Malawian fishing villages in the southern and central parts of the lake. Our comments are preliminary as the data have not yet been completely analyzed.

LAKE MALAWI AND ITS FISHING PEOPLES

Lake Malawi, one of the Great Lakes of Africa, southern end of the rift valley and is bordered is situated in the by Malawi, Mozambique and Tanzania. The lake is approximately 350 miles long and varies between 12 to 48 miles in width (Alimoso et al. 1990). Fish stocks are most plentiful in the shallow southern end of the lake and decline toward the north asi the lake increases in depth and the coastal shelf decreases in size. The lake has a very diverse fauna. Having perhaps the greatest number of cichlid species in the world, it is ah important source of aquarium fish for the international market. In addition, representatives of the fish families tilapia, oreochromis (chambo), cyprinidae (including barbus), barilius (mpasa), clariidae, haplochromis (utaka) and others are important for human consumption. The largest portion of the lakeshore is claimed by Malawi, a densely populated country with a per capita income of under $200.00 per year. Malawi has one of the highest rates of malnutrition in southern Africa, with one out of three children dying before reaching the age of five.

Annual fish catch from the Halawian side of the lake is estimated to be approximately 40,000 metric tons.

Most of this fish is caught by small-scale fishermen; the so called artisanal or traditional sector lands nearly 90% of the catch using an estimated 5,038 dugout canoes, 1,285 plank boats and various types of nets and lines in their operations.

Few of the craft are motorized.

The remaining 10% of the catch comes from what are termed semi-commercial and commercial operators. There aro a total of fifteen pair trawlers (of which ten are operational) in the semi-commercial sector and three trawlers and three Iring net vessels (in various stages of disrepair) in the commercial sector. The commercial operation, MALDECO (Malawi Development Corporation), is fully owned by Press Foods, Ltd., a subsidiary of Press Corporation Ltd., the president of the country':S company (Alimoso et al. 1990, FAO/World Bank 1990).

While the lake is jointly shared by three nations, only Malawi has a functioning system for the lake's management.

The Fisheries Department (in the Ministry of Forestry and Natural Resources) has primary responsibility for the QJake. This responsibility is partially shared with National Parks (also in the Ministry of Forestry and Natural Resources), the Ministry of Commerce, Industry and Tourism and the Ministry of Transport and Communications. Other government ministries such as Agriculture also have interests in the lake and their actions effect water quality and fish and human health. :

One "underwater" national park, Cape MacClear, was established in the 1970s. Located at the boundary between the southeast and southwest arms of the lake, Cape MacClear is regulated by the National Parks Department which imposes limits jon inshore fishing during certain seasons. In addition, the Ministry of Transport and Communications is responsible for inspecting and taxing boats, while the Ministry of Commerce promotes tourist development along the lakeshore.

The Fisheries Act of the Laws of Malawi provides the framework for regulation of gear and licensing, imposing minimum allowable catch sizes and closed seasons for particular fish species. Fisheries has also divided the lake into zones for trawler operations, and prohibits these craft from operating after dark. In addition, Fisheries limits the number of licenses issued to fishermen in the semi-commercial and commercial sectors.

The small-scale commercial fishermen arc regulated by Fisheries as well. While no system of licensing or zoning exists for these fishermen, taxes are imposed on various types of nets, and the use of certain nets is limited by season, time size.

Our findings (which are consistent with consultants' reports) and our discussions with Fisheries Department personnel indicate that enforcement of Fisheries, National Parks and other regulations cannot be carried out effectively under the current budgetary constraints faced by the respective ministries. The Fisheries Department lacks vehicles, boats, extension and regulatory personnel to fulfill its mandate to protect the fish species most susceptible to over-fishing. Thus, despite a series of laws and regulations, little enforcement occurs.

There are strong continuities in fishing policy between the colonial and independence periods. During the |colonial era, fishing was regarded as a domain principally for Africans. Limits were placed on white commercial fishermen who attempted to enter the fishing business. While some larger scale, white-owned commercial ventures did exist, these did not dominate fishing (McCracken 1987). Since independence, the Malawian government has continued to support the smaller-scale fishing enterprises while beginning to develop a larger-scale commercial sphere. The Fisheries Department, as noted earlier, currently divides fishermen into three categories: the artisanal or traditional, the semi-commercial and the commercial sectors. Our surveys reveal that fishermen in the southern and central portions of the lake are commercially oriented-that is, although they do provision their families with fish, they fish primarily to sell.

The difference among fishermen has to do with scale-the number and size of craft, nets and other gear owned significantly influence the amount of catch. We therefore consider all fishermen as belonging to a single commercial sector which is differentiated internally by size of fishing operation. Most fishermen who were interviewed in our study did not own boats, canoes or other gear but instead worked as crew members. They think of themselves as fishermen (nsodzi).* Many of the boat owners we surveyed did not go out with their craft, choosing instead to remain on shore and engage in other.businesses. Crew members do not consider these owners fishermen, and, in some instances, the boat owners themselves have never actually fished.

USE-RIGHTS TO THE LAKE

In addition to gathering information on the organization of the fishing sector and formal systems of control and regulation, one of the purposes of our investigation is to examine community-based systems of lake tenure and other ways in which the lake and its resources are managed by local groups.

In his introduction to A Sea of Small Boats. Corde suggests that small bodies of water are more amenable to tenure arrangements than is the open sea. Our surveys indicate, however, that the southern and central portions of Lake Malawi are an exception to this generalization.

In our studies in six fishing villages in these areas conducted during July-September, 1990, we sought to examine local-level mechanisms limiting fish catch and beach use. IThese surveys revealed an absence of community-level systems of lake tenure, no limits on the movement of small-scale fishermen and few restrictions on use of beaches. In the areas we have examined to date, then, it appears that a system of open access prevails. At this point, we do not know if this has always been the case or if it is a result of the expansion of small-scale | commercial fishing.

Discussions with older fishermen injthe southern and central lakeshore villages indicated that lake jtenure, if it previously existed, has been absent for many decades. However, a brief reconnaissance survey in the north (Nkhatia Bay District) did suggest that tenurial arrangements for certain types of gear (gill nets) exist in some communities there, so it appears that forms of tenure may be present in other parts of the lake. Host small-scale fishermen keep their boats on land at the various beaches, although there are some areas,in the southeastern and southwestern arms where boats can be anchored off shore. Anyone is free use the beaches for fishing purposes.

These areas are subject to the authority of village headmen, Malawi Congress Party leaders or, in one instance we found, a Beach Committee made up of the boat owners. While fishermen do not need permission to use the beach, they are jexpected to inform the headman or other appropriate official of their presence. In doing so, they place regulation of their social behavior under local authority. In one case we found, the headman had asked a group of fishermen to leave the village because of their unacceptable social behavior.

Conflicts among fishermen reportedly develop over entangling of nets in fishing grounds or from efforts by several boats to follow one school of fish. Fishermen state that these disagreements are usually short lived, but, where they are not, they may be taken to the village headman, Malawi Congress Party head or beach committee for resolution.

More detailed information and first-hand observation are needed to fully explore the role and extent of local officials' authority in conflict resolution. Although systems of lake tenure were not found in the southern and central regions, there are social and economic mechanisms which limit fish catch and entry into fishing.

Subject to further analysis of our data, these include:

(1) The high cost of boats and gear. The costs of boats, and especially nets, prevent many people from becoming owners of these means of production and limit their participation in fishing to that of crew members. Plank boats made at the two Fisheries Department boat yards cost between 2,400 and 4,000 Malawian Kwacha.

Boats can be purchased from local carpenters for less, but these craft are usually made of softwood and are not as durable as the hardwood boats produced by Fisheries. While canoes, the most numerous craft on Lake Malawi, are much cheaper than plank boats (generally under 200K), suitable woods for their construction have become scarce. The softwood canoes made nowadays must be replaced every two or three years. The costs of nets are equally, if not more, prohibitive to entry into fishing. Almost all nets in use today are constructed from nylon thread and are usually partially made by.the Blantyre Netting Company. Nets range in price from a few hundred Kwacha to 3,000-4,000 Kwacha. They undergo a process of continuous repair using nylon thread which also requires a steady income to purchase. While boats may be rented from other fishermen, nets are not, reflecting both their high value and their centrality in the fishing operation.' :

(2) Lack of access to credit. Small-scale commercial fishermen do not have access to formal systems of credit. Typically,

they purchase boats and equipment through savings generated from migrant labor abroad or from fish-trading in Malawi (Chirwa 1989). Others have inherited their gear from relatives. In some cases, fish traders may lend money to boat owners for the purchase of nets. They are reportedly paid back through preferential access to catch.

While there is an institution for lending funds to small-scale enterprises (Small Enterprise Development Organization of Malawi, SEDOM) we found no examples of small-scale fishermen obtaining credit from this organization. Discussions are reportedly underway with donors about extending credit to small-scale operators. Two sources of credit are available to larger-scale trawler operators: the Investment and Development Bank of Malawi and INDEFUND, Investment and Development Fund.

(3) Skill and knowledge of fishing. Most fishermen come from families whose members also engaged in fishing. Those who do not have this background have either spent many years learning the skill or, in the case of some boat owners, leave the fishing to hired managers. However, it appears that there are a growing number of crew members and boat owners who come from inland areas and who have little lake experience. As noted below, they are attracted to the occupation by the relatively high earnings it offers and the lack of other employment alternatives.

(4) Willingness to leave the fabric of ones own community. The best fishing is found in the southern, shallow portions of the lake. Many Tonga from the north have moved to the Chewa and Yao dominated south to take advantage of this situation. In addition to this long-distance and usually long-term migration of northerners, there is considerable movement of fishermen from beach to beach on a daily or weekly basis in the southern and central parts of the lake. Many fishermen, especially crew, spend the greater portion of their time living in temporary shelters on beaches away from the main part of the village and from their homes.

Although constraints on boat and gear ownership exist, many people are drawn to fishing because of the relatively high incomes it generates. Our interviews indicate that boat owners and even crew members typically earn more money in a week than the average Malawian does in a month. Crew members report earning up to 100 Kwacha on days when the fishing has been good, while boat owners' incomes are significantly higher (Seymour 1988, 1989). In the south and central portions of the lake the small-scale fishing sector is fully commercialized-people fish to sell and almost all crew are paid in cash (although they may also receive a ration of fish).

Figures on the number of people entering fishing in the last decade are not available, but the number of boats is growing, suggesting an increase in the number of fishermen. At the same time, however, it appears that decapitalization of the small-scale fishing sector has occurred. The number of motors has declined by nearly 1/4 and nets are being repeatedly repaired rather than replaced. While the costs of fishing-boats, nets, petrol and engines-has increased, the price of fish has not kept up with these increased costs, in part reflecting the low purchasing power of the population (Seymour 1989).

In summary, although there are significant capital requirements to becoming boat or net owners and although other important constraints to entering fishing exist, it appears that the number of fishermen is increasing, thus placing pressure on fish resources. In at least one village where we worked, fishermen reported this situation was aggravated by trawling operators who did not observe the one mile off shore limits imposed by Fisheries.

In addition to constraints on entering fishing as an occupation, there are also factors which limit catch in the small-scale sector. As discussed earlier, the Fisheries Department, the Ministry of Transport and Communications and National Parks impose a series of restrictions on the fishing operations of the small-scale fishermen. Although enforcement is very spotty, presumably these rules, and the fines imposed for breaking them, act in a small way to regulate catch. Other limitations at the local level include:

The Nature of the Equipment Used: Given the high costs of motors, the difficulties in getting spare parts and the increasing costs of petrol, almost all craft are now powered by hand, thus imposing some limits on the range of fishing operations. In addition the small size of craft-usually 16 feet or under-limit fish uptake.

The types of nets employed also influence catch. Use of nylon netting material became widespread on the lake during the 1970s and has all but replaced use of local fibers in the southern and central regions. Presumably the effect of this switch to stronger more durable netting, coupled with the introduction of plank boats which occurred in the 1960s, has been to increase the amount of fish caught, although at this time we are not aware of documentation to support this. The British Overseas Development Administration (ODA) Traditional Fisheries Assessment Project does provide information in current fish stocks but, so far as we know, does not correlate this information with changes in gear. While nets have been improved by the introduction of nylon, some commonly used ones may impose limitations on catch during certain seasons of the year. For example, gill nets are placed in a stationary fashion in the lake. During the cold season when fish are less active, people employing this net catch fewer fish than they do during the warmer season when the fish are more mobile.

The Weather: Winds and rains often prevent the small boats from going out. Fishermen report that strong southeasterly winds-called mwera-prevent them from fishing for days at a time. Mwera are especially common during the months of June through September, but they may occur at any time. Storms during the rainy season also limit fishing and reduce catch. While bad weather and the type of gear used by small-scale fishermen to some extent reduce the quantities of fish caught, this effect may be countered by the growing number of people attracted to fishing as an occupation. The issue of whether or not the maximum sustainable yield has been reached is much debated. There are reports from the 1930s and 1940s which suggest that at that time the lake was nearing its maximum sustainable yield and was facing an impending crisis (Lowe 1948).

At the present time, relatively little is know about the magnitude of fish catches on the Tanzanian and Mozambican sides of Lake Malawi. This lack of information, together with the difficulties in estimating the catch of a small-scale diversified fishing industry in Malawi itself, means that it is difficult to accurately state what the yearly harvest from the lake is.

At this point in our study, we suggest that although constraints both to entering fishing and on the amount of fish caught do exist in the small-scale sector, as the number of fishermen increases, these limitations may not be sufficient to prevent overfishing. The government of Malawi is facing some difficult decisions regarding the appropriate scale of fishing operations.

ADDITIONAL PRESSURES ON AND THREATS TO FISHERIES RESOURCES

In an analysis of artisanal fisheries in Africa, Bacle and Cecil (1989) describe the principle underlying one fisheries project in Senegal:

> *...the set of technical-socio-economic elements that make up artisanal fisheries in a country or a region, constitute a system in equilibrium with its environment. If a change is introduced, which theoretically should be an improvement, the system becomes unbalanced, and a long complex process is required for it to regain its equilibrium.*

We do not view the small-scale fishermen on Lake Malawi as being in equilibrium with their environment because they continuously alter their fishing strategies contingent on changes in fish availability and economic opportunities. Nonetheless, we do think the caution Bacle and Cecil sound regarding induced change is well-placed given what we consider to be the major pressures on Lake Malawi.

To date, fully commercial fishermen, although small-scale, have not dangerously depleted fish stocks nor are there indications that they have diminished biological diversity. Where this has occurred, there are suggestions that other factors-such as trawlers and increased water salinity resulting from irrigation schemes-are responsible.

The Government of Malawi has been highly protective of the lake. For many years it has opposed efforts to introduce exotic fish species as a means of increasing yields. Most recently, it has sought to limit species introductions for aquaculture, fearing that these may escape and threaten existing indigenous lake stocks. The government also has prevented the construction of a pulp paper mill even though several thousand hectares of pine had been planted to supply the mill. This operation would have seriously polluted lake waters. In addition, the government created Lake Malawi National Park designed to preserve cichlid and other fish species diversity.

Despite this promising history, a constellation of factors suggest that there are growing risks to Lake Malawi's role as the supplier of a major source of employment and of animal protein to the population. We have already indicated that growing poverty coupled with the lucrativeness of fishing is driving more people into this occupation, thus increasing pressures on fish stocks. While this is an important process, the following factors have an equally if not more significant impact on the lake and its peoples:

(1) A series of risks, in the form of development projects and other types of technical assistance, are posed by those who are benignly called "donors". While many donors currently espouse local community participation in decision making regarding management of natural resources in practice their plans are the opposite.

For example, the World Bank and the FAO have recently proposed a large-scale, long-term project, Malawi Fisheries Project (1990), to the Fisheries Department. The project provides support to the commercial fisheries sector (i.e. HALDECO, a privatized company), the semi-commercial sector (to increase the number of pair trawlers) and the Fisheries Department itself (for a new headquarters, other infrastructure and expatriate staff). Only a small part of the budget (4.4%) is directly allocated toward meeting the needs of the artisanal fishermen responsible for 90% of the catch, and they appear to have had little voice in setting the project agenda.

This proposal reinforces an existing bias toward large-scale, capital intensive ventures and centralized marketing structures as hallmarks of development and progress. One pair trawler operator we interviewed succinctly reflected this bias. When we asked if a new plank boat we had seen on the lake was his,he stated: "No,that one is a toy,my boats [10 meter craft with inboard motors] are ships." It is difficult to overcome the view, held by many donors and recipient/beneficiaries alike, that those who use mechanized equipment are progressive even if such equipment and the scale of operations it embodies are neither equitable nor economically viable.

(2) Another series of threats to the lake and its fishing populations originate from internal and external actors seeking to develop the tourist or vacation potential of Lake Malawi. In these cases, hotel owners are lobbying government to move fishing communities from potentially lucrative locations, and middle and upper class urban dwellers are purchasing lake-front property for the construction of cottages, thus sealing off beaches used by fishermen. In one case near Salima in the Central Region, there is a long (and beautiful) beach used by about forty boat owners and their crews. If the hotel company is successful, the fishing village will be relocated to an as yet unidentified site, and the entire beach will become the private property of the hotel.

Simultaneously, donor funds would be used to build a jetty and the pair-trawl operator owning the "ships" would be able to continue fishing from the location.

(3) While we hesitate to include conservation efforts in a list of potential threats to the lake and its people, such efforts do pose risks if they fail to link conservation measures with development initiatives.

Much biological research on Lake Malawi fish has focused on the cichlids and the high value commercial species such as chambo. Important food fish like usipa and utaka have received little study. Thus, biologists/conservationists ought to conduct more broadly based and socially sensitive research on catch and conservation issues than has occurred to date. A case needs to be continually made for why a poor country like Malawi should preserve biological diversity when it could introduce new species like kapenta, the sardine-type fish found in Lake Tanganyika and Lake Kariba, and increase fish yields.

Conservationists need to address the issue of how maintaining diversity in the fish population can benefit small-scale fishermen and other populations dependent on the fish they catch. Many of the arguments currently supporting the maintenance of crop genetic diversity may apply to fish (Ferguson and Sprecher 1987). These include the possibility that fish diversity offers a form of yield stability. For example, if the catch of utaka is reduced during one season or year, fishermen may be able to switch their efforts to usipa. Also, it is known that certain fish flourish in some ecological niches while others do better in different locations. We suggest that introducing a new species like the nile perch or the kapenta is similar to the risks which result from promoting monocropping in agriculture. Although yields may increase, these may fall primarily to wealthier fishermen who can afford the equipment necessary to catch the new fish."

In this sense, maintaining diversity may be a better food security and equity strategy than aiming for higher yields alone. While many fish biologist/conservationists in Malawi have focused their work on the aquarium fish, a recent article by Tweddle (1985) represents an important exception to this trend. He draws attention to the role of the national parks in providing breeding grounds for food fish. Tweddle clearly links conservation with development by pointing out why and how the preservation of forests and rivers in the national parks and elsewhere in the country helps conserve the breeding grounds for some important food fish. Conservationists in National Parks and other government departments could also work more closely with the Fisheries Department and with communities of fishermen than they have in the past. In the long-term, all parties have a common and vested interest in maintaining species diversity. Conservationists could assist fishing communities and the Fisheries Department not only in maintaining diversity but also in devising ways that fishing peoples, in addition to hotel operators, could benefit from the development of the tourism industry.

Some Preliminary Thoughts on Policy Implications

One motivation for undertaking the present study is that the fish in Lake Malawi have been better studied than the fishing peoples themselves. For a range of reasons, lakeshore dwellers have not been subject to social science enquiry. Given the importance of Lake Malawi both to the surrounding countries and as a part of the much larger Zambezi River Basin, it is important to begin obtaining empirical information on these communities. We anticipate that such information will be useful to policy makers as they engage in a series of important debates about the lake's future. Our assumption is that smaller-scale systems of fishing are more equitable, provide livelihoods for larger numbers of people (both directly through fishing, processing and marketing, and indirectly through boat-building, etc.), require less outside assistance, use less fuel, and probably are more efficient than large-scale trawler operations. This possibility needs to be seriously considered when engaging in debates with donors regarding the appropriate scale of fishing operations to be promoted on the lake.

One way the government can demonstrate its long standing commitment to the small-scale fishermen, fish processors and traders is by making loans and other services readily available. For example, it appears that very few people can generate enough money from working as crew members to buy nets or boats. Entering fishing by starting at the bottom is no longer a viable route of advancement-if it ever was. It seems reasonable to encourage and reward small-scale fishermen's and crew members' knowledge and skill by making loans available to them rather than offering credit solely to those larger-scale operators with existing collateral. In addition, the government, possibly with donor assistance, could fund research to develop improved, longer lasting canoes, the most numerous craft on the lake.

Deforestation is proceeding at a rapid pace in Malawi, and the best trees for canoes have been cut down or are not readily accessible because of transport and costs. Most fishermen interviewed in the course of our survey reported declines in fish availability. For example, the majority of fishermen interviewed in five of the six villages we visited stated that their catches had declined and that there were increasing numbers of fishermen using the lake, while the majority fishermen in only one village reported improved catches. This information, coupled with Fisheries Department and donor reports, suggests that the issues of stock depletion and overfishing are of growing concern and will need to be addressed in the near future. If more people enter fishing or improve their gear they are likely to catch greater numbers of fish. If resources are shifted into the large-scale commercial sectors and trawling intensifies this may diminish fish catches for small-scale fishermen operating particularly in the shallow portions of the lake in the south. A debates continues regarding whether or not there are deep water fish resources that can be commercially exploited on Lake Malawi. This issue is to be examined by an ODA funded-research team beginning in 1990. Large-scale commercial fishing might make sense in areas of the lake-such as the north-where there may be deep water fish stocks which cannot be harvested by those using canoes and plank boats, but such large-scale operations may not be justified in the south where they directly compete with small-scale fishermen.

It is clear that in the near future, the Fisheries Department will have to effectively limit the number of fishermen on the lake. However, they will not be able to do so on their own, without community support and understanding. In the short term, Fisheries will have to place emphasis on outreach and extension activities to provide fishermen with a way to communicate their needs to the Department as well as a means for Fisheries to explain regulations to fishermen. These regulations need to be simplified, and they should have demonstrated positive consequences for fishermen. Many of those interviewed were concerned about violations of regulations which resulted in declines of fish stocks.

We envision (although more extensive research is necessary) the possibility of creating community or beach based groups that can enforce rules or at least inform Fisheries when they are being violated. Policing the lake without fishermen's support will only lead to hostility and conflict. Our brief investigation has also indicated the need for collaboration and coordination among ministries, department and donors concerned with the lake and its fisheries. The competing demands placed on lake resources by different scales of fishing operations, tourist industry developers, conservationists and agriculturalists (the last, a topic hardly explored in this brief paper) mean that an integrated plan for the lakeshore is needed. Further, such a plan will ultimately have to be coordinated with the interests of the surrounding nations which also claim access to the lake and its resources.

CONCLUSIONS

The research has revealed a dynamic, small-scale, highly commercialized fishery which was initially protected by the colonial government and now is supported by the Government of Malawi. However, as pressures build to increase the scale of fishing and to develop international tourism, the livelihood of fishing communities and their associated processors and traders is jeopardized. While we would have liked to report that there were systems of lake tenure which could be built upon to manage the resources, we find that the lake, although technically state property, functions as an open access regime subject to the constraints enumerated earlier. Although there are clearly dangers to the lake's fish and ecology from the small-scale fishermen, there are equal or greater dangers to fishing communities in many donors' plans to increase the scale and intensity of fishing and to concentrate such efforts in the hands of large-scale operators. In addition, conservation biologists have an important role to play in protecting endemic fish species, but they have not yet linked these efforts to those aimed at improving the well being of the populations dependent on the lake for their livelihood.

This research on Lake Malawi is part of a larger study, "Fragile Lands, Fragile Lakes" funded by the John D. and Catherine T. MacArthur Foundation. The purpose of the investigation is to explore the social science dimensions of the ecological health of Lakes Malawi and Victoria and to consider means by which the lake-owning nations can coordinate their efforts with regard to lake management. We use the term "fishermen" instead of a gender neutral term such as "fishers" in this case because we found no evidence of women taking part in fishing itself. However, we do not want to imply that such is impossible in the future or does not exist in o other areas of the lake not yet surveyed. Women do currently play an important role in fish processing and trading, aspects of the fishing industry which we have not discussed in this paper, and with access to resources they could play an expanded role in other aspects of fishing and management of the lake. There are no reliable estimates for the Tanzanian and Mozambican catch nor for what might be landed by Malawians on the non-Malawian shore.

7

Second-generation Cognitive Anthropology and the Problem of History

This study was conducted to address a methodological and theoretical gap in cognitive anthropology. It represents one possible way to apply a historical approach to cognition, illustrated through a comparative case study of Middle Eastern herbalists' folk medical knowledge, beliefs, and practices.

Since the late 1950s, cognitive anthropologists have investigated numerous cultural organizations of mental and material phenomena, centering their work on questions of meaning, knowledge, and concept formation. These cognitive studies can be divided into two distinct types of inquiry which have been variously labeled by adherents of the field. For the purposes of the present discussion the two main versions of cognitive science may most conveniently be labeled "first-generation" and "second-generation" studies.

First-generation cognitive studies, noting the "language-like" nature of cognition (Tyler 1969), borrow their basic ideas by analogy from Saussurian synchronic linguistics. Cultural categories (or "taxa") are thus seen as arbitrary signs best defined by the presence or absence of selected contrastive features. Such taxa are ordered into hierarchical "folk taxonomies" by relations of inclusion and contrast, which are contingent on the presence or absence of these necessary and sufficient features. In the 1970s, cognitive anthropologists discovered that not all cultures clearly delineate categories based on the presence or absence of only a few minimum features. Nor do they necessarily order their categories into hierarchical "kinds of" relationships. Rather, second-generation studies reveal that categories frequently have "fuzzy" boundaries and are primarily based on the Gestalt apprehension of perceptual attributes. Category members "belong" because they are perceived as similar to prototypical "clearest" or "best-case" exemplars which possess the highest average of properties in the pool of attributes present in the larger category. Taxa are gradient categories, and their members share Wittgensteinian "family resemblances" expressed at varying levels of intensity.

Until the present study, only first-generation studies have entertained the possibility of using the tools of historical linguistics to analyze cognitive systems from a diachronic perspective. Second-generation studies have been more concerned with questions of intracultural variation and consensus than of history. However, their focus on variation parallels a shift in historical linguistics to an approach that looks at variable "developmental" patterns and mechanisms of language in diachronic motion. These developmental studies define "lects" (i.e., languages, dialects, or sociolects) as evolving, complexive, constellation-like webs of implicationally-ordered features. Other linguists, while not focusing so much on variation as the developmentalists, have undertaken language and dialect classifications based on global investigations of similarities through "mass comparison" of their features. Some have also attempted to recognize patterns of relationship through numerical classifications based on the presence or absence of lexical, morphological, and syntactic items.

Linguists are not the only researchers who have developed methods for classifying their objects of study based on "family resemblances." Practitioners in several other fields of scientific inquiry have also been working on the same kinds of classificatory problems. Biologists, linguists, and archaeologists have all used variations on phenotypic (or, more properly, "phenetic") and cladistic approaches to categorize cases and clarify historical relationships in their respective domains of study. The "fuzzy" nature of folk categories suggests that a profitable way to engage the problem of history in second-generation cognitive studies might be through an analogical approach. Such an approach classifies cognitive variants (i.e., cognitive dialects) based on "family resemblances" in how similar their similarity judgments are to one another.

TOWARD A SOLUTION FOR THE PROBLEM OF HISTORY

This project is an attempt to develop quantitative mechanisms for making accurate inferences about historical relationships of descent and influence among cognitive systems. More specifically, the example of drug-plant prescription in Islamic societies will be used to confirm or refute the accuracy of phenetic techniques (also known as "numerical taxonomy") when applied to similarity judgment data. Numerical taxonomy is, at its simplest, a method for quantifying similarity of overall form. I will test the usefulness of phenetic techniques for examining cognitive history through the application of a five-point process to recipes for compound drug-plant prescriptions and statements regarding drug-plants' medicinal properties that I have selected from fourteen different sources. Six of the sources derive from late twentieth-century Islamic societies (e.g., Egypt, Syria and Morocco) and the others from historical antecedents in the region (e.g., Ancient Egyptian), as well as from one neighboring non-Islamic society chosen as an "out-group" (namely, India). The process involves the following:

1. The use of a hierarchical clustering computer program to model use-based similarity judgments for the drug-plants present in each source's prescriptions or descriptions of drug-plant properties.
2. Comparison of the individual sources' results using a "sort table" technique developed by Agar (1996), modified to convert the similarity judgments into "features."
3. Calculation of the degree of similarity among the sources, based on the features derived in this manner.
4. Use of the resulting similarity ratings to compare the sources and to create classifications for them based on overall family resemblances in the way the sources group their plants.
5. Examination of the classifications and historical inferences generated from the above method, in light of the geographic and historical facts of the case, as they are known from

other non-cognitive approaches to the history of Islamic medicine.

In an effort to take a first step toward filling the "historical void" in second-generation cognitive anthropology, this study will (a) provide an overview of the geographic and historical facts of the case study (i.e., Islamic medicine in its geographic, historical, and cultural context), (b) review the development of theory in cognitive studies and of classificatory and evolutionary theory in other domains, (c) discuss techniques that have been used to look at similarity and variation in cognition and describe and evaluate methods that have been used to look at the evolution and historical relationships of systems in other scientific fields, and (d) apply modified versions of some of these techniques to the second-generation problem presented by the case study.

NECESSARY ASSUMPTIONS

Several assumptions underlie this study. These will be presented, with their justifications, in the paragraphs below.

First and foremost:

It is assumed that one can speak of "Islamic societies" or "the Middle East" (and therefore, of "Islamic" or "Middle Eastern medicine," as well) as real, researchable entities.

According to Eickelman, the term "Middle East," "encompasses the region stretching from Rabat to Tehran... [and] is often extended to include Afghanistan and Pakistan" (2002:2). While there is significant cultural and linguistic diversity across the region, there are strong general trends of commonality in many domains of culture (including medicine, cf. Ullman 1978 and Ushmanghani et al. 1986). Some historians and social scientists have also referred to societies in this region by the adjective "Islamic." While not all members of these societies are Muslims, non-Muslims constitute a socio-politically dominated minority in the region, and have been profoundly influenced in their worldview and lifestyle by the habitus of the people they live among. As Esposito (1999:x) observes, "Islam... is the dominant symbolic and ideological force" in the part of the world under investigation. In this study, the terms "Middle Eastern" and "Islamic," will be used interchangeably, with the understanding that non-Muslims participate, to varying degrees, in what may be termed "Islamic" societies.

Second:

It is assumed that the sources selected are representative of other contemporary herbalists and other drug-plant-prescribing medical practitioners in the locality where they ply their trade. While it is clear from prior studies that specialized cognitive knowledge is variable and distributed throughout a society, it has also been shown to be shared enough that professionals can be said to take part in a common knowledge and belief system with each other and their clientele (Garro 1986). From a purely economic perspective, herbalists could not last long in the profession without meeting expectations for the provision of relevant prescriptions to their clientele.

Third:

It is assumed that named entities identified as the same plant (at the generic level of classification) by professional herbalists, botanists, or lexicographers may be treated as the same entity. While ethnobotanists have shown that different cognitive systems may partition the world in sometimes radically different ways, they have also found that "generic taxa often approximate in their content the genera and species of Western biology" (Berlin 1992:25-26). Therefore, given a plant named x in society A and a plant named y in society B, both identifiable as representative of the same genera in Western biology, x and y may be conceived of as "the same plant." In addition, even though plant names occasionally vary across the culture area under study, natives of the region have long recognized many terms as synonyms for the same entity. If a term used by one source has been historically identified as synonymous with a different term used by another source, then these two terms can be conceived of as equivalent.

Fourth:

It is assumed that the drug-plants most often prescribed together for the same illnesses will be thought of as more similar to one another than drug-plants prescribed together less frequently (or not at all).

Cognitive anthropologists have demonstrated that named members of highly useful domains (such as medicines) may be organized into taxonomies by their "distributional similarity" (the degree to which the items occur in the same environments or have the same practical uses), as much as by a purely intellectual classificatory "search for order" in the world.

Finally:

It is assumed that cognitive systems evolve in ways that are analogous with other evolving systems and may therefore be fruitfully studied in analogous ways.

Cultural knowledge systems (such as Islamic medicine) exhibit the basic features necessary for evolutionary change: variation, selection, and transmission. They consist of co-adapted idea units or "memes" that vary, are selected, and are transmitted in ways that are analogous, though not identical, to other replicators such as genes and "linguemes."

They are therefore most appropriately examined with analogous classificatory and historical methodologies, such as numerical taxonomy.

The five primary assumptions constrain and direct the kinds of hypotheses that can be formed regarding the history and interrelationships of cognitive structures in the culture area under study.

GENERAL RESEARCH HYPOTHESES

Two main hypotheses were formulated in regard to the application of numerical taxonomy to the history of Middle Eastern ethnopharmacology. They are tentatively advanced as a guide for the research methods to be developed in this study. The following research hypotheses were generated:

1. A numerical taxonomy approach to Islamic medicine will show that there is a relationship between (a) the proximity and shared history of the localities where two or more sources (i.e., collections of prescriptions for drug-plants or descriptions of drug-plant properties) were produced and (b) the degree of similarity between the overall use-based similarity judgments of drug-plants by those sources.

2. A numerical taxonomy approach to Islamic and pre-Islamic Near Eastern medicine will show that there is a relationship between (a) the relative strength of antecedent-successor relationships of sources and (b) the degree of similarity between the overall use-based similarity judgments of drug-plants by those sources.

SIGNIFICANCE OF THE STUDY

First-generation cognitive studies of historical questions continue to become more scarce. Researchers undertaking second-generation studies have yet to ask historical questions of their data. It seems to be an opportune time to draw on models from other disciplines that use variation to explore issues of diachrony and evolution as inspiration for the development of a fresh approach to cognitive classification systems.

If a phenetic approach proves to address the problem of diachrony in second-generation cognitive studies in a way that allows for the classification of "cognitive dialects" based on their overall gross similarities, then this will open the door for a wide range of future projects.

The development of methods for cognitive dialectometry will dramatically broaden the scope of second-generation cognitive science. Such an approach would constitute the basis for a powerful new discovery procedure and serve as a useful tool for case history-specific hypothesis generation.

It would also provide a foundation for the future elaboration of second-generation reconstructive techniques analogous to those used in the comparative method of linguistics. Unlike first-generation techniques, a phenetic approach would be able to make accommodation for the fuzzy boundaries of categories and their prototype-centered nature.

A valid quantitative approach to the classification of cognitive dialects would provide ancillary means for supporting and illustrating previously posited historical "hunches" regarding inter- and intracultural intellectual influences and relationships. The scholarly study of Islamic medicine has been characterized by a rich tradition of translation, interpretation, and comparison.

However, where primary historical records lack explicit statements of descent or borrowing, claims for inter-relationships have often been put forward in the form of unsystematically examined, anecdotally supported conjectures.

The present study may quantitatively support some of these claims for historical influence, help lay others to rest, and, more generally, help to clarify the relative strengths of antecedent-successor relationships.

In the event that the study's results do not prove to reflect the basics of the known historical and geographic facts of Islamic medical practice (a negative result, i.e., a Type I error), then, at the very least, the project will have served to narrow the possible approaches for future solutions to the problem of history in second-generation cognitive studies by excluding some or all features of this particular approach.

In either case, it will provide a more elaborate portrayal of the diversity of the system(s) of Islamic medicine and its/their antecedents in the region than has been heretofore presented.

DELIMITATIONS

Attempting to understand cognitive systems in historical terms is a broad problem. It was deemed necessary to set some boundaries for the scope of this study in order to achieve a usable result (in a realistic time frame) with the resources available.

The first delimitation made was the narrowing of the problem to a second-generation cognitive study. First-generation studies attempting to reconstruct proto-cognitive systems based on componential feature analyses have previously been successfully undertaken (insofar as semantic feature-based analyses and taxonomic hierarchies may be said to represent actual cognitive structures). With first-generation approaches already established, an additional first-generation-style study seemed less interesting than moving the discipline's historical perspective forward into a second-generation approach.

While it would have been theoretically possible to test the hypotheses for this project with data from any domain of knowledge in any well-defined culture area (or even beyond and across culture areas), it did not seem expedient to attempt the initial trial with any randomly selected domain or culture area. Instead, Middle Eastern medicine was selected as the focus for the case study on the grounds that it has a better documented history of greater time depth than is found elsewhere or in other domains of "traditional" or "folk" science.

Taking into account its ancient Near Eastern antecedents in Egypt and Mesopotamia, the records of Middle Eastern medicine go back over three millennia.

Another necessary delimitation was the restriction of the theory and methodology to evolutionary approaches that do not necessarily distinguish between formal, phenotypic similarities in outward appearance and behavior and those that result from purely phylogenetic relationships of descent.

Cladistic approaches and other reconstructive techniques that base their classifications on subjectively selected characters "known" to represent genetic descent were excluded as too problematic at this early stage of inquiry.

From a second-generation perspective, there is no way (yet) to distinguish between similar cognitive characters or features deriving from descent with modification, evolutionary convergence, or diffusion through areal influence.

However, since phenetic classificatory results might reveal something about phylogenetic relationship, the identification of similar tendencies in classification by different sources or subjects is a first step in the direction of discovering how researchers might be able to identify genetically inherited characters in the future.

Finally, in terms of the sources and data selected for analysis, the modeling of distributional similarity judgments was limited to the utility of drug-plants as presented in previously published sources. This delimitation can be understood as consisting of three related restrictions: first, the restriction to plants only; second, to utility only, and third, to previously-published sources only.

Islamic and pre-Islamic medical systems in the Near East exhibit a broad range of pharmaceuticals, including animal and mineral products as well as plants and plant-derived materials.

However, the names of animals, minerals, and the medicinal drugs derived from them have proven particularly difficult to identify and translate, especially in earlier sources.

They were therefore excluded. In addition, some plant-derived products (such as olive oil, crystallized sugar, and cotton wadding) were also excluded on the grounds that the degree of processing to which they are subjected before they ever reach the herbalists is so extreme that they may no longer be conceived of purely as "plants." Only those plants and plant products that remain in their original morphological shape until the herbalists (or other traditional medical practitioners) themselves modify them were included.

While it is feasible to model similarity judgments based on the gestalts generated by attention to an extremely wide range of possible attributes (the author previously conducted such a study on ancient Egyptian "trees," Pittle 2002), this exhaustive approach seemed inexpedient for the problem at hand.

The present study was limited to utility only (or the named properties that ultimately determine utility, where the utility derived from them is not presented by a source). It was not feasible to collect all known attributes for all of the drug-plants used in all of the locales under study.

Published sources were selected as the only appropriate basis for this initial trial. While a fine-grained, region-wide, fieldwork-based collection of relevant data might ultimately yield more nuanced results, the monetary expense and cost in personnel and time resources were prohibitive for the initial application of this previously untested model.

However, once the approach has been successfully demonstrated, there would be sufficient reason to seek the funding and resources to undertake a similar study with a large number of "live" subjects, over a broad area, in an effort to further develop and validate methods for elaborating the emergent field of "cognitive dialectology."

PRELIMINARY DEFINITIONS AND OPERATIONAL TERMS

The following definitions are presented to provide an early clarification of some of the key variables, constructs, theories, and models used in this study. They may also be used as a reference guide to these concepts.

Variables and Constructs

Drug-plant: Drug-plant (or plant drug) is operationally defined as a botanical entity used with the intent to cure or improve the health of an ill person. More specifically, it is defined as entities that are most familiar or useful to healers (herbalists, etc.) in the least modified form possible. For the purposes of this study, drug-plants given alternative names in different locales are measured as the same drug-plant if they have been identified as representative of the same botanical genera or have been historically recognized as synonymous terms for the same entity. Drug-plant Property. Drug-plant properties are features of a drug-plant describing its healing qualities in terms of a limited set of dimensions belonging to a traditional system that dictate how the plant is to be prescribed (such as Galenic humoral qualities of "hot," "cold," "moist," and "dry," or Ayurvedic qualities and actions).

Prescription: Prescription is operationally defined as a list of two or more drug-plants to be compounded or used together as a remedy for the same illness or negative condition (such as spirit possession).

Proximity: For the purposes of the present research, proximity entails a consideration of both the geographic nearness of two or more locales to one another and the geological and constructed structures that impede or facilitate interaction between those locales. While locales A and B may be geographically proximate in the normal sense of their relative adjacency "as the crow flies," mountains or large bodies of water may significantly impede the interaction of their populations. Additionally, two locales may not be proximate in the traditional sense, but may have heavily-trafficked trade or pilgrimage routes connecting them. For the purposes of this study, localities so linked will be treated as having greater proximity.

Shared History: In this study, shared history refers to historically documented periods of interaction and influence or to specific indicators of direct or indirect borrowing of cultural ideas or features (especially explicit primary source statements).

Antecedent-Successor Relationship: Antecedent-successor relationships are inferred from the presence of intervening links between the systems of medicine practiced by two or more temporally removed sources. More specifically, such relationships are characterized by the influence of one extinct cognitive system upon a later system, either directly or by means of one or more intermediate systems to which both are related. For example, system A and system B are contemporaneous and mutually influence one another. System A becomes extinct, while system B persists. System B later interacts with and influences System C. System C is therefore the successor in antecedent-successor relationships with both systems A and B.

Similarity: According to D'Andrade, "Terms that share many features will generally be judged to be more similar than terms which share few features" (1995:64). One important kind of similarity judgment used in this study, "distributional similarity," represents "the degree to which sets of items are found to co-occur in the same environments."

This study will examine the distributional similarity of a set of items, namely, "drug-plants." Following D'Andrade et al. (1972), the distributional similarity of drug-plants is conceived of as being determined by their environments, i.e. the "prescriptions" that they occur in or the "properties" that they co-occur with. The global set of distributional similarity judgments for a source will ultimately be transformed into "features" (items representing tendencies to distributionally group a particular set of plants into the same cluster) using a statistical computer program's hierarchical clustering tree-generation capabilities. The overall similarity of the sources will then be measured in terms of the number of these derived features that they share in common.

The "degree of similarity" between sources will be quantified by means of one or more of several measures, including the arithmetic mean, the geometric mean, and the usability index.

THEORIES AND MODELS

Cognitive System. First-and second-generation cognitive studies operationalize the idea of "cognitive system" differently. From a first-generation (G1) perspective, a cognitive system is a structure made up of units that can only be defined in relationships of contrastive or complementary distribution with one another (typically modeled as a hierarchically arranged taxonomic structure or paradigm). From a second-generation (G2) perspective, a cognitive system consists of a set of related gradient categories centering on prototypic objects and including the extended set of more or less prototypical objects that share the highest number of attributes, on average, with them.

Memetics. Memetics is a newly emerging scientific approach founded on an "analogy between cultural and biological contagion". "Memes" are "units of cultural transmission" or "idea units" that are carried by "vehicles" (humans, their behavior, and the artifacts they produce) and "evolve via differential replication." Groups of memes that are replicated together (such as a cognitive system, like Islamic medicine) are called "coadapted meme complexes," or "memeplexes," for short. Like genes, memes are formally expressed in phenotypes that are sometimes referred to as "memotypes."

Phenetics. Phenetics is "the mathematical assessment of similarity" (Heywood et al. 1964:iii) through "an extension of genetic approaches and principles to... forms that are difficult or impossible to study [otherwise]". Phenetic classification (also called "numerical taxonomy") is based on similarity of form in multiple traits. Since the numerical categorizations of pheneticists are based only on similarities in phenotype, they yield "taxa in which members of [a higher level] taxon are in some sense more similar to one another than any of them is to members of any other taxon."

Hierarchical Clustering. Hierarchical methods involve the sequential joining of objects, by similarity, into clusters, ultimately forming a tree-like structure where families of clusters "higher up" on the "tree" incorporate smaller families lower down.

This chapter served to introduce the study, delineate the problem under consideration, provide an exposition of the assumptions underlying how it will be approached, and present the general research hypotheses to be tested. In addition, it included an argument for the significance of the study, a description of its delimitations, and a collection of brief definitions of key concepts and operational terms relevant to the research at hand. The next two chapters, the background of the case study and the overview of relevant theoretical and methodological literature, involve an overview of selected literature related to the problem of applying a numerical taxonomy-based second-generation approach to the elucidation of the cognitive history of Islamic medicine. More specifically, they entail a review of literature pertinent to the general background of the study, the theory necessitating and underpinning it, and the instruments previously used to study related phenomena in other domains and disciplines that have been modified to undertake the present research.

8

The Contemporary Context of Carib Revival in Trinidad and Tobago

The problem addressed here is the putative resurgence of an indigenous community and traditions (in a region widely and long perceived as lacking either) within a context of extreme socio-economic change. Included in this process of change is the apparent crisis of official Creole nationalist ideology emerging within the conjuncture of the 1970 Black Power 'Revolution' in Trinidad which challenged the outward-oriented cosmopolitanism and inward-oriented provincialism of Creole Nationalist ideology. The crisis can also be seen as gaining further momentum in the 1980s (into the present) with the shocks engendered by neoliberal structural adjustment, plummeting social expenditure, high unemployment, the reworking of patron-client networks, the withdrawal of the state from a leading role in development, and the acute upsurge of racialism.

The questions treated here are: Why is there a renewed interest in Carib (re)identification now? Is this an outcome of "de-hegemonization" in the centre of the world-system? The resurgent Carib Community, organized as a limited liability company and connected to the state via its leader, has read and sifted prevailing local and global trends in defining and establishing itself. This can be seen in terms of its position towards Creole/Trinidadian identity (and its demise), the ethnic segmentation of the society, and neoliberal developmentalism with state technocrats' emphases on community development, self-reliance, and the improving of the balance-of-payments in part via marketing ethnic products and cultural tourism. The Carib Community's ability to read and sift these trends also extends to its perception of, and relation to, the global organization and construction of aboriginality. This paper examines how the terms and processes of social incorporation are reworked in a context of heightened crisis, with special reference to the reworking of indigeneity as a multilateral enterprise involving the vesting of interest by numerous actors and institutions.

INTRODUCTION

The resurgence, reorganization and reconstruction of indigenous communities and traditions in the Caribbean within a context of socio-economic crisis poses a problem for our understanding and explanation of ethnicity and culture. First, the Caribbean has long been perceived, both within and without, as region where indigenous peoples and their traditions are extinct or nearly so. This raises the question: why do we see this resurgence of indigeneity now? Second, the context is that of a twin set of crises: one, the crisis of Creole nationalist ideology of a "Mother Trinidad and Tobago" which was believed by its upholders to have largely overcome its internal "recalcitrant others," and; two, the crisis for state-led development occasioned by neoliberal structural adjustment. A second question arises when we consider how these crises not only constrain but even enable the emergence of sub-national or even alter-nationalist ethnic and religious communities throughout Trinidad. The specific focus of this paper is the Santa Rosa Carib Community of Arima, Trinidad, its development as a business enterprise, its reorganization as a distinguishable community, and its forging of international connections and relationships.

In general terms, the crisis of a national creolized identity entails the ethnic segmentation of the society along the lines of increasingly polarized, rigidly exclusive, essentialist and oppositional categories of ethnicity and racial identity. A significant portion of the society is the product of an ongoing history of miscegenation-a mixture that is as often denied as it is celebrated, and, as often overtly proclaimed as it is covertly sifted for the most congenial elements of an individual's chosen/imagined racial genealogy (a process not immune to the occasional fabrication of fictitious, racially favoured ancestors). In the eyes of ethnic partisans, the national is at best a potential state, at worst an imaginary abstraction. Many, if not all of these movements and communities have themselves assiduously developed working alliances, friendly ties and other relationships with a plethora of global institutions, transnational actors, and relevant diasporic partner communities. Ironically, the latter are not always considered as "global" but as internal or lateral to these reconstituted communities. I believe that the profusion of revitalization movements in Trinidad itself acts as an accelerant to the formation and development of further resurgences of sub-national identifications. I would also agree with Immanuel Wallerstein and Ulf Hannerz who suggest that revitalization movements stem, in large part, from both the pressures and possibilities emanating from the world-system.

The crisis of state-led development under a regime of neoliberal structural adjustment has resulted in Trinidad's technocrats developing policies that promote community development, self-reliance and tourism. The first two of these policies were especially the concern of the National Alliance for Reconstruction government of Prime Minister A. N. R. Robinson (1986-1991), the first government to begin concerted and sweeping structural adjustment. Tourism promotion, at the community level, has been the hallmark of the United National Congress government of Prime Minister Basdeo Panday (1995-2000) and the state's Tourism and Industrial Development Corporation (TIDCO), the latter seemingly ever-present in local political machinations. I see these developments as key influences on the form and dynamic of many of these newly emergent and redefined micro-communities, regardless of their sometimes-open rejection of the state and national institutions.

Thus a major question at the back of this research is: what happens to ethnic identity and cultural expression under neoliberalism in the Caribbean? My hypothesis is that "marketing the cultural product," in the official pronouncements of technocracy, is a powerful stimulus and framework for the (re)creation of ethnic groups as business organizations.5 This points to the possibility of there being a symbolic mode of accumulation, embedded in a wider political economy of tradition, where traditions are valued for their developmentalist potential and global significance, as well as being heralded as cornerstones in the building of the nation. Brackette Williams in similar vein has explained that the "boundaries that mark identity distinction also mark ownership of cultural products and the symbolic significance they have in civil society;" moreover, she instructively observes that, "no ethnic group can afford not to measure its accomplishments against those of others. In search of a legitimate place in the nation, each group must guard its gains and insist on all credit due." Ideas of credit and value thus become in actuality more than just metaphorical constructs, and attain multiple levels of meaning from the economic, to the political, to the cultural, developing along a local-global continuum. Strategies of legitimacy thus become central expressions of the struggle to establish value, strategies that often resort to what Bhabha calls "the artifice of the archaic."

By the "symbolic mode of accumulation" I mean literal capital accumulation derived from: the establishment of the value of products on the basis of their symbolic importance-emblematic (in the case of the Caribs) of environmentally-friendly practices, of self-reliance, and of basic ways of satisfying basic needs; the value of the products of traditional practices in terms of their representation of symbols important to the nation, that is, an Amerindian ancestry of the modern nation thereby indicating a long-term, European-like national history; the value of the traditional material culture of "endangered indigenous minorities" that requires preservation, and thus, inevitably, funding; the value of indigeneity-on-display for cash-in-hand foreign visitors, thereby contributing to "national development" by helping to address the balance-of-payments crisis. To use Michael Moerman's terms, we see that even the most seemingly inane, insignificant or trivial practices can take on special value in multiple ways given the right context. This symbolic mode of accumulation dwells within a larger political economy of tradition, which recognizes the ways in which cultural property is produced and presented and the conscious and purposeful transformation of the symbolic into capital, aided by an array of actors and institutions of political and economic nature, operating within a local-global continuum.

GLOBALIZATION, CREOLIZATION AND THE CRISIS OF HEGEMONIC CREOLE NATIONALISM

While miscegenation, linguistic creolization, and religious syncretism have been and continue to be ongoing historical processes (however muffled or denied at present in the increasingly audible assertions of Trinidadian ethnic activists), only particular crystallizations and ideological formulations of the "right mix" have been dominant at different times.6 An Euro-Creole society, dominant for most of Trinidad's history, involved a hegemonic notion of creolization involving a pattern of upward (towards the "white") identification and a downward (away from the "black") distancing. Some argue that the Afro-Creole successor, dominant from the 1960s to the 1990s, also has an inherent bias against "African consciousness" (let alone East Indian culture).8 Creole nationalist principles attempted to work against a history of ethnic division, but were charged with having "only fostered difference" insofar as Creole nationalism preserved, perpetuated and yet harshly judged racial and ethnic "otherness." By preserving and perpetuating otherness, whilst denouncing it, I mean Dr. Williams' fashioning of a vision of a "Mother Trinidad and Tobago"-"No Mother Africa, No Mother India, No Mother China, No Mother Syria, No Mother Europe...just a Mother Trinidad and Tobago and mother does not discriminate among her children"-which came to be seen as being a Mother with children of "different fathers." When calling people to the nation, Williams and other Creole nationalists chose to call them via the vehicle of their separate racial and ethnic identities. Recently, artist and poet Le Roy Clarke wrote:

> If we were to seriously examine our claims that we prosper as a harmonious 'society' [on another occasion he argued there is no Trinidadian society and no Trinidadian]; that, as diverse as we are, we have managed to create a model, 'where every creed and race finds an equal place' [a verse from the national anthem], we would find that our claims are merely boasts in which we excel

by fooling ourselves and others for any of many reasons that may be revealed under real analysis.

Dominant configurations of "Creole culture" thus involved a continuation of a colonial ethos of hybridity, i.e., as a relation between the "mixers" and those to be passively "mixed in." The emergence of what often seems to be a "pervasive lack of mutual knowledge and communication between the various ethnic groups of Trinidad," has also been referred to as "negative indifference" and "plural acculturation" and leads to the preservation and rigidification of racial and cultural differences. Moreover, it is also a "major ingredient in the middle class Creole ideology" which emphasizes the society's cosmopolitan mixture while pronouncing the alienation of the East Indian half of the population an "aberration."

Whilst proclaiming itself a cosmopolitan blending of especially European and African cultures, an almost mystical/mystifying "new national culture" that was to overcome divisive particularisms, in many ways it revealed its basis as a micro-spatial specification or localization of the power culture of the core of world-capitalism. The central institutions thus were Christian churches, schools, the plantation system, the labour market and the national educational system based on European colonial models of pedagogy with a high volume of European and North American content. Michael Lieber (1981: 86), similarly argued that, "in the Caribbean politically powerful and usually white bourgeoisies have laid down the rules, invoking and enforcing those rules through the schools, churches, courts, newspapers. This elite had imposed a cultural design...upon a politically subordinate black majority."

At the same time capitalist social relations worked effectively through the labour market in helping to effect ethnic segmentation-effectively establishing the polar identities always referred to in Creole ideology-and this was often elaborated through the use of space, creating and reinforcing social worlds under Creole or East Indian "control." Colin Clarke also amply details the extent to which increased racial segregation, socially and spatially, is now "typical of Trinidadian society." We see then contradictory tendencies in the development of hegemonic creolisms:

pronouncing unity and assimilation yet unable to undo the daunting social structure bequeathed by colonialism. Colonial institutions in the history of Trinidad are thus found to have kept the immigrant groups residentially, occupationally and culturally apart to the extent that, "a body of shared values did not emerge to weld the disparate peoples into any sort of coherent community."

Where I may disagree concerns the view that absolutely no shared values emerged, at least insofar as we recognize capitalism as also being a system of values, a system very widely adhered to by people in Trinidad, along with a pronounced and generalized preference for individualism and luxury consumption. What locals refer to as "Americanization," remains regardless of any and all ethnic conflicts, the dominant and shared way of life. Indeed, some local intellectuals see the root of ethnic conflict in Trinidad as being a battle over negotiating different avenues and special access to the "white, North American ideal."

Internal processes of putative "decreolization" (or anti-Creolism, to be more accurate) have begun to emerge via globalized ethnic revitalizations and the development of local alter-nationalisms. Observers note that ethnicity has become, now more than ever, "implicated in the power struggles of everyday life," permeating all of Trinidad's political, socio-economic and cultural institutions and practices. Ralph Premdas (1997: 1) also observes that numerous ethnic identities are now being (re)asserted, even invented, all of which he sees as serving to undermine the state as a carrier of a dominant cultural core and as an exclusive unit of loyalty. Premdas also stresses that these newly (re)assertive ethnic groups and movements are engaged in a quest for security, status and resources, "in a sea of cachophonic [sic] contestations over shares, equity, redress, rights, wrongs, etc."

Selwyn Ryan (1997: 11) goes as far as to say that in a situation where scarcity obtains, "culture is being imagined and invented to be used as a resource to capture public and non-state resources." Ryan (1997: 13) adds that, "much of what is currently being identified as Hindu, African or Orisha culture in the context of the Caribbean are little more than collective fictions or myths manufactured by political and cultural entrepreneurs who seek to use them as part of their political, social or economic stock of capital." Friedman makes the argument (1994: 199) that the heightening presence and representability of groups such as Fourth World peoples is the outcome of de-hegemonization at the centre of the world-system, the same centre which formed a major defining part of local Trinidadian creolism. Trinidad has reached a stage where the dominant paradigms of Creole identity are openly challenged and contested along lines of renewed and reinvented ethnicities, linguistic decreolization, and changing gender relations that deny "the nation" of its "mothers" and even of its "manly men." Provincialisms have become globalized, paradoxically, and with the aid of ever-improved communications technology, are having a serious impact on the restructuring of loyalties and envisioned possibilities in countries such as Trinidad.

It is interesting to note not only the number and names of the new "African" organizations in Trinidad ("African" never having been as common and popular a designation as is currently the case), such as the National Association for the Empowerment of African People (NAEAP), the Organization for the Preservation of African Culture (OPAC) and the African Diaspora Unified Movement of Trinidad and Tobago (ADRUM), but also the fact that they all involve some measure of international diasporic connections, inputs, assistance and encouragement. Many of these are viewed as very recent reactions to similar organizations among the Indian population. It is also interesting to observe-and this has been widely commented upon both locally and abroad, by ordinary individuals and academics-that a pronounced "West Indian" and "Trinidadian" identity seems to have evolved more among migrant communities in North America and Britain, indeed even the racial tensions that prevail back home subside abroad if not rendered altogether irrelevant and redundant. This may be case of being more at home abroad.

I see these developments as inevitably bound to the socio-economic crisis that mushroomed following the end of Trinidad's oil boom and the rise of neoliberal ideology and practice.

THE CRISIS OF THE DEVELOPMENTALIST STATE

Under the "guidance" of international institutions such as the IMF and World Bank, Trinidadian governments and all the dominant parties have accepted, domesticated and implemented neoliberal structural adjustment measures in both philosophy and practice. The outcome has been the withdrawal of the state from an active and central role in fostering development via state ownership of the "commanding heights" of the economy. Furthermore, plummeting social expenditure, rising unemployment, and increased poverty had all served to alert the population to the "scarcity" of valued material resources (that is, the inequitable distribution of resources). Albeit a sketchy description, how does all this amount to a "culture of crisis" and what are its dynamics?

Analysts, such as Emile Sahliyeh (1990), locate the roots of ethnic and cultural revitalizations in a pervasive "crisis atmosphere" that stems from:

1. The inconclusive modernizing efforts of secular elites in the Third World;
2. the growing disillusionment with nationalism;
3. problems of state legitimacy and political oppression in many Third World countries;
4. problems of national identity;
5. widespread socio-economic grievances; and,
6. the erosion of communal traditions.

Furthermore, with regard to the engineered scarcity of resources, Abner Cohen's situational "interest groups" approach seems to have some validity when we begin to speak about the impact of material scarcity on ethnic organization and resurgence. For Cohen the, earning of livelihood, the struggle for a larger share of income from the economic system, including the struggle for housing, for higher education and for other benefits, and similar issues constitute an important variable significantly related to ethnicity.

I must agree with this to some extent since all ethnic groups in Trinidad-literally without a single exception (and I can make this seemingly absolute statement with some confidence)-have either an explicit and formally structured economic agenda, or have actual economic interests and enterprises, or at the very least bear serious economic gripes which at times burst forth in their members' monologues. Cohen further explains that, "in the perennial request for livelihood in a divided labour market, competition for a greater share of income results in the formation of interest groups," and that one can look at the role of ethnic identities in the "formation of self-help organizations focused primarily on enhancing the group's economic competitiveness."

Both supranational and infranational processes arising from economic and cultural globalization have aided the transformation of the state as a central unit of loyalty and social relevance. The state has seemingly retreated into its own exclusive identity-making, aggravating popular perceptions that those who govern serve themselves and their supporting elites: public service as 'serving oneself to the public.'

Perhaps never before the 1990s has one heard so many declarations of the "sanctity of parliament," of "permissible displays of behaviour in this august chamber [parliament]," about "the dignity and integrity of Ministers," etc. This reinforces the view that the state is almost daily called upon to justify and promote itself, a subtle and dangerous admission of the decay and growing irrelevance of Trinidad's fossilized and arcane version of Westminster democracy.

The rise of a state technocracy, distanced from the mass of the population, and the state's increasingly evident inability to solve problems within its borders, mark a growing crisis-driven redefinition of the state. Party politics have also entered into crisis: the threat to post-oil boom patron-client networks has led parties to increasingly appeal to race in order to win or maintain constituencies. Simultaneously, however, when in power these same parties appeal for stability through national unity. Added contradictions emerge from the state's encouragement of a global economic orientation while expecting national political allegiance from citizens, many of whom have important multiple ties with agents and institutions in other countries.

Globalization and the crisis of Creole nationalism have acted as both medium and outcome of the development of sub-national micro-communities whose local legitimacy, in a society with such pronounced external orientations, is validated and enforced by supportive global networks, institutions and trends.

Yet, the state has retained a commanding position as broker amongst communities and interests in this crisis. Its position has changed rather than being rendered altogether obsolete. These transformations have also had a cultural impact: the language of technocracy has entered popular discourse: almost all organizations in Trinidad, of all types seemingly, embrace terms such as "coming on stream," and speak of "project evaluation," "coordinating officers," "meetings of council," "articles of association," "revenue earning potential," and call for new "policy modalities." The language of private sector business has long had a cultural impact, possibly from the time that corporate theatre in the form of CBS' "The Young and the Restless" became so vastly popular in Trinidad. The onus is placed on ethnic associations to organize formally, with their own bureaucracy, elected officers, mission statements, and are required to register formally as corporate bodies, and draft legal "articles of association," in order to receive state recognition, funds and other resources.

Observations of these phenomena lend credence to Brackette Williams' thesis that, "how the distribution and legitimation of the power some groups have in the state to constrain the actions of other groups...shape both their [ethnic groups'] need to organize and the character of their organizational efforts" (1989: 406). Williams views the state as a set of power-broking apparati intervening among competing groups, which seems to be the case here, and sees such intervention as a factor in establishing the material and symbolic conditions for the production of ethnic groups (1989: 427). Williams' analysis stresses "the state as the purveyor of the policies and constraints that both formally define and informally direct politically and morally acceptable forms of competition and cooperation" (1989: 405-406).

Where I might disagree, if I have understood all of Williams' propositions, is that nationalist precepts and principles continue to guide, inform and condition the claims, demands, and formational practices of ethnic groups. I think it may be useful to think more about statist precepts, principles, and models of organization, and to try to better understand how globalization alters and shapes Williams' nationalist precepts. The problem then is that, like the ethnic groups it manages and governs, the state itself has difficulty in establishing and maintaining continuity in a changing world-system. Moreover, accepting everything Williams argues still leaves us with the need to carefully elaborate the sources of the state's centrality, especially in the very new nation-states such as Trinidad and Tobago, and to understand the implications of change in the world-system. Does the state's power rest on coercion? On manipulation of the public purse strings? On symbolic power and prestige? On patronage? On the gullibility of a duped populace?

For a state whose cultural make-up is questioned, all such ethnic groupings feel the need to proclaim their value to the development of the nation, both symbolically and economically, even while they may challenge the contents of established perceptions of the "true nation." Very important also is the state's heightened role in funding various groups' cultural events and festivals (always with conditions attached) and the various groups' competition to secure these funds. Ryan (1997: 19) reveals the tremendous sums of money, in some cases hundreds of thousands of local dollars, are spent by the state on groups' cultural festivals and in subventions to ethnic and cultural associations.

This is happening even while public bodies plead that they have no funds or resources to adequately provide services to large parts of the population, including areas that go without any water supply for months. Ryan notes, to cite one example, how Emancipation Day activities, now observed by many more Afro-Trinidadians than ever before, received $419,000 TT as opposed to $67,000 in previous years (Ryan 1997: 20), regardless of the fact that an Indian-dominated party is in power (or perhaps, more accurately, because of it). This is important for as Brackette Williams (1989: 435) explains: "Designated ethnic celebrations provide forums for such [ethnic] groups to display colourful proof that they too have contributed to the national foundation," however, "[e]thnics...are not the autochthonous ancestors who have the power to turn feathers and flourishes into brick and mortar."

THE RE-ENGINEERING OF INDIGENEITY

Having set out the rudiments of an outline of the context of crisis and its manifestations, we can now explore the specific phenomenon of a resurgent indigeneity in Trinidad, although I do not provide here a satisfactory ethnographic description of the group concerned. The Santa Rosa Carib Community (SRCC), based in the city of Arima, numbers 30 regular members, at most, and is led by a return migrant from Detroit who is also an elected Councilor on the Arima Borough Council, in charge of Culture, and is a member of the Peoples National Movement (Arima is often cited by PNM politicians as being a "traditional" PNM stronghold).

The community was organized as a limited liability company in 1976 and, along with its plans to preserve, retrieve and symbolically reclaim national traditions as being Carib, is also hoping to build a cultural tourism facility in Arima, with the support of public funds and the involvement of private interests. The Carib Community is allocated $35,000 TT annually for preparations involved in the Santa Rosa Festival, a Catholic feast for St. Rose held every August 23rd, funds provided by the Ministry of Culture and the Arima Borough Council. The Caribs are to receive private lands to be used in partnership with a prominent local political figure. The Mayor of Arima, Elvin Edwards, says that the presence of the Caribs' leader on the Borough Council has been both instrumental and beneficial to the Carib Community, even though he represents a mostly non-Carib constituency.

The Carib presence in Arima is deemed by almost all the local powers-that-be to be of special significance in highlighting the uniqueness of Arima and its people. Identified by the state in 1990 as the only legitimate representative of the indigenous peoples of Trinidad and Tobago, this effectively gives Arima a monopoly of indigeneity, one that may also have economic benefits for key interests in the city, whilst bestowing legitimacy on the Carib Community. The fact that prominent nationalist intellectual and leader, Dr. Eric Williams, spoke of Amerindians as 'ancestors of the nation', adds the weight of nationalist legitimacy. The temporality of this resurgence is important to note, seeing that this group really gained prominence and support from local and foreign sources in the 1990s though it began its "rebirth" in the mid-1970s. The SRCC is also a member of the newly formed Caribbean Organization of Indigenous People, founded and first chaired by a Belizean anthropologist, and boasts of its ties to large North American indigenous bodies, such as Canada's Assembly of First Nations.

I refer to this case as one of "re-engineered" indigeneity. By indigeneity I mean a generalized sense of being or becoming indigenous, or acknowledging an indigenous heritage, the act of making claims to being indigenous, and purposefully acting on those claims. By re-engineering I mean to highlight those aspects of this phenomenon such as formal, bureaucratic, business organization; internal shareholders and external stakeholders; multilateral connections; internationalization; and, marketing and commerce-all designed to achieve security, stability and special recognition for the given group. I see this phenomenon as a case of "neo-traditional development," harnessing custom to commerce (see Sahlins 1994), and developing traditions for both material and affective gain. The value of such traditions is determined in the local and global economic and cultural marketplaces. This value is further enhanced when endorsed and defended by powerful international organizations and by indigenous bodies elsewhere in the world.

I have also been looking at how, at the international level, United Nations agencies (to name one example) have played a critical role in the formulation and organization of a new and globalized aboriginality. At the local level, UN bodies can act as "guarantor" of the legitimacy, importance, and authenticity of a group's identity and organization as indigenous. Significantly, UN commissions in Trinidad have held events in association with the Santa Rosa Carib Community. Indigenous perspectives and concerns are being increasingly voiced in many United Nations fora, and the UN has become very important in indigenous peoples' struggles to organize, define and advance themselves. The UN's role has been symbolically and politically heightened with the International Year (1993) and Decade (1994-2004) for Indigenous People, in addition to an array of UN projects centred on indigenous people and the drafting of important declarations. Often, indigenous people world-wide are cast in an homogenous manner as people knowledgeable of valuable traditions and as victims of discrimination.

The activities of the UN and large transnational indigenous bodies may well have the outcome of producing a global aboriginal "imagined community" (to use Benedict Anderson's concept), the creation of a "global ethnoscape" of indigeneity. In the process, UN agencies have by their own admission been drafted into the process of cultural preservation: "strengthening cultural identity" of indigenous peoples is an established goal; setting up networks of indigenous communities and organizations for the sharing of information and experience is another established goal (and a process the SRCC has itself already participated in); promoting an international "trade fair" for indigenous products was also a declared goal of the UN; and, the "right to be different," the "right to development," and the "right to revitalize" of indigenous people was made into a matter of international concern and responsibility.

Re-engineering thus occurs in a local-global continuum: the construction, organization and transmission of symbolic resources (images, motifs of indigeneity) and material resources (funds, international conferences, projects) legitimizing, supporting and aiding the re-creation of indigenous communities. The "reinterpretation of tradition" is a defining feature of this case, with the role of "culture brokers" selecting and interpreting traditions for a particular clientele whilst operating in conjunction with political, economic and religious hierarchies within a given "social organization of tradition." Antoun defines the "social organization of tradition" as a "universal process found among all societies at all times once particular hinterland communities become linked to overarching political, economic and religious structures and implicated in the concomitant processes of debt, politics, social control, and the quest for salvation."

Chaos' Capital: Brokering New Terms of Social Incorporation.

In brokering and negotiating new terms of social incorporation, no longer as atomized and faceless nationals, but as organized and distinctive ethnics, it is of vital importance to a group such as the SRCC to be able to appeal to established precedents and recognized categories in order to legitimize itself and make itself intelligible to the public, in part because they require public recognition and assistance. By these precedents and categories I mean, to name some, the general preservation of "race" as an accepted construct, and its heightened emphasis in popular discourse within Trinidad's crisis context; the preservation of "Carib" as colonial racial category; the acknowledged legitimacy of ethnic forms of organization; and, the international attention to indigenous peoples. As Brackette Williams explains, addressing the work of A. Cohen, most individuals "are 'only too happy' to give definite expression to their uncertain ideas and feelings through the symbolic conventions of their society." For groups such as the SRCC, the past is a resource, the present is a platform, and the future is a project.

The SRCC's ability to sift and read the global cultural scene for useful and established ideas of indigeneity and tradition is of central importance. I rely here on Roland Robertson's observation that, some of the most significant cultural phenomena of our time have to do with responses to and interpretations of the global system as a whole. More specifically, globalization involves pressure on societies, civilizations and representatives of traditions, including both 'hidden' and 'invented' traditions, to sift the global cultural scene for ideas and symbols considered to be relevant to their own identities.

The SRCC constitutes itself not only within a diaspora-like regional Carib network but also defines itself, in part, in and through a network of globally organized aboriginality. Where their public presence is asserted, and even marketed, I believe that the act of presentation is itself an act of constitution, and must conform to certain demands and expectations.

In the end, my intention was to indicate not only the continuities made salient by the crisis of Creole nationalism and statist developmentalism, but to also point to those aspects that render crisis an opportunity for certain groups and agents. Moreover, I believe that the temporality of these new ethnic resurgences in Trinidad, their organizational forms and political orientations, are not just coincidences of crisis, but constructs arising in and from crisis.

9

African Gender Research and Postcoloniality: Legacies and Challenges

INTRODUCTION

Much African gender research draws extensively on the disciplines of anthropology, and the predominant emphasis in many gender initiatives on the continent remains technocratic and narrowly developmentalist. Alternatives to traditional anthropological and technicist methods and ideas have been developed by feminist scholars in a variety of fields. In historical research from the late 80s, for example, Fatima Mernissi (1988) and Bonlanle Awe (1991) explored the need for "herstory"in African historiography, with their comprehensive accounts of women's agency and subordination transcending the limitations of insular anthropology and developmentalism. Developing these themes in more recent work, Cheryl Jonson-Odim and Nina Mba in For Women and the Nation (1997) link the texture of historical process to a Nigerian woman's narrative of her life to approach issues of gender and development from a holistic and humanist point of view.

Certain recent studies of the state have gone especially far in extending theoretical and empirical material for understanding women and African politics. Scholars like Azza Karam, dealing with Egypt (1998), and Sylvia Tamale (1999) and Ailai Tripp (2000), focusing on Uganda, examine postcolonial states in terms of gendered institutional structures, relations and cultures. In so doing they question restrictive notions of development and enlist a much wider range of theories and subjects than those examined in traditional anthropological accounts. In the sphere of economics Aderanti Adepojou and Christine Oppong's Gender, Work and Population in Sub-Saharan Africa (1994) draws together a range of case studies in which women's work is explored with detailed reference to gender roles, kinship, conjugal relations and the connections between reproduction and production. Collectively showing how governments and donor agencies, ignoring the minutae of women's labour, usually base development programmes on skewed notions of what this labour actually entails, this anthology offers a powerful critique of liberal women in Development approaches and also implicitly questions traditional anthropological biases.

With many contributions to recent cultural studies, African feminist scholarship has encouraged attention to the everyday, the ordinary and the seemingly insignificant. Here "culture", seen to encompass all socially-inflected exchanges and mediations, is viewed as the site of localised struggles and transformations. Before the nineties, work on culture in relation to women and gender tended to fix or reify culture, or focused primarily on literature, visual art and music as examples of formal cultural expression; recent research has been enriched by confronting the enormous varieties of cultural communication. With this recent cultural studies work, broad attention to voice, communication and agency enlarge conventional understandings of women's agency and transcend the "resistance"models that have often constrained understandings of women's roles as political and historical actors. The attention to popular culture and social history in particular opens up ostensibly self-evident or neutral forms of women's lives as fertile sites of self-expression, cultural creativity and political rebellion. Marking a departure from scholarship's traditional "serious" subjects, these studies usefully depart from conventional anthropological projections of culture as static and unchanging.

The range of innovative and radical feminist work on gender in Africa today is therefore considerable, with earlier models often providing the basis for recent exploration. Yet despite the steady upsurge of ideas and publications, the field of women and gender studies in Africa today continues to bear the imprint of traditional anthropology and developmentalism. This impact is often insidious and indirect. It can affect, for example, students' perceptions of gender, or biases in particular gender sources, or the orientation of gender research, or the donor specifications with which many feminist initiatives need to comply. In other words, these conservative traditions have continued to obstruct progress in African gender research and advocacy even though many feminist scholars have successfully mapped alternative paths and goals. It is a key argument of this paper that the dominance of anthropology and developmentalism need ongoing scrutiny in order for us to fully consider how to take progressive postcolonial agendas forward.

The paper starts with a survey of research trends that undermine the radical trajectories identified above. I focus mainly not on the details of particular approaches, but on the epistemological and political patterns thrown up by research to date, as well as the challenges they pose for future research. In the sections that follow I draw on my conclusions for a recent review essay of African women and gender studies to describe innovative emerging patterns.

This paper stems from research work for a project driven by the African Gender Institute at the University of Cape Town. However the opinions expressed reflect my own views, rather than the "collective beliefs" of the project, one of whose main aims is to encourage debate and conversation, rather than to establish consensus.

The Impact of Anthropological Studies of Women

A tradition of scholarly research on African women first surfaced with studies like Denise Paulme's Women of Tropical Africa (1963) and Sylvia Leith-Ross' African Women: A Study of the Ibo of Nigeria (1965). These works were powerfully shaped by the structural functionalist approaches initiated by Claude Levi Strauss. Paulme, in her introduction to the collection, describes the variety captured in the essays as follows: The first thing that strikes one on reading these contributions is how widely varied the modes of life are which they describe. There are agriculturalists of more or less permanent settlement, pastoralists living in straw huts and following their herds from one grazing land to another, or again a complex stratified society with masters, servants and slaves and a strict clientage where subordinates provide subsistence products for a patron who is bound to protect them from the exactions of others, this being the mode from the bottom of the pyramid to the solitary sovereign at its apex.

The tone and language reflected here as well as the subjects focused on immediately signal a particular anthropological fixation with customs, modes of life and cultural difference, an over-riding feature of which is a tendency to present African women as frozen in time and place and subjects with static rituals and customs but lacking any real history. The character of this work has been traditionally ethnographic in the sense of offering a window on non-western worlds by defining these as the complementary projections of western ones. Discrete units of analysis like the family, lineage, marriage or kinship indicate an effort to demonstrate (or inscribe?) the radical difference of African from western societies. The particular focus on women's social roles, their situations within marriage and their cultural roles in many ways conjures up a sense of all-pervasive "strangeness".

The codification of African women's "difference" in scholarship did not necessarily result in their being denigrated, an effect usually attributed to much western scholarship. On the contrary, scholarly imagining of African women in texts like Paulme's are often ennobling and even iconic. These portrayals continue to be a marked feature of the present, and the shrouding of African women in an enigmatic "difference"is a significant feature of recent seminal work produced by certain African scholars. Among these is Ifi Amadiume's voluminous oeuvre. In her Reinventing Africa: Matriarchy, Religion and Culture (1997), a work in which she outlines concerns in her output as a whole, she shows that a strong matriarchal legacy throughout Africa has allowed women to acquire unique powers and positions of authority, these distinguishing them from women in the west. Amadiume's recourse to anthropological legacies originating in structural functionalism is registered especially clearly in her preoccupation with topics like kinship, family, lineage and ethnophilosophy. Pat McFadden acutely pinpoints the political effects of this connection when she writes: "The academic language of lineage, the family, and notions of hierarchy and status are drawn largely, in methodological and conceptual terms, from the stock of traditional ethnographical and anthropological sense making, different only in that it is applied via a claim that because it is an African female academic who is using the language, it therefore assumes a different meaning and implies different and previously unknown features and characteristics about those societies and communities."

McFadden concentrates on the political effects of this "strange consonance" of "old European appropriational practices of studying Africa"and the "claims of indigenous African anthropologists" dealing mainly with how problematically the latter feed off the former. What primarily concerns me here, though, is the extent to which early anthropology has functioned as a discourse for producing particular research agendas and establishing interpretive frames for ongoing study and representation of African women. In other words, the problem is that the overwhelming impact of a particular tradition within anthropology has been registered not only in anthropological work on African women and gender relations, but more pervasively-in the way that early anthropological concerns have filtered into and defined an authoritative lens in fields ranging from feminist theory and politics to gender advocacy.

The overdetermining impact of anthropology is evident in the way that certain theorists have essentialised African women in terms of binary oppositions between western and African women. A theorist like Catherine Acholonu, for example, in her Motherism: the Afrocentric Alternative to Feminism, uses the term "motherism"as a "multidimensional Afrocentric theory" (1995: 110) to define what she sees as being "the essence of African womanhood"(1995). Writing more recently, Gwendolyn Mikell (1997) claims that "African feminism is distinctly heterosexual and pro-natal"and grants a pivotal place to the distinctively supportive roles of African as opposed to western women. For certain theorists, then, African women's ascribed roles and identities are seen to constitute the basis for their radical "alterity", with difference being imagined through the available signifiers and images offered by structural functionalist anthropology.

Another manifestation of the traditional anthropological bias in research is the leaning towards a fetishisized "culture", seen to be self-contained, coherent and neatly bounded. References to culture infiltrate discussion and debate in various ways to codify and entrench the binarism of Africa and the West. Here, the fixation with an imagined "africanicity"in relation to women and gender in many ways reproduces the dominant discursive construction of Africa, constantly described in terms of everything that the west is not. This is not to deny the importance of ongoing attention to Africa's unique situation in global politics or culture, or to reject the relevance of metaphorically using terms like 'the west"or "western"to decode power relations. What is disturbing, however, is the fixing of these categories as absolute entities, with meanings about Africa being formulaically measured on the basis of their being antithetical to projections about the west. In the same way that colonial discourses have imagined Africa in terms of its antithetical difference from the west, so does much recent intellectual thought and politics fixate on a binary impulse-ostensibly in an effort to contest western dominance, but often with the effect of reproducing western modes of misrepresentation and projection.

The preoccupation with cultural difference often colours the tone of debate, the kinds of agendas that define conferences or workshops, orientations in teaching and curricula design and various forms of gender advocacy. The focus of this work and politics often appears extremely radical insofar as inherited terms like "gender"or "feminism"are jettisoned in favour of a new language which seeks to register distinctively pre-colonial or postcolonial agendas.

One difficulty with the assumption that language can be overturned in favour of an entirely new lexicon and world outlook is the problematic assumption that words and their meanings can be neatly separated from a globalised cultural repertoire pervasively underwritten by centuries of western discursive dominance. The effort to salvage past modes of thought, or to invent an entirely new language, seriously underplays the extent to which current language use, terminology and theory have become irrevocably creolised. This means that what we understand, from the vantage point of the present, to be pre-colonial and what we currently imagine to be postcolonial will always be deeply implicated in western discursive practices. This dilemma seems to me best confronted not by attempting to transcend hybridisation as "contamination", but by squarely acknowledging and working with it in order to develop "new"contestatory modes and theories.

Another problem with efforts to salvage or recreate entirely new meanings by codifying a pristine "Afrocentrism"concerns ways in which organicist notions of African identity feed into conservative gender and class hierarchies. Throughout Africa, the reification of African difference has been marshalled in a variety of ways to build a sense of African unity that mystifies class and gender divides. Evidence of this abounds in the strategies and pronouncement of postcolonial political elites, in the philosophies of heads of state, and in the defensive reactions to radical women's agendas of many male politicians. Thus, the effect of Afrocentric nation-building in debates about gender on the continent is often to foreground alliances between formerly colonised black men and women to the extent of underplaying the very urgent divisions and struggles around resources, power, dignity and self-expression associated with inequalities between men and women.

This seems to me a key drawback of the extremely important intervention made several years ago by Chikwenye Ogunyemi. In a seminal work published in Signs "Womanism: The Dynamics of the Contemporary Black Female Novel in English", Ogunyemi launches a radical critique of the extent to which white and western women have ignored the realities and locations of African women. She goes on to coin the term "womanism"as an alternative to feminism, arguing that African women and men have been united in a common struggle against colonialism. I believe that this intervention, made in 1986 remains a crucial milestone in the efforts of radical African women to name themselves independently and to contest the appropriative ways in which many western feminists have spoken for them. But the argument about the congruence of African men and women's struggles can become tricky when a critique of colonialism and neo-colonialism and white feminists'dominance is pitted against an analysis of gender hierarchies in Africa. There seems to be no reason why one form of oppression should be privileged above another, and why it should not be possible to critique western feminist discursive dominance while simultaneously disavowing patriarchal oppression in Africa.

When we consider the repercussions of privileging racial or national identity to the extent of ignoring structural inequalities between men and women in postcolonial African politics, it is disturbing that a celebrated "Africanicity"can muffle and displace crucial power relations and challenges for change in Africa. Consequently, the reification of Africa or an essentialised African identity can mystify political consequences in ways reminiscent of earlier constructions of Africa. Traditional anthropology, and in particular the legacy of structural functionalism, can therefore be seen to have had a major impact not only on anthropological work on women and gender, but on the debates, discourses and frames that are sometimes generally deployed within African women and gender studies and advocacy. As such, anthropology has exercised the force of a regime of truth, a discourse with which observation and description are anchored in language and interpretive methods with the force of irrefutable objectivity or scientific scholarly accuracy.

DEVELOPMENTALIST APPROACHES

Women in Development has been a feature mainly of donor-driven activity and research for NGO's, handbooks, consultancies and so on. As such it has been sidelined within academic scholarship and publishing. Despite this, the impact of developmental paradigms continues to make an enormous impact on, for example, the drawing up of gender courses, university lecturers'selections of readings, the political focus of workshops or postgraduate research and thesis-writing in addition to much advocacy work and policy-making in Africa. Originating with Esther Boserup's Women's Role in Economic Development (1970), this paradigm defines as its aim the liberation of third world women from their entrapment in African patriarchy and under-development. The paradigm of women-in-development that was current in the seventies has been augmented in the present, with gender experts couching their prescriptions in the form of knowledge specially attuned to practical agendas for African women. This has resulted in a deluge of "accessible"and "relevant"material that sets guidelines for African women's "development". The limitations of this paradigm have been extensively critiqued by Rudo Gaidzwanwa (1992), Ruth Meena (1992), Amina Mama (1996), April Gordon (1996) and others. What still seems to warrant scrutiny is the ongoing appeal of this paradigm as one that most compellingly answers the need for Africa's gender-related developmental problems.

In other words, it does not seem sufficient simply to identify why WID approaches have been inadequate. What is important is the question of why, despite the abundant evidence of its inadequacy and the many examples of rich, innovative work on women's labour and involvement in the economy, it remains so prominent, and what this implies for the climate of progressive gender research and politics in Africa. In a climate that prioritises an urgent pragmatism, issues of intellectual development and the need for building a critical intellectual culture that exerts an influence on state and donor-funded gender work have been consistently underplayed. While it is therefore noteworthy that developmentalist approaches have been steadily critiqued, the mindset and bias that makes these approaches, rather than any other, such major contributions to Africa's dilemmas are noteworthy.

One result of the emphasis on technocratic and functional development has been to limit the intellectual quality and range of gender research. From a WID perspective, gender research and advocacy can be reduced to neatly defined gender issues, while analysis and rigorous intellectual work is marginalised as secondary, not of pressing importance, the luxury of intellectual elites.

The hegemony of developmentalism has been to sever scholarship from the agendas and priorities facing African women and to delimit issues of development to narrowly economic and donor-related concerns. Stephen Arnold, in his Preface to Culture and Development in Africa (1990), describes this situation as "technocratic balkanisation" (1990:viii). "Technocratic balkanisation" has had a major impact on university teaching and the ethos of intellectual debate and scholarship throughout Africa, with the trend being to displace the relatively militant and independent intellectual activity of the immediate post-independence period (during the sixties and seventies) with a growing focus on Development Studies, technologies of development and intellectual agendas driven by market forces and conservative political strategies. With gender research, technocratic balkanisation has had an especially restrictive impact because "gender" has a long history of being reduced to a peripheral "hands-on" concern. The broad and wide-ranging field of gender analysis has easily been reduced to clearcut "gender issues", technical points that can be easily identified and resolved in line with transformation driven by structural adjustment and conservative postcolonial state-building.

Another effect of the functionalist emphasis driven by WID is the bias towards policy-making rather than intellectual activism in gender advocacy. This means that short-term problem-solving and immediate action takes prior place over the careful analysis and political insight that could shape radical programmes and projects for long-term transformation.

In a highly suggestive article on Ghana, Dzotsi Tsikata (1997) identifies a schism between policy activism and intellectual activism on gender in Africa, a situation that has meant that "research has not had a fundamental impact on the work of activists, organisations and on state policy formulation"(1997:381). She goes on to claim that "while analysis has shown that state action is often both gender-blind and gender-biased, both independent and state-sponsored activists have sought to rely solely on the state to outlaw gender discrimination, with limited success" (1997). The systemic and structural nature of the problem presents difficulties that cannot easily be remedied. Tsikata's historical approach to policy is extremely valuable, since it develops more than a critique of existing state policy and considers how patterns develop, how pervasively they have affected gender research and activism and, implicitly, how they can be changed. Reviewing historical trends helps to explain the constrained dialogues between critical feminist scholarship and gender activism and the reasons for the highly visible, yet remarkably ineffectual state-inspired gender policy-making throughout Africa.

STATE AND DONOR-DRIVEN INITIATIVES

The emphasis on women in development has fed easily into the state-controlled developmentalist orientation that, throughout Africa, has helped to erode independent feminist initiatives in Africa. This orientation has a number of causes that vary from region to region and from country to country. Its key causes, however, are very similar throughout Africa. With the transition to independence, new ruling parties rapidly set about consolidating the diverse and militant women's organisations that had mushroomed during the struggles against colonialism The militancy and independence of women's movements in countries like Algeria, Ghana, Zimbabwe and South Africa rapidly dissipated as women's wings were yoked to the new ruling parties. With this co-opting of many grassroots and local women's movements, political lines of difference (which might have sparked off important realignments, mobilisation and consolidation for radical women's organisation in the post-colonial period) were reduced to personality struggles and petty conflicts.

Tsikata demonstrates this situation in Ghana (1997: 393) while Gaidzanwa reflects on the co-option of the women's movement in Zimbabwe and South Africa (1992). Extending the argument to Kenya, Tripp shows how the Kenyan African National Union steadily increased its grip on women's organisations to turn the dominant Maendeleo ya Wanawake into a party wing eventually declared the sole representative of Kenyan women (2000:9-10). Lazreg develops similar conclusions in her discussion of how women involved in Algeria's armed struggle were later confined by the patriarchal agendas of post-independent Algerian nation-building (1994). In an important contrastive study, Tripp shows how Ugandan organisations were able to elude state co-option. Focusing on the concept of "societal autonomy", her study is an important discussion of conditions shaping the independence of Ugandan women's movements, a position that has generated the vigorous gender struggles in the country today (2000).

A final consideration in explaining the general impact of state policy on gender concerns the fragmentation and conservativism of postcolonial policy-making. Generalising about state policy on gender in the third world, Haleh Afsar writes: Third Word states in general... do not have coherent policies abut women, nor do they usually have structural facilities for co-ordinating their decisions. Given the tension within bureaucracies and the almost total absence of discussion between the separate branches of the executive, it is not surprising to find the introduction of policies which have radically opposed implication for the lives of women and make at one and the same time contradictory demands of them. (1987:3)

Many of the pioneering feminist studies of African state policy today, including Tsikata's (1997), Tamale's (1999), and Tripp's (2000) demonstrate that it is often liberal or WID approaches that frame state policy and generate funding. Post-colonial governments, under pressure to democratise from donor agencies and an international community, have been quick to embrace ad hoc, piecemeal and uncoordinated gender initiatives. This creates situations where gender is arbitrarily woven into policy-making in the absence of any long-term vision or context for meaningful gender transformation. At times, legislation may be surprisingly radical. Yet this is often not connected to legislation in all areas, so that concerted policy-making in certain areas may be out of step with its absence in others, or particular pieces of progressive legislation may be undermined by unmonitored gender discrimination in the wider society. Tripp expands this bleak picture of state control over gender advocacy by showing how many African government's have regulated funding sources for progressive activism and planning (2000:10-11). By monitoring NGOs, many African governments have sought to ensure that funding potentially aimed at progressive and state-independent gender initiatives is channelled through the state's agendas for development and policy-making.

The coordination of gender advocacy mainly under the impetus of indigenous patriarchal anxieties about meaningful gender equity, external pressure and western prescriptions has had far-reaching consequences for women. Although the picture that emerges is of vigorous and high-profile gender activism, planning and policy-making, the reality is often evidence of government's nominal engagement with women's rights. Many African women scholars have critiqued postcolonial state initiatives in relation to the economy or health, implicitly offering guidelines for radical planning and policy-making in particular regions or throughout Africa.

Yet it is usually the legacies and patterns traced above, rather than this insight and rigour that infiltrates policy-making. The salience of the state in gender initiatives can easily create the impression that it offers a flourishing site or models for gender research and scholarship. It is easy to assume that the voluminous research, mechanisms and information generated by different governments creates an adequate climate for future work, especially when these are linked to donor support and international mechanisms. The fact that they have not done so poses a crucial challenge to African feminists seeking to forge connections between their work and radical activism, and to ensure that initiatives from civil society, rather than from the state, take responsibility for conceptualising and driving transformation and development in post-colonial Africa.

POSTCOLONIALITY AND AFRICAN FEMINISMS

The situation mapped above raises the importance of strategising for feminist capacity-building and research on a number of levels. Of importance here are not only efforts to enhance the quantity of the enormously important feminist work on the continent. Possibly even more urgent is the need to develop capacity-building and networking projects that address the entrenched discursive and structural legacies traced above.

The legacies I have described indicate that levels of networking need to be qualitatively transformed in order to foster strong communication and fruitful cross-disciplinary exchanges. To challenge the fragmentation of knowledge and representation originating in anthropology's dominance, it is crucial to encourage communication among scholars, students and researchers who are often confined to their different niches. Secondly, reinstating an ethos of critical debate and intellectual rigour is a vital way to forge fruitful exchanges between activism and academia, to contest the current separation of activism from academia, and to undo the misconception that gender advocacy and activism can dispense with rigorous intellectual work.

Already there have been a number of exciting collaborative and networking initiatives that contest the legacies and elements reviewed above. Development organisations and research networks such as CODESRIA, the Southern African Regional Institute for Policy Studies (SARIPS) and the Association of African Women for Research and Development (AAWORD) have been hugely influential in shaping regional intellectual, cultural and political agendas.

Specialist networks and organisations dedicated to particular areas for women's empowerment, like Akina Mama wa Afrika (AmwA), the African Women's Leadership Institute, Femmes Africa Solidarite (FAS), which concentrates on peace-building), ABANTU for development, dealing with organisations and development, the Council for the Economic Empowerment of Women in Africa (CEEWA), Women in Law and Development in Africa (WILDAF), AMANITARE, a recently launched organisation concentrating on reproductive rights and gender-based violence, and the Association of African Women Scholars (AAWS), which has consolidated scholarship in Africa and North America, have considerably strengthened the work of those formed in the eighties. This tradition has allowed feminist intellectuals to "institutionalize their presence, to articulate agendas for African feminism by facilitating research and activism by African women scholars [through organising] workshops on methodology, women and rural development, reproduction, the mass media and development assistance" (Mama, 1996:6).

These networks have also offered foundations for the much-needed debate and conversation likely to address the structural legacies traced above. One of the key effects of this conversation would be to instil a strong ethos of cross-disciplinarity in African feminist scholarship. Another effect would be to strengthen traditions of intellectual rigour and so invigorate the politics, research and advocacy hat have been insidiously undermined by technicist and state-or donor-driven developmentalism.

Cross-disciplinarity and boundary-breaking have long been celebrated as keys to the success of feminist intellectual intervention. A definitive characteristic of second-wave feminism was the way it questioned the conventional schism between activism and academia. Moreover, disciplines blended and fused in rich and exciting ways, resulting in a pattern that made gender and women's studies in the seventies and eighties extremely difficult to place in disciplinary terms. Women and gender studies teachers were frequently drawn from a range of disciplines, while course-work and research were often emphatically and proudly situated inbetween conventional boundaries.

Although it has become increasingly clear that understanding gender dynamics and promoting gender transformation requires us to explore intersections in terms of connections between disciplines, fields, power relations and identities, enthusiasm around interaction and interdisciplinarity has not developed as far as it might in the field of African women and gender studies. There are clearly a host of reasons for this, reasons that must include the constraints on African feminist scholars to sustain inter-disciplinarity in universities with very different priorities, insufficient time for exploratory research beyond conventional disciplines or limited opportunities for conference travel and scholarly collaboration. Located in disciplines where we are often constrained by heavy teaching loads or administrative duties, sometimes unaware of each other's work because of the relative paucity of African conferences in our field; unable to visit other countries and universities because of limited funding from our universities for research and conference travel; and pressured to take up important yet exhausting ideological and political battles in unsupportive institutional environments, as African feminist scholars we have far fewer opportunities to network effectively and consistently than many feminist academics in the West.

The positive impact of interdisciplinary conversation is attested to by trends in gender research that draw on a variety of fields and marshal a range of theories or genres to bring fresh insights to bear on particular subject. Laetiticia Mukurasi's Post Abolished (1991) springs to mind here. Exploring the iniquitous mechanisms preventing and circumscribing women's access to higher paid economic activities Post Abolished is a powerful autobiographical account of the author's battle against gender discrimination in Tanzania despite this country's progressive postcolonial policies. Appraising the discriminatory landscape that women workers confront, the book uses testimony and personal narrative and so enlists a genre that is often marginalised in mainstream scholarship.

A study which is similar in orientation but which has the advantage of incorporating a concise introductory analysis of patriarchy and feminist research methodology is Ngaiza and Koda's The Unsung Heroines: Women's Life Histories from Tanzania (1991). Contributors include both established and new writers dealing comprehensively with the experiences of women ranging from migrants and peasants to urban housewives. These works are notable both for the ways in which they draw on different styles and genres and for their holistic appraisals of African women's experiences. It is clearly demonstrated that economic activity, politics and interpersonal or domestic relations are inextricably linked, even where the focus may be on a particular facet of women's social experience.

Other important developments have occurred in research with strongly literary or cultural orientations. Of importance here are ways in which a cultural or literary focus is deployed to shed light on broader questions of subjectivity and political expression. A pivotal subject here has been motherhood, with many literary critics focusing on the centrality of social and symbolic motherhood for African women to raise general concerns about ways in which women have been defined in ideologies of domesticity and to explore women's subjectivities and self-perceptions. The anthology edited by Susheila Nasta, Motherlands and, more recently Nnaemeka's edited collection, The Politics of (M)othering: Womanhood, Identity, and Resistance in African Literature (1997) are highly suggestive here.

In the studies of diasporic African women's writing in these key anthologies, a range of critics bring different political perspectives to bear on their reading of women authors'concerns. At the same time, they unravel the contours and histories of the looming mother motif in African women's subjectivities. Much cross-disciplinary research reveals an emphatic commitment to the transformation of gender relations. It is acknowledged that power relations between men and women are complex, multi-dimensional and pervasive, and that a diversity of tools and angles are needed to disentangle and contest them. Rather than simply registering women's locations and identities, or narrowly compartmentalising "women's struggles", this work intricately explores and challenges gender dynamics as the confluence of networks that shape men and women's relations vis-à-vis numerous past and present circumstances of power and control.

Having highlighted networking and conversation as the basis for strategic interdisciplinary work, it seems significant to raise a caution about interdisciplinarity for interdisciplinary's sake. bell hooks (1994) trenchantly observes in her discussion of the boundary-crossing in recent American cultural studies that it can easily define a new orthodoxy, with critics, researchers, students and scholars enthusiastically speaking the language of contestation and border-crossing, yet making very little effort to connect their ideas to practice. Our networking needs to be informed by the priorities and legacies that have thus far shaped the singularity of progressive feminist scholarship on the continent. While it would ideally enhance our research output and opportunities to grow, effective networking need not only lead to career consolidation and individual academic achievement. The agendas, priorities and directions that have thus far shaped progressive women and gender studies on the continent, especially the important collaboration and conversation between advocacy and women's movements and academia, would therefore be a crucial dimension of progressive exchanges and networking for activist-oriented interdisciplinary work.

CONCLUDING REMARKS

We have singled out three major constraints in women and gender studies and gender advocacy in Africa today. At one level, these have led much African gender research to become overly preoccupied with endorsing a "difference"predicated on colonial imagining of Africa. At another level, the content of research and politics has often been constrained by technicism, state interference and the role of developmentalist discourses in shaping technologies of gender, rather than fostering critical intellectual debate. By way of conclusion, I want to highlight the paradigm shift which largely informs the radical work and focus on interdisciplinarity traced above. Many radical third-world feminists have extensively deployed post-structuralist methods and theories, while insisting on the "postcolonial"as opposed to the"post-structuralist"or "postmodern". The use of post-structuralism in the work of certain feminists in Africa signals a major re-orientation away from earlier structuralist emphases in theory and methodology

For example, Pat McFadden, in a recent article on culture and resistance, draws on Said and Gramsci to explore discourse as a site of post-nationalist African feminist struggle (2001). Amina Mama has focused on subjectivity as an entry point into cross-disciplinary explorations of women's experiences and struggles in Africa. This approach informs much of her work on politics and the state, but it is most clearly outlined in her Beyond the Masks (1995), a study of black diasporic women's subjectivity that yields important comparative insights into the articulation of race, imperialism and gender n Africa. Marjorie Mbilinyi's work is similarly inflected by a critical engagement with post-structuralism. Defining her origins as "European/American" and redefining herself as a "critical Third-World feminist", she writes that "Identities or positions are the product of struggle and they represent an achieved, not an ascribed trait... 'Third World Feminist'connotes a critical analysis of the imperial relations, not a geographical location or physical trait'"(1992:35). As her comments suggest, much recent work registers an emphasis on self-reflexivity and positioning for feminists. Increasingly, scholars are acknowledging that all representation and knowledge production are mediated, and that feminist research and practice, if it is not to betray its progressive thrust, is always relational and partial. Azza Karam's work on the Egyptian state (1998) is especially noteworthy in the way it directly brings Foucaldian analysis to bear on pressing questions of power in relation to postcolonial gendered practices and relations. Drawing on discourse analysis and demonstrating that power is not simply imposed from above, but infiltrates the way in which social subjects routinely police themselves, Karam offers important insights into understanding the tenacity and complexity of oppressive relations in postcolonial Africa.

The shift to post-structuralism has therefore focused on power at a range of levels, rather than on entities and constants clearly observable in real life. Efforts have been made to consider how the naturalised language and tools of scholarship are themselves implicated in multiple networks of power. The emphasis has also been placed on acknowledging how multi-layered oppression usually is. Overall, postcolonial interventions have the potential to expand work in some of the key growth areas for African women's studies and to open up for scrutiny hidden facets

Structuralism here would include not only structural functionalist anthropology, but also Marxist, Nationalist and many early feminist paradigms that assumed singular causes of oppression and that were often insensitive to the multiplicity of power relations and the encoding of power in theory and discourse of power, subjectivity and society. The recourse to post-structuralism therefore, indicates a strategic, self-conscious and extremely selective borrowing of progressive resources in order to address specifically African concerns with gender and substantive development. Far-from signalling hasty efforts to "keep up"with the theoretical orthodoxy of the west, they are highly politicised and distinctively African forms of intellectual engagement. By way of conclusion, it seems important to reflect on the role of modern ICTs in relation to the impact of poststructuralism in African gender research. What is postmodern is generally considered to be uncontainable, without boundaries, fluid, what upsets the securities that we have long cherished about knowledge, information and text.

The internet is characteristically "postmodern" in the way that it opens up limitless opportunities for communication, writing and thought, in the way that it galvansies the proliferation of text freed from the mastery of authors, and in the way that-hypothetically-it makes all information the ownership of everyone. The internet is often equated with an apocalyptic postmodernity, with the impact of the modern information revolution being seen as an anti-humanist movement that has, in comparison with the industrial revolution, taken the world by storm. From this point of view, the internet seems to occupy a place in an amorphous, dispersed and post-humanist global culture that is at worst hostile to and at best impervious to the agendas of culturally, socially and politically marginal groups. Yet to stress the generally postmodern effect of the information revolution can also mean ignoring the way that information technology is always used for particular political goals. ICTs are fundamentally a resource, requiring human agency and political intention in order to be used. In this sense, ICTs afford enormous possibility for the networking, reflection and rigour that can continue to invigorate African feminist thought. In devoting our energies to challenging conceptual and research work, therefore, we cannot risk ignoring the exciting resources and possibilities made available by a globalised "postmodern"world.

10

NGOs, Anthropology, and the Encounter with Cultural Knowledge

INTRODUCTION

Among the practices of "alternative develop-ment" for rural people of the Third World, it is now considered important that nongovernmental devel-opment organizations (NGOs) understand and value the local culture and knowledge of target pop-ulations. Indeed, it is now the case that Northern donors often insist that their Southern counterparts devise projects "compatible" with local culture.

The resources available to NGOs wishing to deepen their understanding of the cultures of the people they seek to develop are substantially greater than they used to be, particularly with the wide dissemi-nation of anthropological ideas, the proliferation of anthropologists and other social scientists in devel-opment careers, and the influx of works document-ing and strategizing the usefulness of indigenous or folk knowledge for development and conservation. Yet despite the best intentions of donors and NGOs, cultural knowledge frequently lacks rele-vance and applicability to the planning and opera-tionalization of projects, and for their part, development anthropologists can be frustrated in their attempts to draw development staff out of their received notions of what development means with its characteristic emphasis on modern technol-ogy transfer and attendant notions of efficiency and progress.

The tendency to overlook cultural or local knowledge is due to the persistence of common assumptions that pervade agricultural development and comprise its interventionist ethos. In particular, development expertise lays claims to an objective view of the prob-lems of target populations, which serves to legitimize the developmentalist agenda while underrating the potential contributions of local knowledge.

This pro-motes a skewed situation where in many development projects worldwide, NGOs provide the "technical as-sistance" while locals provide the labor. Development workers point to local or "traditional" knowledge as part and parcel of the problem of low productivity, gender inequality, poverty, etcetera, in the expectation that these adversities will be alleviated given the right technology and expertise (Shepherd 2004). This not only encourages an ignorance of local knowledge (Hobart 1993) but also reinforces a prevalent attitude that development experts understand the problems of target populations in an objective fashion while the latter fail to see themselves as they "really are" and lack the capacity and know-how to exit the cycle of poverty in which they are immersed.

Within this context of asymmetrical knowledge re-lations, attempts to meaningfully incorporate local knowledge tend to be weak. In this article I argue that NGOs cannot succeed in utilizing local knowledge without challenging some of the fundamental tenets of development, not only in terms of development's re-liance on external or foreign technologies but also in terms of the kinds of narratives that are invoked to de-fine the problematic of the local environment.

To illus-trate these ideas, I draw on fieldwork carried out in the southern Peruvian Andes in 1997 and 1998, focusing on the experience of one NGO and the connections it forged between gender, locally held knowledge, agri-cultural production, and environmental sustainability. Without the dissemination of anthropological views of knowledge and culture, and indeed without the direct influence of a group of actors who understood knowl-edge and culture to be intimately related, these changes to the NGO's practices would never have been realized.

KNOWLEDGE AS CULTURE AND THE CULTURE OF AGRICULTURE

Ever since the "functionalist turn" in anthropol-ogy, local knowledge and technology have played a prominent if analytically varied role in discussions of culture. With the mid-century arrival of the ethnosci-entific tradition in particular, the limits of relativism were stretched by a methodology that proposed that the cultural knowledge of anthropology's subjects was knowable on its own terms, promising to uncover a people's cognitive system and their subjective expla-nation of the world. In the rural agricultural context in particular, it has been demonstrated that local knowl-edge is not simply an isolated matter of possessing a cognitive capacity to achieve a given task. Rather, it is intrinsically related to the broader gamut of social re-lations and relations with nature. In farming commu-nities, local knowledge has as much to do with the division of land and labor, sociopolitical formations, and worldview as it does with the technical aspects of tillage, sowing, and harvesting. Indeed, in the Andes as elsewhere, technical knowledge and cosmology are intimately related.

One of the most important contributions of an-thropology has been not only to reveal the actual con-tent of local knowledge but also to provide a counterbalance to the scientific universalism of mod-ern discourses on the Third World (Escobar 1995) and to guard against the temptation, prevalent in ethno-science itself, to pit local knowledge against Western scientific knowledge under the asymmetrical assump-tion that the latter offers the objective measure useful for assessing the "accuracy" of all other knowledge systems. As such, Western epistemology stands out as the only sys-tem to have established a notion of "objective" knowl-edge in the form of modern science (Latour 1993).

These theoretical advances in comparative anthro-pology are important for the way we understand the "cross-cultural encounter" in any Third World context. In the Peruvian highlands, an autochthonous or Andean knowledge system intersects with a Western knowledge system now operationalized as much through development as through the "natural" diffu-sion of knowledge and artifacts. Notwithstanding the new postcolonial critiques of pure and territorially de-marcated cultures or forms of knowledge

(Gupta and Ferguson 1997), Andean ethnographic studies continue to locate a distinctly Andean stock of knowledge, technology, and cultural practices (Gelles 2000). Murra (1972), Golte (1980), and Morlon et al. (1992), among others, have shown how agriculture in the topograph-ical verticality of the Andes has been, and remains, in-timately tied up with political control, communal organization, crop diversity, and risk management. In various ways, these authors have emphasized the nexus between aspects of knowledge and culture.

Other researchers, notably Apffel-Marglin (1994, 1998), have gone further to examine the role of knowledge in its comprehensive ontological domain, thereby ques-tioning the philosophical split between epistemology and ontology and, concomitantly, the divide between nature and society (Latour 1993).

Yet the narratives we routinely encounter in the Andean development world continue to reveal an "in-efficient" and "inadequate" indigenous technological capacity in the Andes. In order to construe indigenous knowledge in such deficient terms, development has historically dismissed the relativism of knowledge in the production of an overarching development discourse according to which Andean agriculture could be assessed on supposedly technical grounds to de-termine its levels of productive output and efficiency. Despite the visage of neutrality, the fact that Andean knowledge has "measured-up" unfavorably has been built into the very criteria by which different efficiencies have been compared.

Another stream of anthropological studies has docu-mented the effects of this asymmetry in the everyday practices of development, which, it has been argued, have accelerated the erosion of local knowledge. Some critics have extended this epistemological prejudice to an analysis of the social relations and power dynamics that prevail between development workers and target populations in arguing that the marginalization-or "invisibility"-of local people and local knowledge are one and the same under the auspices of an au-thoritative development praxis.

As in many parts of the rural Third World, agricultural development in the Andes has been of equivocal value. In Peru, development programs have enabled the state and coastal mestizos to in-crease their control over Andean highlanders to expedite the assimilation of the peasant economy into the national economy.

While the success of these programs has been questionable in terms of economic returns to beneficiar-ies, particularly to women, the ecological impacts have been indubitably ad-verse. In particular, the sustained attempts to bring intensive agricultural practices to highlanders by way of hybrid seeds and their attendant inputs have occasioned a rapid diminution of genetic diversity in the Andes as elsewhere in the world. Whereas environmental degrada-tion is now generally cited as a primary cause of underdevelopment and poverty (for which the solution is "sustainable development"), it is rarely acknowl-edged that development has contributed enor-mously both to loss of biodiversity and to the loss of cultural knowledge. Indeed, biodiversity in the Andes is intimately connected to the agricultural practices and knowledge of the indigenous farmers of the Andes. As the following case study of one NGO reveals, looking for new ways of drawing on local knowledge for development and conservation has far-reaching implications for how knowledge is understood and framed by anthropol-ogists and practitioners of development alike.

THE CULTURE OF BIODIVERSITY

Alongside hundreds of other agricultural develop-ment NGOs, Centro de Servicios Agropecuarios (Center for Agricultural and Livestock Services-henceforth CESA) was established in 1984 for the peasant com-munities of Abancay and soon moved its operations from there to Paucartambo with its headquarters in Cusco. Conventional development models, in particular Integrated Rural Development and Community Development, were followed for several years until a reevaluation of CESA's activities revealed that agricultural projects based on the introduction of high-yielding seed, irrigation technology, and inputs were falling short of expectations. In 1994, a new pro-gram called "The Culture of Biodiversity" was inau-gurated under the guidance of another NGO, based in Lima, which strongly criticized standard development models while promoting alternatives that affirmed campesino culture and agriculture.

The objective of that program was the conservation and extension of genetic diversity within communal spaces in Cusco's northeastern province of Paucartambo. The impressively high density of diver-sity in plants in this region has been typically attrib-uted to its geographical location on the fringe between the Andean highlands and the Amazonian lowlands and to the preponderance of multiple ecological niches. Thus geographical and climatic determinants have tended to organize knowledge of biodiversity in scientific terms, thereby underrating the import of local people in this process. In contrast to this view, CESA began to treat biodiversity as a cultural phenomenon, acknowledging the role of peasants as a fundamental part of the regeneration of that diversity.

CESA proposed that diversity was closely connected with, even indistinguishable from, peasants' agricul-tural and communal practices and rituals and with their ongoing communications with each other and with the Pachamama, the Mother Earth. It emphasized the centrality of the vigorization of strategies proper to peasant experience and defined its relationship with the peasant communities as one of "accompaniment." CESA accompanied communities in their recourse to their own knowledge, technologies, and cultural tradi-tions to conserve diversity as well as to maintain or in-crease production. Accompaniment reimagined what development was about. It underpinned, firstly, the view that indigenous knowledge was an innate poten-tial rather than a deficiency justifying an intervention-ist ethos and urging replacement technologies.

Secondly, accompaniment informed a nonhierarchical knowledge relationship between extension workers and campesinos such that the former no longer framed themselves as those who delivered expert advice, know-how, and new technologies to "inexpert others." CESA understood the intrinsic importance of Andean knowledge to agro-diversity in two primary ways: the distribution of seed and the nurturing of the chacras-the cultivated plots of land.

Distribution was not the contractual and commercially regulated mode of distribution that transpires in Western economic life. Rather, it was governed by in-formal and flexible networks that exist between fami-lies and communities-the ayllu-according to relations of reciprocity. Peasants described distribution in terms of seed paths-los caminos de las semillas. In so speaking, they treated seed not as inert cargo trans-ported by humans, but imputed a measure of agency to seed itself, as if that seed were alive and self-motivated.

This is indeed the case within the Andean worldview, where all entities from rocks, rivers, trees, and seed are imbued with life. The first part of CESA's engagement with local knowledge was descriptive. CESA mapped the caminos of the seeds by learning from campesinos in which com-munities which type of seed was circulated. Each com-munity revealed a distinct seed distribution "map," which was conveyed through oral communication. The maps of peasants were marked by a combination of their knowledge of the phenotypic traits of various seed as well as by the physical action, experience, and mem-ory of carrying seed from one place to the next.

CESA's maps were docu-mented translations thereof, interrelating standard geo-graphical representations of physical space with peasant "maps." The aim was not to specify or quantify spatial requirements (and so the maps appeared as sketches) but rather to determine how and where seeds came and went. Mapping seed paths required that CESA find out what range of seeds were available in any given community or region. CESA made counts of different varieties and identified them according to the local taxonomy in Quechua, ordering the data into charts. Accordingly, agro-diversity became known to CESA as an approximation of agro-diversity as it was experienced by the campesinos.

Maps and charts were derived from peasant testi-mony, which characteristically linked knowledge of seed circulation with other aspects of cultural knowl-edge. Translated from the Quechua, the following testimony of Don Quintin Quispe of Sipascancha Alta appeared in CESA's annual report:

The potato seed movement takes place at three levels. Firstly, the seed moves internally and between families from one plot to another. This continues to be practised by sale, by exchange and by ayni.

1. Secondly, seed moves from the loma (high altitudes) to the q'ata (lower altitudes)
2. and vice versa in order to 'refresh'
3. the seed-the preferred seed should be sown under chuki
4. so that the harvest is clean and healthy. Thirdly, seed moves between communities, especially when the season is not so favorable in our community so we need to resort to neighboring communities like Chahuaitiri and Colquepata and to the Cusco market where we look for seeds that have come from Chincheros and Urcos.

The report went on to list the 51 varieties of potato in Sipascancha Alta. It identified the community as a locus of genetic agricultural diversity and maintained that the informal seed exchange practices by peasants were critical aspects to maintaining and enhancing agro-diversity and well-being.

In all, some 250 varieties of potato-one-third of the estimated total-in the province of Paucartambo were known to CESA at the time of research. Diversity was concentrated in the higher regions of Paucartambo, and numerous varieties were restricted to specific ecological niches. It appeared that some varieties were few in number and extension, a phenomenon that CESA at-tributed to the disproportionate degree to which hybrid seed had been promoted and to imbalances brought about by commercialization.

The second dimension to CESA's accompaniment was proactive. It was concerned with recuperating native varieties of potato as well as other cultivars and medicinal plants to communities and families where they were now inexistent. The lack in diversity in a community was not seen to result from an absence in technology or know-how but rather from a reduction in the local practices of seed exchange. Thus CESA en-couraged peasants to exchange seed and plants along routes so that a distribution favorable to diversity was foreseeable. Ultimately, the goal was not to create the reliance of peasants on the organization as a distributor of seed and plants but to support peasants in taking responsibility for their own distributions. CESA understood its task as going beyond the facilitation of seed distribution. Seed and diversity were construed not in reductionist terms but in terms of the totality of peasant experience. The following excerpt expresses how "technical," agroecological, and so-cioreligious matters were treated not differentially but concurrently.

> Seed lives in the chacra. The chacra constitutes home, and it is a space of convergence where seed, the Pacha, and people come together in dialogue. For this reason, the condition of the chacra influ-ences the social relations in the community. And it is in this sense that it is important to dedicate time and effort to the upkeep of the chacra: we take care that her fertility does not diminish, that she re-ceives the water that she needs at the right mo-ment, and we watch that communication with the Apus is not interrupted.

Although the success of CESA's accompaniment was judged on diversity counts, "the culture of biodiversity" aimed to embrace the broader context of peasant life, building on practices that were inherently knowable for local people within the parameters of local knowledge, local technology, and existing social relations. Campesinos taught CESA not only about seed paths, local taxonomy, and landraces. In addition, CESA learned of peasant knowledge of agroecological levels, crop rotation and intercropping, tillage and har-vest practices, seed and food storage, food processing, climate prediction, agricultural tools, and the commu-nally organized dimensions of agriculture. When workshops took place in Paucartambo, these were not "training courses" that instructed peas-ants in new technologies and productive techniques. Rather, they were generally directed toward collecting, transcribing, and translating Quechua testimony such that CESA could immerse itself in local ways and per-ceptions of the world, in view of which the organization devised its accompaniment strategies.

With time, CESA also came to understand gender and its relationship to knowledge differently from how it was conceived within the mainstream of devel-opment. Whereas development organizations custom-arily perceived the duties of women to be congregated in the domestic sphere with limited and subservient engagement in the broader productive processes, CESA found female gender roles to be complementary to those of men, especially in what concerned conser-vation of genetic resources. The stability and sustain-ability of ecosystems, livestock, and cultivars depended on the practices and knowledge of local women. Moreover, women possessed specialized knowledge of cultivars and crops and had historically played a critical role in the transmission of knowledge over generations. Rather than stereotyping women as victims (or perpetrators) of environmental degradation, women proved to hold valuable and broad knowledge that attenuated the severity of that degra-dation. Concomitantly, women's labor was executed in light of that knowledge with rather than under the menfolk. During the entire process of agricultural pro-duction including tillage, tending, harvesting, food processing, and exchange, women were involved in important ways, and in many instances (for example, in agricultural ritual and ceremony) their contribu-tions of cognitive and physical labor were central.

Rather than assume that women were subordinate and held no valuable knowledge, CESA looked carefully at the complementary roles of women and men in the productive cycle.

Whereas development typically justifies its inter-ventions on the basis of a deficient (inefficient, unpro-ductive, traditional, gender differentiated) Andean agriculture, and more recently, a degrading environ-ment, CESA manifested the curious position of estab-lishing its role in seed distribution vis-à-vis a problematic of conventional intervention:

For various reasons, among which can be mentioned the strong impact of external organizations, the flu-idity in the trajectories and exchange of seed has di-minished. Consequently, it is necessary to direct efforts at revitalizing this practice. If "external organizations" are properly under-stood as development organizations, CESA worked to counter the impact that hybrid seed programs and agricultural modernization have had on biodiversity and indigenous practices, including the complementary relations of knowledge and labor that sustained that diversity.

DISCUSSION

From a developmentalist standpoint, CESA was likely to be exacerbating the very causes of poverty and underdevelopment rather than alleviating them. Asked about the impact of CESA on the communities of Paucartambo, an observer from a neighboring

NGO said he had failed to see any improvement in Paucartambo's communities over the past decade. Certainly, by development's criterion, an "improve-ment" or vitalization of traditional farmer knowledge would have remained invisible.

A visiting representative of a Dutch sponsor to CESA saw CESA as being involved in an environmental program (of enhancing biodiversity) and not a develop-ment program. This coincided with the rubric under which CESA was assessed externally: CESA's activities acquired their legitimacy (and therefore funding) through their appeal to environmental concerns. Understandably, CESA's indigenous knowledge orien-tation arose at a time when considerable funds became available for proposals framed within "sustainable de-velopment" and, in particular, the conservation of bio-genetic resources. Despite the recent and not unstrained marriage between sustainability and development, CESA pushed for a version of "the sustainable" as lodged in local knowledge, while rejecting development as a force that failed to affirm campesino culture and knowledge.

CESA's critical posture vis-à-vis develop-ment was tolerated by donors while an external assessor reported that CESA was "excessively ideological." At a reunion in Paucartambo, the mayor of the province spoke of CESA in glowing terms as an or-ganization that was "developing" our backward and impoverished communities. The mayor seemed to miss the point completely and placed CESA's activities among a whole conglomerate of praiseworthy initia-tives: to pave the Paucartambo-to-Cusco road; to pro-mote the region's tourism (he spoke of a five-star hotel in Paucartambo); to turn bleak valleys into a flourish-ing greenery of crops and fruit trees; and to envisage and help construct the planned highway linking the Brazilian interior to Peru's Pacific coast, a trajectory that should place the small forgotten township hap-pily in the midst of international trade.

It remains to consider the campesino response to agricultural development and to CESA. First, the claim could be advanced that campesinos were empowered by an institutional strategy such as CESA's that called upon campesino knowledge and the epistemic and ontic content of that knowledge. This would fit neatly within the counter-discursive space that CESA occu-pied, with development construed as a hegemonic discourse (Escobar 1995). However, the campesino farmers of the southern Peruvian Andes rarely adopted a counter-discourse. Their resistance to development was frequently expressed as a disapproving expression or a "turning away," a lack of interest, complacency, or an unwillingness to partake in proj-ects in the way organizations expected of them.

Indeed, the task of the development anthropolo-gist is often understood as one of mediating between development workers and campesinos in order to in-duce a greater level of participation in projects. As most development anthropologists appreciate, devel-opment projects can flounder for a myriad of reasons; it is too facile to hold that campesino resistance is rooted in a commitment to traditional knowledge and ontology. The resistance of project beneficiaries is cer-tainly more complex than the way it is framed by de-velopment organizations who invoke the charge of peasant irrationality. In practice, campesinos not only reject technological interventions as much as they ac-cept them. They also redefine them according to their own will, aspirations, knowledge, social organization, and the productive constraints of the ethnic economy.

As CESAengaged the local communities, it was evident that many campesinos responded favorably to the institutional agenda. Moreover, it appeared that CESA's modus operandi gave way to less conflictual relationships with campesinos than did those of more standard agricultural NGOs. CESA did not typecast campesino communities according to their "level of development," and it desisted from the racial stereotyping of campesinos that proliferated in other development organizations. And given that CESA was not trying to transform local agriculture, resistance to the organization was both expressed differently and interpreted differently by CESA itself. Sometimes campesinos wished for inputs, inter-ventions, or incentives that were clearly off-limits for CESA as these were too akin to the technological pack-ages of Integrated Rural Development.

The desires and needs of campesinos, however, presented a much more ambiguous picture than the parameters of discourse and counter-discourse would have us believe. There were no stable or unchanging alliances. Campesinos, too, fractured or disregarded the division between the internal and the external, between the traditional and the modern, between states of underdevelopment and development. Whereas a developmentalist view of CESA was inclined to see CESA as evading the root causes of poverty and underdevelopment, in particular if those are to be equated with low productivity and the per-sistent use of traditional technologies, CESA empha-sized the disruptions brought about by development and construed difficult local livelihoods as the histori-cal effect of development, the market, and other interventions. Both views attempted to speak for campesinos, but neither was spoken by campesinos in such terms. Campesinos tended to stand aside from the discourse of development and underdevelopment and from the causal assertions embedded in that discourse.

Their explanations were not framed within discursive packages, and explanation was rather transmitted through comment and gesture, embedded in actions, and situated in local experience. Agriculture, for them, was lived experience rather than packaged knowledge. As scholars repeatedly assert, the peasantry is not a homogeneous entity. Even within the province of Paucartambo, a great amount of diversity exists among and between the campesino communities. These differ-ences touch on socioeconomic distributions, on the de-gree to which social and agricultural change has taken effect over past decades, and on the proximity of markets, the existence of road access, and the level of institutional intervention from outside organizations. Within this context of heterogeneity, CESA instituted a very dif-ferent politics to that of a standard development organization. First, CESA contributed to the making of a category called indigenous or local knowledge. Although that local knowledge certainly did (pre-) exist uncategori-cally in campesinos' experience, it was modified episte-mologically by CESA, who drew it into a category that was dualistically objectified against Western or external knowledge. Curiously, some campesinos began to mirror to CESA's narratives, and that mirroring was in turn taken up in the form of campesino testimony to add weight to CESA's claims. In CESA's communities, I heard campesinos talk eloquently of their Andean knowledge in ways that I never encountered in other areas. It was also evident that CESA's approach was more appropriate where indigenous knowledge was already alive and well. To undo development where development had been performed with greater vigor might have invoked campesino resistance in much the same way as a stan-dard NGO encountered greater resistance in its suppos-edly more "traditional" communities.

CONCLUSION

The desirability of development is seldom ques-tioned, and local knowledge and technology are seldom considered as anything but obstacles to progress. For this reason, Andean peasants, like most other rural peo-ples of the Third World, are seen to be in need of development, of new technologies, technical know-how, and practices. Although still in the minority, international and southern agricultural development organizations are increasingly turning their attention to the potential of local knowledge-it may be particular knowledge of the soils, of climate, of animals and plants, and of the types of practices as well as the social relations and worldview that accompany that knowledge.

Thus a tension has emerged between, on the one hand, development interventions whose le-gitimacy stems from a perception of inherent weak-nesses or inefficiencies in local productive modalities and, on the other, "development" that takes local knowledge as inherently or potentially valuable. It is precisely this latter image of "development" that im-plies a reconsideration of conventional development's strategies, and it is the tension between the two that in-spires constructs of ethnodevelopment (or ethnoagricultural development), ecodevelopment, "alternative development," mutual learning, postdevelopment, and accompaniment, among others.

For many development organizations who err on the side of conventional agricultural development mod-els associated with the technological style of the green revolution and the precepts of Integrated Rural Development, the very narratives they deploy to de-scribe the pitfalls of local productive forms serve to pro-hibit a more balanced perspective of the possible strengths and weaknesses of local knowledge. In the day-to-day world of campesinos, there are many reali-ties that cannot be fairly represented on a scale from tra-ditional to modern, from persistence to change. I further suggest that such notions along with our few other or-dering modes (poverty maps, literacy maps, agricultural assessments, productivity assessments, etc.) simplify rather than enrich our appreciations of the Andean farmers and their knowledge, that of both men and women. Conventional development organizations draw heavily on such simplifications. As a consequence they run the risk of pursuing strategies that are out of touch and dangerously incongruous with the cultural values and knowledge extant in the targeted communities.

Although development anthropologists are engaged in a broad spectrum of developmentalist initiatives, they are valued-and employed-precisely for their expert knowledge of the interrelationship between the world of development and that of those "being developed." They are called upon primarily to assist and harmonize that in-terrelationship. Often this implies a challenge to some of development's fundamental assumptions, and thus the job of the development anthropologist can be a tenuous one involving careful negotiation, juxtaposition, and reconciliation of differing viewpoints. Without assuming that indigenous knowledge is good simply because it is "indigenous," the development anthropologist must examine the possible value of local knowledge vis-à-vis development knowledge and seek points of intersection and reciprocity.

This is precisely what CESA has done. CESA's work rests on the categorization of an Andean knowledge system and sees that knowledge as a potential and innate resource rather than as an ob-stacle for development to transcend. CESA has done interesting work in bringing local knowledge into the purview of development and environmental conserva-tion. Such a view mitigates the dominant penchant to dismiss the import of local knowledge. One of the more creative challenges for development anthropol-ogy is not only to seek to account for local culture and knowledge but also to find ways to incorporate the particular narratives and understandings of local peo-ple into development strategies. As revealed through CESA, these narratives are intrinsic to particular, and disparate, ways of organizing knowledge (epistemol-ogy) and being in the world (ontology). I offer CESA's example not as a blueprint for development anthro-pology but as an encouragement for them to think about local knowledge and not only explore the way it is excluded by the dominant development wisdom but also find novel ways of drawing local knowledge and development together such that development can pro-ceed in ways more sympathetic to local knowledge.

Development anthropologists are well placed to identify peculiarly local livelihoods and understand-ings of the world, to appreciate the complexity of so-cial life and intercultural interaction, and to aim for fairer knowledge-power relations. This is what I have wanted to show in CESA: it has creatively shaped its projects to attempt shared knowledge relations, such that "power over" (epistemic warrant) has strained to-ward "power with" (epistemic/ontic negotiation).

While I would not claim that CESA represents the es-sential voice of the indigenous highlanders, it speaks to them in ways that are more approximate to their lived experience and lived knowledge than do its more developmentalist counterparts.

By refusing to adopt a priori the position that local knowledge is necessarily regressive and constitutes part of the problem of poverty, low productivity, and so on, de-velopment anthropologists shoulder the responsibility of translating development knowledge into terms that agree with the particular cultural values and knowledge of the targeted communities. These issues are especially perti-nent to regions such as the Andes where there remains a strong and readily identifiable stock of local knowledge. In reconsidering the role of culture and cultural knowledge, one of the critical questions to ask is to what extent devel-opment's enduring economic assumptions and expertise-based methods restrict and constrain alternative forms of development that genuinely value local knowledge and other ways of being in the world different from our own.

11

Anthropology and Global Environmental Change

Anthropologists have always been concerned with the relationship between the people they studied and the natural environment. Since the late nineteenth century, the first professional anthropologists focused their research on tribal peoples who were directly dependent on natural resources for their survival. The environment was obviously too important to be ignored. Initially, anthropologists studied how people exploited the environment, then they asked how culture might in turn be shaped by the environment, or by the nature of the human-environment relationship. Nine-teenth century anthropologists were often natural historians, and it was common then, and still today, for them to be very broadly interdisciplinary, with interest, and sometimes for-mal training, in geography, geology, zoology, and botany. During the first half of the twentieth century the anthro-pological interest in environmental issues led to the identification of cultural ecology as a distinctive sub-discipline. Contemporary prehistoric archaeologists often maintain a focus on environmental issues.

Most early academic anthropologists rejected any simple environmental determinism, but they grouped similar cul-tures into large culture areas that often reflected underlying common cultural adaptations to generalized natural areas. Before 1950, pioneer cultural ecologist Julian Steward, cau-tiously observed that over time people tended to organize themselves in similar ways to exploit similar environments, thus producing broadly similar cultural types in widely separate areas of the world. By the late 1960s, cultural ecologists began to apply equilibrium models to small-scale cultures, treating them as human systems in balanced, adaptive relations with natural ecosystems. These function-alist approaches were largely abandoned because they could not explain how systems developed and changed, and they often treated cultures as artificially closed systems. Since the 1980s, cultural ecologists have increasingly situated the peoples they study within the national and international political economy, and interest has shifted to approaches that will help local peoples defend their resources and sub-sistence economies. Many contemporary anthropologists continue an environmental focus, but it has broadened to include contemporary commercially organized, and global scale cultures, as well as existing indigenous peoples with small-scale societies.

CULTURAL EVOLUTION AND HUMAN ADAPTABILITY

One of the longest-running theoretical debates in anthropology concerns the nature of cultural evolution. The orthodox view as originally developed by Morgan (1877), and refined by White (1949, 1959) and others, was that general cultural evolutionary progress was an inevitable and beneficial process of growth and devel-opment leading stage by stage to more complex societies, using more energy more efficiently, and with greater adapt-ability and security. Cultural evolutionists thought that evo-lutionary progress was such a self-evident human benefit that they did not demonstrate it. White (1949) emphati-cally declared that culture evolved "as the amount of energy harnessed per capita per year increased." The assumption was that cultural evolution gave people greater control over nature, and this was good for people. However, it is significant that the most enthusiastic anthropological exponents of these measures of cultural progress wrote before the energy shortages of the 1970s, and before the United Nations Brundtland Commission (WCED, 1987) report on sustainable development. Thoughtful reconsideration of all the standard measures of cultural evolutionary progress sug-gests that it must be a maladaptive process.

Leslie White attributed the most recent step in cul-tural development to the switch to fossil fuels and nuclear energy, but it is now obvious that the advantages of this may prove illusory. Cultures can be arranged in a progres-sive general evolutionary sequence of increased energy use running from 5000 to 12 000 kcal per capita per day in small-scale band and village societies, 26000 kcal in pre-capitalist agrarian civilizations, and 230000 kcal consumed by Americans in the 1970s (Cook, 1971). However, critics pointed out that this sequence does not account for the eventual depletion of fossil fuels, the serious deficits in using non-renewable energy to produce food energy, or the costs of the waste by-products of energy production and con-sumption.

Hubert (1969) predicted that global petroleum production would peak in 1995, and that the supply would be virtually exhausted by 2075. The most telling criticism was the calculation that if energy consumption increased at 5% a year for 200 years, the waste heat produced would equal the heat of incoming solar radiation and the earth would burn up. Fortunately, before such a Sun Day the polar ice caps would melt and rising sea levels would flood out most of the power plants (Luten, 1974). Human repro-ductive success would also be an unattractive measure of human evolutionary progress. If the production of larger, more complex cultural systems is the measure of evolu-tionary success, then the process still seems maladaptive for long-term human survival, because fewer, larger, more homogenous, and less durable cultures have replaced more numerous, more diverse, and more durable small cultures.

Greater cultural complexity creates a human survival prob-lem in part because larger, more complex cultural systems incorporate and subordinate smaller systems. Some of the evolutionary theorists recognized that small-scale cultures might actually be better adapted to particular local ecosystems than large-scale cultures. White (1949) observed that foragers, with the simplest cultures, may have had "the most satisfying kind of social environment that man has ever lived in." Sahlins (1968) noted that for-agers were successful because they limited their wants to the consumption levels that their environment and tech-nology could support and they lived satisfying and afflu-ent lives. As the contemporary environmental crisis began to unfold, many anthropologists commented on the con-nections between self-sufficient small-scale societies and greater social equality, and relative equilibrium with the environment (Bodley, 1975). This suggested the possibility that increased social scale caused inequality, poverty, and global environmental change.

More recent biocultural evolutionary theory shows how cultural evolution could become a maladaptive process that would undermine the resiliency of both natural and human systems. From the biocultural perspective, cultural evolution is produced by changes in culture, which is conceived from the ideas that human behavior is directed in the same way that genes create biological organisms. Cultures change as shared symbolic information changes. The important difference between genes and culture is that individuals intentionally produce and transmit culture, and they can borrow from many sources. However, the scale of culture influences how it is created and transmitted. Cultural transmission is frequently biased, because people emulate the beliefs and behavior that appear to be most successful. Cultural emulation is easy and efficient, but it can lead to maladaptive runaway economic growth and power aggrandizement, which in turn cause global environmental change.

In small, domestically organized societies the members of each household are daily making cultural decisions about technology, production, and consumption. In larger scale, politically organized societies, cultural evolution becomes a political process in which a single ruler can direct the actions of thousands, or even millions of people. Household-level decision making is inherently more responsive to local social and environmental conditions, but it can be over-ridden by political rulers who may be far removed from the environmental consequences of their decisions. Thus, it is not surprising that large scale agrarian civilizations directed by political elites, frequently collapse because they exhaust the resource base, generate social conflict, or become too costly to maintain.

THE UNIQUENESS OF THE CONTEMPORARY ENVIRONMENTAL CRISIS

Bennett (1976) describes a seemingly inevitable ecological transition from environmental equilibrium to disequilib-rium.

From this viewpoint there is nothing particularly unique about global environmental change. Bennett placed small-scale, tribal societies at the equilibrium end of the continuum, but argued that all people had the same behav-ioral propensities that would lead to drastic environmental change. However, this mixes human means, ends, and secondary consequences. Biocultural theory maintains that all people are driven by a human nature that seeks domestic security and the future welfare of one's children. People living in small-scale societies achieve these human ends cooperatively by remaining small, consuming resources sustainably, and resisting aggrandizing individuals who would promote security-reducing growth in consumption. Some people in commercially organized cultures compet-itively elevate their consumption levels in order to obtain these same ends for themselves. Bennett argues that equilibrium cultures are "only pauses in the overall historical tendency toward exponential increases in environmental use and impact." However, historical tendencies are not inevitable; they are the outcome of particular events and individual decision-making.

By the 1980s, as global economic growth and environ-mental problems intensified, some anthropologists began to argue that people have never been in equilibrium with the environment. For example, Rambo (1985) called Malaysian shifting cultivators "primitive polluters," because they put carbon dioxide into the atmosphere and lived in smoke-filled houses. He declared that primitive and civilized soci-eties interacted with the environment in essentially the same way. In a similar vein, Krech (1999) maintains that Native Americans were not always conservationists, and were in the process of exterminating the bison before Europeans arrived. These revisionist anthropologists, and many oth-ers (Headland, 1997) were reacting against the widespread tendency of some environmentalists and deep ecologists to attribute a mystical oneness with nature and an ecological nobility to tribal peoples.

The mistaken implication of such romanticism of the human past, would be that our only salvation is a return to the Stone Age. This is a mislead-ing issue because anthropologists have abundant evidence that tribal peoples were pragmatic materialists who burned on a large scale, sometimes killed more animals than they needed, felled trees to harvest fruit, and were not always guided by the spiritual sanctity of nature. There is also evidence that prehistoric humans hunted some animals to extinction, and may have contributed to the extinction of the Pleistocene megafauna, such as New World elephants, although there is much controversy on the details.

These facts need to be viewed in a larger perspective. The reality is that until 8000 years ago, when the world was still domestically organized and inhabited by only 8 million people living mostly in mobile bands at extremely low densities, there was no need for deliberate conserva-tion practices. Likewise, optimal foraging theory suggests that intentional over-hunting would have quickly proven unproductive, because as prey species become scarce, hunting them becomes inefficient. Archaeological evidence that Australian aborigines successfully lived as hunters and foragers for at least 60 000 years, and aboriginals in Southern Africa success-fully survived as a people for 130 000 years leaves little doubt that people living in very small-scale societies produced resilient cultural systems able to successfully maintain very long-term balances with their natural resources. The archaeological record needs to be compared with the estimates at the end of the twentieth century show-ing a high proportion of plants and animals threatened with extinction, or nearing threatened status. Nothing in human prehistory or history compares with the present rate of global envi-ronmental change.

It is remarkable that the scale of global change corre-sponds directly with increases in the scale of culture. This was dramatically confirmed by the ARCHAEOMEDES project, an interdisciplinary investigation of 30 000 years of environmental change in the Mediterranean region initiated by the European Union in 1992. Researchers found that the measurable rate at which land degradation could be observed from land clearing, erosion, and dessication incr-eased progressively by orders of magnitude from tens of millennia during the Paleolithic, to millennia during the Neolithic, to centuries during the Roman era, and to decades under industrial capitalism since 1850. In one region of Spain, researchers found that half of all the erosion over the past 10 000 years had occurred in the past 500 years, and it had accelerated over the past 150 years.

THE DRIVING FORCES BEHIND GLOBAL ENVIRONMENTAL CHANGE

The most widely accepted anthropological explanation for the rise of cultural complexity and intensified environmental problems has been population pressure on carrying capac-ity. Carrying capacity must be defined in relation to partic-ular environments and technologies, and is not a constant. Population pressure is also a variable that can be different under different con-sumption demands and distribution patterns. Nevertheless, population pressure remains a powerful explanatory model. It is a variation on Malthus' (1895) observation that pop-ulation has the potential to grow at a faster rate than food production. Population pressure and subsistence intensifi-cation have been used to explain the Mesolithic to Upper Paleolithic transition, the domestication of plants and animals leading to the transition from the Upper Paleolithic to the Neolithic, increased energy input and technological innovation in agriculture, and the origin of the state and civilization. All of these changed the environ-ment. Population pressure has also been explicitly linked to contemporary environmental problems.

The problem with all of these population pressure expla-nations is that often they do not explain population pressure itself, and they do not deal with the social inequality that also produces scarcity. The archaeological record demon-strates that for most of human prehistory population growth was minimal, not because of high mortality, but because fertility was culturally limited. In domestic-scale cultures in the absence of political pressures women opted for small families, because extra children were a disadvantage. Only in politically organized and commer-cial societies are there strong externally imposed incentives for population growth. When anthropologists have looked at extreme examples of supposed population pressure pro-ducing environmental stress and human misery, whether in Bangladesh, Brazil or El Salvador, they have found that social inequality, not population, was the problem.

Viewed from a culture scale and biocultural evolutionary perspective, the driving force behind global environmental change is the natural human desire of individuals to improve the material security of their households under cul-tural conditions of economic scarcity produced by social inequality and competitive striving. The important point is that economic scarcity and environmental problems are produced culturally by social inequality, they are not natural conditions.

ANTHROPOLOGISTS, INDIGENOUS PEOPLES, AND ENVIRONMENTAL CHANGE

Cultural ecological researchers have often helped indige-nous people defend their ecosystems and natural resources against deterioration caused by the uninvited intrusion of outside commercial interests. The most important anthro-pological support, from both archaeologists and cultural anthropologists, has been in helping indigenous communi-ties document their long-term use of particular places and resources, in order that extensive, traditionally owned and used territories can be legally titled to communities and protected. In some cases it has been useful to document that traditional uses were sustainable. Anthropologists have also helped demonstrate that indigenous communities have highly developed knowledge of their ecosystems, includ-ing the names and natural histories of plants and animals. Some indigenous communities have asked researchers to help them with the difficult problem of managing natural resources for both subsistence and commercial uses. Other communities have sought to protect portions of their terri-tories for eco-tourism.

LOCAL KNOWLEDGE IN GLOBAL ENVIRONMENTAL ASSESSMENTS AND CONVENTIONS

Second, I consider the constitution of "knowledge," showing how scientists interested in local/indigenous knowledge have focused overwhelmingly on environmental knowledge and ignored other domains of knowledge that are salient in the effort to link scales of analysis The 1980s and 1990s showed remarkable growth and proliferation in indige-nous movements worldwide. Much of the momentum for this movement was built around opposing the presence of extractive industries on indigenous lands, and the indigenous movement forged alliances with, among others, the global rainforest movement. Somewhat later, as the term indigenous knowledge began to appear on international agendas, the issues of bioprospecting and intel-lectual property rights became central concerns around which indigenous activists organized (Brush 1993).

Shifts in the conservation field have been equally significant. As global envi-ronmental change proceeds at an unprecedented pace, conservation has emerged as a central element in civic and political debates in the nations of both the North and the South. Responding to these debates, new forms of con-servation practice are continually emerging.

In the early 1990s, we witnessed the proliferation of bottom-up models under the rubric of community-based conservation. Since then, the "requiem for nature" argument has questioned the effectiveness of community-based approaches and called for stricter enforce-ment of protected area boundaries (Terborgh 1999). Simultaneously, we are seeing a host of new strategic priority-setting approaches that fall under the rubric of ecoregional conservation. Taking developments such as these into consideration, I conclude by offering an alternative approach to integrating local/indigenous knowledge into global scientific assessments that is premised on distinguishing several forms of mediation of local perspectives, and that incorporates a more expansive definition of knowledge.

THE CONSTITUTION OF THE LOCAL AND THE POLITICS OF TRANSLATION

What counts as "local" when we speak of "local knowledge"? I want to sug-gest that when we invoke the "local," we might in fact be speaking about two distinct things. On the one hand are the voices of peasants, farmers, fishers, or indigenous peoples, often living in out-of-the-way places, frequently marginalized politically and economically. These are people we have come to valorize as possessing richly detailed knowledge representing generations of observation and experimentation about medicinal plants, crop varieties, trees, the habits of animals, and much more.

On the other hand are the voices of those who are delegated to speak for local or indigenous communities in national and international fora. They are no less local-it is more the context in which we encounter them. We do not go to them; they come to us. These are actors who have much to say to the scientific community and to decision makers. In an effort to counter long histories of oppression and dispossession, they are forthright in challenging national and international conservation or development agendas, conventions, and assess-ments and in asserting their rights to lands and livelihoods. These are relatively new actors on the global stage. Though local and indigenous peoples have mobilized in many times and places over the centuries, it has really only been since the 1980s that we have witnessed the emergence of a global indigenous rights movement-what Friedman has referred to as "the rise of the indigenous voice."

These are the people who have increasingly made such a dramatic impression at such international events as the Fifth World Parks Congress, the CBD/COP7, the MA Bridging Scales and Epistemologies conference. Over the last few years at these and similar events, representatives from indigenous and local communities worldwide have appeared in large numbers. At plenary sessions, on panels, and in workshops, indigenous and local community representatives speak of conservation initiatives undertaken without their consent, and of exclusion from ancestral lands. That indigenous issues are increasingly on the agendas of such international events is in no small part the result of extensive preparatory work by indigenous organizations and their allies. They have lobbied to secure prime speak-ing slots and seats on drafting committees for indigenous representatives, sought funding for indigenous participation, and coordinated regional and preparatory meetings. As a result, indigenous and local representatives have been well prepared to make their voices heard and to ensure they are included in the final outputs of these events.

What this indigenous presence represents is a challenge to many basic assumptions about conservation. Indigenous representatives are suggesting that conservation can be done without externally imposed models, management plans, or monitoring and evaluation. They are also challenging assumptions about the roles of both Western science and major conservation organizations, asserting that conservation goals can be accomplished outside circuits of transnational expertise. Their message is that indigenous and local communi-ties must represent something other than a "transaction cost," that threat assessments that classify their land use practices as disturbances are unacceptable, and that participatory methods that define them as just one more cate-gory of stakeholder have no place in their vision of conservation. Though both kinds of actors-"local locals" and local/ indigenous advocates-get coded as "local" in international fora, important differences exist between them. When we consider how their words, their insights, and their knowledge move between scales in the process of translation, we must recognize that both are mediated, albeit in very different ways. Making an effec-tive link between local knowledge and policy requires that we recognize these different forms of mediation.

For researchers interested in local or indigenous knowledge, it is those "local locals" that we usually work with the most. After all, these are the people who exist "on the ground" as repositories of the knowledge that interests us. The point, however, is that their knowledge enters circuits of global knowledge pro-duction in mediated form through us. Most of us who conduct research on local knowledge are able to do so because powerful institutions are interested in sup-porting our research, and because these institutions are increasingly interested in what we have to say about particular peoples and places. When they want to learn about local realities and local perspectives, they turn to the social sci-ences. This is what Gledhill was getting at when he reminded us that "intellectuals are contributing to new regulatory strategies being pursued by states and transnational agencies.

There is a particular danger that anthropologists will reinforce a politics of containment where this offers a new market opportunity for peddling our services as experts on 'culture,' either to the national state as an employer of specialists in the administration of ethnic difference or to the wider world of transnational agencies and NGOs" (1998, 516-17). The key to understanding this process of mediation lies in an understand-ing of the tools we use. As an anthropologist, I believe in the value of ethno-graphic research methods. Other social scientists rely on more rapid, formalistic, survey-based methods. Whichever methods we prefer, the social sciences get positioned as speaking for the local. In so doing, the danger is that the repre-sentations of those who possess expertise in making the local legible and intel-ligible to those working at other scales are conflated with local voices themselves. These are not the same thing; we must never conflate data pro-vided by those who work at a local level with local voices themselves. We can offer our translations, our mediated accounts, and these can be very valuable, but we must never presume that we actually ever speak for the local.

The voices of indigenous advocates or representatives are mediated as well, albeit very differently. While they may be unmediated by social science con-ventions and formalistic methods, they are mediated by transnational dis-courses of indigeneity. While asserting locality and connection to place, they simultaneously speak with reference to global categories. This does not make their claims any less authentic: there is nothing inauthentic about the solidar-ity that is emerging from a recognition of shared histories of marginalization. Still, the fact that indigenous representatives are compelled to speak in global categories is a form of mediation.

There is yet another aspect of how the local is constituted that deserves our attention: the pervasive distinction made between local actors and "decision makers." This is achieved in part through what I have elsewhere termed the "topology of simple locality" (Brosius 1999c): a topology that defines the task of the ethnographer as one of inscribing and representing for an audience some actually existing place or set of places-our research sites, the communities in which we work. It is a kind of focalizing strategy, drawing our attention to particular places as the most significant loci for the production of knowledge, and diverting our attention from the ways in which those places articulate with other places or with actors working at other scales. The topology of simple local-ity suffers from the same shortcoming that has produced critiques of that other convention of anthropological writing, the "ethnographic present." Anthropologists today are much more alert to the politics and histories that have shaped the communities they study.

However, the "ethnographic pres-ent" is a still-extant convention of ethnographic writing wherein an anthro-pologist describing a particular set of cultural practices writes about them in the present tense, even though their research may have occurred many years in the past and though much of what is described may no longer exist in the same form as it did when it was observed (Fabian 1983). Just as the ethnographic present acts as a distancing mechanism that relegates our research subjects to a timeless irrelevancy, immune from history and from the effects of our ethnographic presence, so too does the topology of simple locality cre-ate a coherent "there" that can be known and represented and kept in its place. As Tawfic Ahmed and Reid (2002, 219) remind us, the Millennium Ecosys-tem Assessment is "designed to meet the needs of decision-makers." Unspo-ken here is an assumption about the inherent distance between local actors and decision makers and, therefore, about the relation between scale and hier-archy. Viewed in this way, indigenous knowledge is provided to those in the policy domain, but it speaks only in the passive voice of science rather than in the active voice of advocacy and it speaks from the subordinate position of knowledge solicited and translated up for the purpose of governance.

Whether our goals are purely instrumental (rendering local voices and local knowledge into forms useful in managerial terms) or emancipatory (rendering local voices into compelling narratives designed to secure rights), those local voices are situated in a subject position.

THE CONSTITUTION OF KNOWLEDGE

Now we turn to the question of what counts as "knowledge" when we speak of "local knowledge." As it is used by ethnoecologists and others, reference to indigenous or local "knowledge"-often referred to by the acronyms IK (indige-nous knowledge) or TEK (traditional ecological knowledge)-is generally applied to knowledge of the natural world: what such groups know about the resources they exploit, how these societies cognize or interpret natural processes, and so forth. In short, when we speak of indigenous or local knowledge, what we generally mean is environmental knowledge.

That we are at last recognizing the value of local/indigenous knowledge, rather than dismissing it as anecdotal, irrelevant, or merely a lesser form of knowledge, is clearly a positive development. But that we limit our valoriza-tion of knowledge largely to that which pertains to the natural world yet again consigns that knowledge to the irrelevancy of the ethnographic present, des-tined forever to fill what Trouillot has termed the "savage slot" (Trouillot 1991), an epistemological backwater distinct from, and subordinate to, the forms of knowledge possessed by decision makers.

Let us, for a moment, consider the domains of knowledge that concern the Millennium Ecosystem Assessment. One strength of the MA is not only that it is firmly science driven, dedicated to producing and synthesizing reliable sci-entific data, but that it goes beyond this to identify trends, scenarios, trade-offs, and response options. Central to the MA vision is that it provide information that is not only scientifically credible but salient and legitimate as well.

According to Reid: "Scientific information is salient if it is perceived to be relevant or of value to particular groups who might use it to change management approaches, behavior, or policy decisions.... It is legiti-mate if the process of assembling the information is perceived to be fair and open to input from key political constituencies, such as the private sector, gov-ernments, and civil society."

But what might happen, we may ask, if these three criteria were applied not only to objective scientific information but to local and indigenous knowledge as well? What if, when we went out to seek information from local people, we not only asked about their knowledge of the natural world but also sought their analyses of the political world? How might their analyses of drivers and their assessments of threats differ from our own? What if we asked them about trends, scenarios, trade-offs, and response options? In other words, instead of treating our informants as reservoirs of local/indigenous knowledge, what if we treated them as political agents with their own ideas about the salience and legitimacy of various forms of knowledge? And what if we made a more sys-tematic effort to incorporate that into MA outputs?

A brief example illustrates what is at stake here. For several years in the 1980s and 1990s, I worked with various groups of Penan hunter-gatherers in the Malaysian state of Sarawak. As traditionally nomadic hunter-gatherers, Penan depend on the forest for virtually every aspect of their existence. They exemplify the depth and richness of environmental knowledge that indigenous peoples hold, with a remarkable knowledge of trees, plants, and animals and of the relations among them. Penan also possess a rich vocabulary for describ-ing landscape and an extensive knowledge of places in the landscape they inhabit. This landscape is more than a reservoir of detailed ecological knowl-edge or a setting in which they satisfy their nutritional needs. It is also a repos-itory for the memory of past events, a vast mnemonic representation of social relationships and of society. For Penan, landscape, history, and kinship-the bonds linking individuals to households to communities to generations past and future-are part of a larger whole.

In the late 1980s, the Penan became the focus of a high-profile transnational indigenous rights campaign concerned with logging. Since the 1980s, timber companies have expanded their reach throughout virtually every river valley occupied by Penan, and Penan have responded with intermittent blockades. During the first wave of blockades in 1987, images of Penan resisting the approach of logging companies traveled global environmental and indigenous rights circuits, producing an outpouring of support. Penan continue to assert their rights to land using every tool of persuasion available to them, though their efforts have largely been futile. The official government view of Penan is that their way of life is little more than a form of vagrancy in which would-be subjects are able to evade the gaze of the state. The only way Penan can be heard, the only dis-course audible to the state, is that of development. The overall effect of the campaign was that the government shifted the debate over logging in Sarawak from a focus on forest destruction and the rights of indigenous communities to an issue of sustainable forest management. The discursive contours of the debate were shifted away from the moral and political domain toward the domain of environmental management. By the mid-1990s, the campaign's momentum had largely dissipated.

The question I want to pose is, in a "policy environment" characterized by dis-possession, where the threats to local communities result from the actions of "deci-sion makers," of what relevance is indigenous knowledge of nature by itself, divorced from its significance with respect to the making of claims? What is needed, I would argue, is a more expansive, less fixed notion of knowledge. What matters is not how much Penan know about the landscape they inhabit but how they posi-tion that knowledge, and themselves, within the broader contours of power. Whether or not they are actively engaged in explicit acts of resistance, the topic of logging is one that consumes Penan and that they discuss endlessly. Their narratives recount confrontations between themselves and state author-ities or company representatives: police, judges, government ministers, camp managers, and others. They recount the arguments put forth by themselves or others: why they decided to blockade, why they should not be blamed for those blockades, and who they believe to be ultimately responsible.

Any effort to understand Penan narratives of dispossession must begin with recognizing the variety of forms they take. Such narratives, and the forms of action they prescribe, exist on a continuum from the concrete to the aesthetic and oblique. Many of the concerns they express are practical in nature-for instance, the simple difficulty of making a living in a logged-over landscape. Penan describe in matter-of-fact terms the destruction of the forest and the hardship this has caused them. They speak of river siltation, the destruction of sago, rattan, and fruit trees, and the depletion of game. At times, Penan make direct claims: they speak of boundaries and of the need to prohibit the entry of outsiders onto their lands. At other times they speak movingly about the qualities of the forest and their life within it.

They speak of the heat, dust, and desolation of logging against the coolness and cleanliness of the forest, the harsh sound of chainsaws versus the squeaking of trees rubbing in the wind. The words and images they employ are contrastive and tinged with nostalgia: what the forest was like before logging and after it. And they speak of loss and pain-at seeing valuable fruit trees destroyed and the graves of loved ones bulldozed. What is further striking about Penan commentaries on landscape and for-est destruction is the degree to which the arguments they put forth are about locality and biography. Penan do not talk about the need to preserve rainforests as a generic abstraction; they talk about the need to preserve particular water-sheds "from which we eat." It is the transgression of that densely biographi-cal and genealogical locality that Penan find to be such a great injustice.

Often too, Penan speak in metaphors-for example, linking the forest to a supermarket or a bank. Such arguments are meant to appeal to what Penan presume is a shared sense of justice and respect. The arguments that Penan are putting forth should be viewed not exclusively as acts of resistance but simul-taneously as efforts at engagement. In making their arguments to loggers, civil servants, environmentalists, and others, Penan are attempting to speak across difference, to familiarize themselves, to frame their arguments in ways that they hope outsiders will recognize. Their purpose is to persuade.

In considering how Penan frame their struggle against logging, it is impor-tant to consider not merely the rhetorical elements of these narratives but the forms they take as well: letters addressed to government officials, verbal argu-ments with timber company managers, maps produced with the aid of local activists, videotaped interviews produced by Euro-American documentary film-makers, and others. What happens when Penan claims are textualized in dif-ferent ways? How do Penan conceptions of their audience condition the arguments they put forth and the forms of knowledge they deploy? What this points to is the need to foreground notions of agency in narratives of landscape and dispossession. The questions of whom Penan believe to be responsible for their plight and whom they believe is in the best position to help them are as central to this whole domain of discourse as are statements about what is occurring and how it effects their everyday lives. These are as much narratives of culpability as narratives of place.

For instance, in asserting claims to land, arguing for the establishment of reserved areas, attempting to demarcate borders, or contesting the claims of timber companies, Penan-often with the help of nongovernmental organiza-tion allies-produce maps or written declarations.

Penan see that loggers bring maps, show them official letters, and try to compel them to sign documents, and that all of these serve to validate company claims to Penan lands. Penan recognize that these methods are the single most effective way to assert their claims in a way that is meaningful to outsiders At the same time they are asserting their own claims to land, Penan deny the validity of maps produced by others. One nomadic headman, referring to map-making practices, described timber companies as "stealing [land] from open places"-that is, from the outside.

He declared government maps a lie because they are made from high above, showing only the shape of the land. The Penan see the fact that these maps are made from a distance as an indication of duplicity. Penan contrast the way companies make maps from a distance with the way they themselves do: by walking through and over every valley and ridge, by filling the place with names, and by sustaining themselves on resources that have been passed down for generations.

As one nomadic Penan man sarcastically told me, he would ask loggers, "If this is your land, why do you always ask us the names of rivers? Do you know the names of places? You and your people are always asking-what is the name of this river?, what is the name of that river? If you don't know these, you don't belong here."

The Penan response to logging is a product not only of the tangible effects of environmental degradation but also of the way Penan perceive themselves to have been treated by those with an interest in its continuation.

They are responding not only to logging as an activity that directly affects their lives but also to the agents of logging. When Penan discuss why they erect blockades, one theme arises more than any other: they say they blockade because "the government does not hear what we say," repeatedly describing the government and companies as being "deaf." Company and government officials do not lis-ten to them, Penan assert, because the officials do not respect them, and they interpret this as a form of insult. Further, because they have made innumer-able good-faith attempts at dialogue, any action they might then take-most often blockades-can no longer be considered their fault. In recent years, we have observed a florescence of scholarship focused on indigenous conceptions of landscape.

This literature has alerted us to the rich variety of narrative forms through which societies inscribe their presence in places. Yet in lis-tening to Penan statements about the forest and its destruction, we should be cautious about assuming that documenting Penan conceptions of landscape as some fixed entity-"indigenous knowledge"-is ever enough. Rather, we also need to try to discern how Penan conceptions of their audience condition the arguments they put forth.

LOCAL KNOWLEDGE, INDIGENOUS PEOPLES, AND ENVIRONMENTAL GOVERNANCE

In the past decade or so, it has become axiomatic to state that indigenous peo-ples "possess, in their ecological knowledge, an asset of incalculable value: a map to the biological diversity of the earth on which all life depends.

Encoded in indigenous languages, customs, and practices may be as much understand-ing of nature as is stored in the libraries of modern science". As self-evident as this may now seem, it does not provide much guidance with respect to how one moves between local knowledge and global science. That is the question that animates this volume and the Millennium Ecosystem Assessment as a whole.

In our efforts to bridge scales and epistemologies, we stand at a critical cross-road. For today we are confronted with two apparently contradictory trends in the domain of environmental governance. On the one hand, we have witnessed a trend toward valorizing indigenous/local forms of knowledge and mobiliz-ing indigenous peoples. The Bridging Scales and Epistemologies conference, the outputs of the World Parks Congress, the World Conservation Congress, and the CBD/COP7-all of which express some form of support for indigenous priorities-are four manifestations of this trend.

On the other hand, in the last few years we have witnessed a decisive move by major conservation organizations toward cartographically enabled regional land use planning approaches under the rubric of ecoregional conservation. Along with this, we have witnessed the emergence of the field of "conserva-tion finance" and the proliferation of social science-based metrics and models designed to monitor and manage social and political processes in conservation.

These three are linked discursively, strategically, and institutionally in a broader process of consolidation, and together they are reshaping the way conservation is conceptualized, planned, and admin-istered. The comprehensive visions being promoted and the proprietary data-bases being produced in the emerging complementarities of spatial planning, investment, and social metrics have the potential to reshape the contours of the relationship between humanity and nature for generations to come.

Events such as the World Parks Congress and the World Conservation Con-gress can be seen, in essence, as exercises devoted to normalizing and reinforc-ing these complementary manifestations of consolidation. Attending these events, one is left with the impression that an enormous weight of managerialism has descended over conservation, much as it once did on development, and that this state of affairs is in large part due to the efforts of major conservation organizations to consolidate their authority over global conservation practices.

They are achieving this consolidation by establishing administrative technologies in which they are taken for granted as methodological gatekeepers. Increasingly, conservation has become a gated community that one can enter only by accepting the methodological terms promulgated by major conservation organizations. This has occurred as tools or approaches that originated as emancipatory moves-stakeholder analysis, participatory mapping, community-based natural resource management-have been incorporated into the managerial apparatus of conservation. Once incorporated, they become tied to the imperatives of funding cycles, scaling up, accountability to donors, and more.

This situation is ironic, and it has major implications for integrating local and indigenous perspectives into conservation. Just when local voices and local forms of knowledge are being invoked as relevant to the setting of global con-servation strategies and local conservation management, the institutional struc-tures of global conservation that are now emerging are preventing them from being meaningfully included. What then becomes of alternative forms of con-servation that are informed by local ways of knowing?

This consolidation of conservation practices by major conservation organi-zations is being achieved by the shift in scale that I have described. As Smith (1992) and Harvey (1996) remind us, scale is always political. Left unspoken in contemporary conservation is the relation between scale and hierarchy. Higher-level scales of visualization require higher-level structures of governance.

Ecoregional conservation is fundamentally about scale-both enlarging the scale of environmental interventions and linking information created at different scales into a single strategic blueprint for the future at an extended temporal scale. All the talk about scaling up in conservation is accompanied by a concern for improving "efficiencies" and reducing "transaction costs." Indigenous knowledge, when it moves up the scale, becomes both simplified and embedded in a range of other agendas.

Earlier I drew a distinction between two forms of locality: that mediated by the research activities of social scientists and that articulated by local/indige-nous activists and advocates. One speaks in the passive voice of science, trans-lating indigenous ways of knowing into forms intelligible to practitioners and decision makers; the other speaks in the active voice of advocacy. Making this distinction draws our attention to the question of how local/indigenous per-spectives and ways of knowing are elicited and translated between scales and how the link is made between this knowledge and the policy domain.

The for-mer reifies the distinction between local/indigenous peoples living their lives in particular places and policy makers who are making sometimes momentous decisions about those peoples' lives.

Local/indigenous advocates, on the other hand, are refusing that distinction. Making meaningful progress in the future will entail a willingness on the part of conservation scientists and practitioners to work with indigenous/local com-munities in new ways, ways in which the tools of Western science are offered in support of local conservation priorities. What that means for how conservation initiatives are planned, implemented, and governed is not yet clear, but it is an effort that we must take seriously. The challenge is to seek productive terms of engagement. We cannot afford to perpetuate the polemic that the goals of con-servation and indigenous rights are at odds with each other, or that indigenous knowledge is something to be packaged and passed up to "decision makers." The fate of biodiversity rests in part on how the conservation community responds to the challenge posed by indigenous and local communities and whether it is able to embrace this as an opportunity to create new alliances for conservation.

12

Empire to Nation, and the Relevance of Reciprocal Understanding to China

It is a special privilege for a social anthropologist from China to be invited to present this personal view of reciprocal understanding. Indeed this is not a personal honor but that of a Chinese scholarly group whose involvement in the Transcultura based in Paris-the prime institution for the promotion of transcultural dialogue--has been recognized as important.1 So I admit that what I will say will concern not only me but also many of our Chinese colleagues. We can thus indulge ourselves in an act of reciprocation--but not academic rivalry as we usually see in the academic institutions within our own Chinese contexts--and we can do so to make our references not merely to ourselves and our own cultures but also to the Western world. The thing to do is to depart from a broader perspective to include the cosmological part of China and to consider the possible trappings from which we-my European and Chinese colleagues--want to find out before we fall into them.

It is what we now call "reciprocal anthropology". As many of you know, our shared definition of it is that it is part of a larger project of restructuring the space between others' and "our" own cultures-"our" meaning either European or Chinese and others in turn referring to "our" respective alternative counterparts. As some human elements of the new intellectual enterprise, we use "reciprocal anthropology"-which has only been called for in the past decade--to refer to an alternative world-view and practice, chiefly consisting of the recognition of the logical and ontological significance of conjuncture and exchange among systems of culture, and to honor the endeavor to create "mutual disposition" or "co-presence" among human cultures. This is a sort of anthropology with an emphasis on the idea of "reciprocity", reciprocity between different points of view of the world. But how can we say that such a pursuit is an innovative quest for knowledge and intercultural relationship?

For almost the whole of the 20th century, anthropologists have engaged in the pursuit of viewing the self "in the other'". Out of what they observe, anthropologists, taking "cultural contrast as a means of knowing", have sought to track the paths of culture in order to reflect on their own "local knowledge." Some exemplary characters are the structural anthropologists such as Levi-Strauss who builds his theories on "alliance theory" and on the conception of complementary opposites and highlights the unconscious model of cross-cultural communication in the "savage mind". There are also anthropologists of other kinds who tell stories of mystics against the market, tribes and castes against individualism, theater states against the "substantial state," and of many other complementary contrasts as perspectives for our reflexive co-presence. More recently, post-colonialist or reflexive anthropologists seek to re-tell the story of how anthropologists themselves departed from their European homes to "classify non-European humanity in ways that would be consistent with Europe's story of triumph as 'progress'." These, though not quite in agreement with earlier structural and interpretive approaches, are producing some works that are also interestingly similar to "mutual disposition".

But the above does not direct us towards a rejection of our efforts. Further to modern and post-modern anthropological traditions, reciprocal anthropology demands certain explicit forms of reciprocation that are only implicitly conveyed in other earlier anthropological perspectives. It is proposed that we should aim to relate our pursuit with Bakhtin's notion of "dialogical imagination", and with a sort of chronotope or the "particular sense of time in relation to space that develops in a human scenarios and gives it special character." Perhaps drawing more or less on

Marcel Mauss's "total prestation", it has also been proposed that we should realize a principle, one that stems from a position that "supposes an approach which respectively engages two subjects or cultures in an equal process of mutual knowledge." Both emphasize that the new kind of knowledge as proposed is only conceivable when we treat it as an alternative practice involving a re-evaluation of anthropology's disciplinary formation. But how can this re-evaluation be distinguished from structural, interpretive, and post-colonialist re-evaluations?

The answer may lie in what seems self-contradictory. Along the culturological line, reciprocal anthropology may be viewed as what is akin to interpretive approaches to ethnographic narratives, and especially with the interpretive anthropology of the others' (or natives') points of view. Nonetheless, the so-defined intellectual pursuit also encompasses a perspective of cross-cultural relationships: it participates in the intellectual protest against the bifurcation of the world as "the West and the rest". Thus we should admit that our endeavor is faced with a sense of ambivalence. On the one hand, so-supposed reciprocal anthropology encourages anthropologists to take the others' cultural differences from "us" as a saliently distinctive system of value and knowledge. On the other hand, the subject itself depends so much on the refutation of modern anthropological bifurcation of the world-and its consequential anthropological "coevalness of time"-that it is directed towards a critique of "othering" practices in modern anthropology. The central problem deserving our consideration is thus how reciprocal anthropology is to make an academic and ontological continuity between the contradictory.

Le Pichon's inspiring idea of correspondence-that "the observation and analysis of the one corresponds to the observation and analysis of the other"--is part of the solution to the problem. Further to this idea of correspondence, he also proposes that we should look at the ways in which different cultures see each other in historical contexts. Following the line of this proposition, I would thus believe that to create the kind of correspondence we need first to avoid the usual reduction of reciprocal anthropology to a kind of Euro-centric vocation. I meant that we needed a kind of multi-lateral communication instead of the usual calling for

"Western culture" to gain their identities and self-knowledge-which often end up as reflexive distinctions--through putting themselves into the much wished equal exchanges with non-Western counterparts. Our problem with the singular lateral pattern of reflection is that a common derivative of "equal exchange" has been to treat it as an one-sided critique of the shortcomings of the Euro-centric hierarchical treatment of the Other: the Other as the object of scientific "high culture" and the counter-mirror of "progress" and Western expansion.

True that conventional Western anthropology which sincerely or politely respects the "noble savages'" often ended up with the paving of the roads of imperialism, and in our context of reciprocation, post-colonialist anthropologists should be credited with their contributions to the discursive critique of discourse in anthropology. However, on both the epistemological and ontological premises, what reciprocal anthropology promotes is not simply the questioning of the "native cosmology" in the West. We regard it as a more effective re-evaluation, a re-evaluation for purpose of improvising a new approach along the line of the critique of "walled university" where universal knowledge including Marxian political economy and power-determinism makes up an equally ethno-centric cultural system of signification. This is a historical and transcultural reflection of the "perfect meta-science language", and a return to the semiotic order of language that was once over-objectified as "blind symbols."

It implies that reciprocal understanding entertain a broader sense of exchange, the exchange between "this" cosmology and "those" other patterns of knowing and representing the world to humanity, to me including the exchange between "your" Western problems and "our" non-Western ones. Furthermore, the purpose of exchange has been defined quite differently from the critical perspectives of colonial modernity (and Enlightenment). Making efforts to rediscover a linguistic and semiotic realm between and betwixt ourselves and the others, we are keenly interested in understanding our possible mutual misunderstandings which do harm to our cross-cultural co-presence and to the peaceful existence of different cultures in a "globalizing world" (Eco 2000). In a word, it is not our purpose to make simple political corrections of Euro-centric politics of socio-economic and power dynamism-e.g., that of the notorious "modern world system".

- In Chinese words that are indeed more vivid, "harmony with differences" (ge er bu tong) has been seen as the central theme of our symphony. Yet the polyphonies of reciprocal reflections of misunderstandings that are to be composed into the symphony of understanding should be even more urgently desired than this futurological theme. Polyphonies involve a non-Western vocation. For theories of post-modernity have given non-Western intellectuals a hope for cultural revitalization, including that of old Chinese perspective of "Unity" (tong). The pitfalls of "human sciences" in the Western expansion, having been proven to be pitfalls, now lead our non-Western colleagues out of their pessimism about their own cultures. In China, "self-awareness of culture" (wenhua zijue) has thus been called for in correspondence with the self-reflexive anthropology in the West-also in front of some Westerners who took part in a conference on cross-cultural dialogue in Beijing (e.g., Fei 1998). What has happened in the past decade has proven the truthfulness of the story of how critiques of imperialism can be narrated into the redemptive discourse of our empire-turned nation's historical identification. One of the Transcultura's tasks is thus to make sense of the transmission of the post-modern worlds, the transmission as translation of a self-reflexive mode of cultural production into self-confirmation of cultural revitalization.

There might be endless cycles in the transcultural transmission of knowledge. But for us, the post-colonialist negation of discourse and its fate in "colonial situations" that have turned into "national situations" validate an important point. Those who misunderstand the others in their own ways are not only the Europeans, Americans, and Japanese (to the Korean and Chinese) but also those who have, in the past few centuries, become objectified as the subjects of colonial historicity. Like understandings, misunderstandings exist in various tribes and civilizations that have often been excluded from our scope of critical reflection, simply for the reason that the scope of our critical reflection often only covers the discourse of the supposed "powerful". But in so doing, haven't you forgotten the fact that examples of misunderstanding can also be found among "indigenous peoples"-perhaps excluding the Chinese whose society was regarded as "complex"--who used to be viewed as "innocent children" by classical anthropologists?

In my view, the mission of reciprocal anthropology should not simply be the recitation of the poetics of innocence. More complexly organized, it is to draw our attention to the development of certain common measures with which our mutual misunderstandings are detected before they are hopefully avoided. Here our specific reference is one such illustrating example. For purpose of making a historical reference, we turn our attention to the history of Chinese perspectives of civilization, including ancient Chinese cosmological patterns and disciplinary anthropology in which we find some similar problems to what you find in modern European discourses. Our scope is as extensive as covering more than two thousand years, extending from the classical period and to the current stage. The extensive perspective is useful as an approach to the "native's point of view" of others, even though its extensive scope is problematic due to its over extensiveness. As a "native" Chinese anthropologist, I have come to have a "embodied awareness" (tihui) of the "evolution" (or degeneration) of our world-views, and that impression bears greatly on my approach. But my brief outline will fit into the framework of a reflexive reciprocation in which my own culture is placed in the correspondence to the others'.

In particular, I will describe the worlds of Chinese cosmology in terms of historical transformation from "empire to nation". Briefly, this is the transformation of the world-view of "All Under Heaven" (tianxia) in imperial periods into the nation's narratives of redemption in the 20th century (for earlier examples, also see Duara 1995). I will try to be modest by limiting my discussion to the general patterns that I draw out from what I know, and especially, to the consideration of one simply issue. So far, an argument has been widely received in both Western and non-Western social sciences that Euro-centrism has done more than enough harm to our quest for knowledge. Because many Western anthropologists, namely "anthropologists of the North", seem to be attributing all the wrong conceptions to the Western mind and its economy, we are in a good position to ask instead an alternative question. Can we simply say that the "truth is out there" among the non-Western peqples? And for our purpose of intellectual pursuits here in this particular context, are Chinese perspectives of "China and the rest"--in correspondence with the West and the rest--distinct from or better than the "native Western cosmology" of the "world system"? In other words, can a distinctive "Oriental convention" satisfy our search for the "reciprocal space" in which the ethno-centricity of knowledge is altered?

CLASSICAL CHINA'S WORLD-VIEWS

We now begin by way of a brief visit to the classical period of China, between the Zhou and the Han dynasties (the 11th century B.C to 24 AD). The complex historical twists and turns of that period are not what we should narrate in this context. We alternatively focus on some textual sources that provide a guide to the world of cosmological representations of Self-Other relations at the time. Although many Chinese anthropologists regard anthropology to partly originate from classical China, we can only agree that some efforts to construct a space for "mutual disposition" among peoples and customs were made. Many Chinese schools of thought were developed in the period. But focusing on the issue that we intend to discuss, we find it more interesting to consider the transformation of the relatively plural perspectives in the Zhou dynasty into a singular sino-centric cosmology in the Han dynasty.

Centuries before the Chinese court encountered the European maritime empires, the Chinese thinkers and officials-perhaps including Confucius himself--were compiling a book called the Zhou Scripture of Rites (Zhou Li). The title sounded like what Victor Turner thousands of years later gave to one of his books, The Ritual Process (1966). Incidentally, in the 1930s, when Radcliffe-Brown was visiting Beijing, teaching in the first generation sociologists in Yanjing [Yanching] Uiversity, he himself made the point that it was the Scripture of Rites and Confucius' Analects (Lun Yu) that enabled him to figure out his structural-functionalist explanation of ritual on the Andaman Islands. Radcliffe-Brown was too deeply engaged in the work of anthropological demonstrations of Durkheim's sociological theory of totality. He was not aware of the fact that although the Scripture of Rites was, like his theory of "comparative sociology", a perspective of structural functionalism, its concern was directed towards the concept of "All Under Heaven" (tianxia) but not a bounded Chinese society. To the Zhou thinkers and politicians, rituals were important devices whereby "All Under Heaven" or the world as perceived by the Chinese could be orchestrated toward a high harmony or the "Great Unity" (datong).

We may still accept Donold Munro's point that the conception of the "Great Unity" in terms of ritual was the core of Chinese perceptions of natural order and human mind, which in effect yielded the orthodox Chinese projection of society and social relations (Munro 1969). Reading Confuciu's interpretations in Analects, we also find that the sense of Unity was revealed as a means of government by ritual. As Confucius said, Govern the people by regulations, keep order among them by chastisements, and they will flee from you, and lose all self respect. Govern them by moral force, keep order among them by ritual and they will keep their self-respect and come to you of their own accord." (Analects: 3).

The conception of the "Great Unity" seemed China-bound or even Zhou dynasty-bound theory instead of a "globalization theory" that has only become pervasive in the past decade in America-centered social science discourses. However, one should not ignore the fact that "All Under Heaven" was regarded as the total square of the earth in the Scripture of Rites and many other early Confucian classics. It was neither a theory of "floating continents" and nor a scientific theory of culture and the state. "Unity" did not refer to a one-world culture. But it did encompass a radiating system of "five zones" (wufu) which were hierarchically organized as a system of layered cultural maturity (jiaohua).

The center of the square-world was the "emperor's capital" or "royal domains" (didu); radiating from it were zones which varied in terms of distance and cultural hierarchy from each other and from the center. Scripture of Rites designated a class system for peoples and cultures whereby the center and the divided outer zones-the zone of feudal lands (dianfu), the zone of princes (houfu), the zone of pacification (suifu), the zone of allied ethnic groups (yaofu), and the zone of wilderness or cultureless (huangfu)--were rendered their respective ceremonial and social institutions. This was also a model for the world, which served not only as the city-scape for the design of the imperial capital and prefectural seats (Wang 1994) but also as a pattern (wen) whereby the worlds of civilization (wen) and wilderness (ye) were constructed in a hierarchically organized pattern. Because all the species and customs included were disposed in a centripetal relationship with the center, the mapping in this scribe could be described in terms of an ethno-centric cosmos-geopolitic.

But the "Great Unity" was not a realized formation. It is better seen as an alternative and a solution to the chaos during the late Zhou dynasty (770-221 BC) when the feudal countries and princes created conflicting states that did not obey the rules set up by the earlier Zhou court (Yang 1997). It should also be noted that the system of the ceremonial designated in the Scripture of Rites was complemented and even altered in other less orthodox texts.

While the Scripture of Rites provided a basic framework for distinguished ritual practices for the zones under the same Heaven, or the "Great Unity", some literati who lived in Confucius' time sought to represent in their texts many strange species, which were certain mixtures of humans and animals distributing around the outer zones of the "central kingdom" (zhongguo), or what China meant to the Chinese. One of these texts was the Scripture of Mountains and Seas (Shan Hai Jing), in which "anthropological geographies" (Needham 1992) were mapped to highlight the wilderness of the uninhabited or uncolonialized spaces. Many others who were less concerned with the wilderness and strangeness were visiting in the countryside. There, they collected folk songs and wrote them into the Book of Poetry (Shi Jing), which to the French anthropologist, Marcel Granet, was the truthful ethnography of communal life and inter-group connectivity in classical China (Granet 1932).

One of the most interesting aspects of the Scripture of Mountains and Seas was that it involved a map of the sacred mountain-residences of spirit-media or Shamans who had closer linkages to Heaven than the Son of Heaven or the emperor. These mountain residences were distributed distantly outside the imperial center. However, the gods and goddesses who resided in them were described as divinities that were personified as the deities for the Son of Heaven's ceremonial sacrifices. Equally interestingly, one of the three collections in the Book of Poetry was about the country songs (guofeng) that were performed during local village and trans-village festivals in the countryside distant from the city of the Son of Heaven. The sociality of these festivals was encompassed in the exchange between the two sexes which was in turn the facilitating mechanism of inter-group connectivity. The "wilderness" of these rituals and songs indicated the liveliness of the countries that were not included in the early imperium of China. The other two collections-the collections of euphonies (ya) and royal praises (song)-were devoted to literati and imperial ceremonies. But the collection of country songs (guofeng) demonstrated to be the perfect example of the "gendered gift" as the structural logic of "mutual disposition", and to be an exemplary space of the peaceful and equal relationship.

Apparently, apart from other available sources that we cannot exhaust here, the three important classics of Chinese cultural ideas respectively provided three different perspectives of the world. The Scripture of Rites was a work of civilization; the Scripture of Mountains and Seas was a thesis of geography, mythology, and racial ethnology; and "country songs" in the Book of Poetry was a collection of communal festivals that defined classical Chinese conceptions of the universe of socio-cosmic rhythms. The "mutual disposition" between Heaven and Earth and between central Chinese ways and other less central ways was in common emphasized in all the three books. However, the interaction was enacted in the texts in rather different ways. The orthodox ideology of ritual in the Scripture of Rites relied on the hierarchical distinctions among the zones on the Earth which were disposed in a correspondence with heavenly compartments and its ultimate purpose was to serve the creation of social order among hierarchically organized human beings. The other two classics were partial reversals of the hierarchical system of "All Under Heaven". The Scripture of Mountains and Seas reversed the relationship between the imperium and Heaven with the intervention of the mountain-residences of the divinities who were masked with the guises of animals. The Book of Poetry reversed the same relationship with the folkloric reciprocity of sexuality and the inter-group alliances. Thus, the three classics constituted several models of producing human relations in the world.

In the Han Dynasty, the diversity of the classical world-views in pre-Qin China was replaced by the ascending unitary orthodoxy that fed on the earlier texts such as the Scripture of Rites. The historical transformation of ceremonial ideology in the Han dynasty involves so great complexities that we cannot provide a full picture of it in this limited space. But a general pattern of the Han transformation can be seen in the observation that the plural traditions of ritual, mythology, and seasonal rhythms in the texts that I mentioned were re-organized into a politic of nature and society. The politic was based upon "a vague belief that there was a connection between abnormal natural phenomena and social life", and it was mainly about the "practice of utilizing this belief as a tool in the political struggle" (Eberhard 1957: 70). However, the politic of cosmology was not confined to the Han court; instead, it was part of a larger project of making cosmology relevant to the restructuring of imperial Chinese world. In this regard, it is possible to understand the politic by way of limiting ourselves to an aspect of the transformation, the turn of the New Year as a cosmological metaphor, that has become familiar to anthropologists.

In his historical anthropology of pre-Han festivals, Marcel Granet draws out a line of the ritual transformation of the spring (Granet 1932). Spring festivals first originated in the rural communal celebrations of seasons, which enhanced the conjunction of sexual orgies, inter-group relationship, and communal renewal. As Granet argues, these celebrations were deeply rooted inter-village contests in which the sexes were divided and put into a oneness to formulate a generic relationship between yin and yang. The conceptual framework of the contesting and mutually incorporating yin and yang further defined the constructive interrelationships between neighboring villages. In a later stage, from the Spring and Autumn period onwards, and especially during the Han dynasty, these celebrations were transformed through "impoverishment and specialization" into an simplified cycle of seasonal rhythms of the royal clan of the regional states. The "royal" cycle of sacrifices, heightened to go beyond the communal confines of festivity. But it actually narrowed it to certain spatially confined celebrations of the dynastic cosmological order. As recorded in the Shi Jing (Book of Poetry), the spring festivals in their original forms were diffused in time, place, and function. Having been "transformed"', they tended to become more and more restricted and specialized. As official sacrifices, they became restricted to short periods of days. Their locations, once extended over rivers, meadows, and mountains, became specialized in particular royal sacrificial altars. The number of performing participants decreased to the handful of the royal clan and its officialdom.

The transformation of the spring ritual was not an isolated accident; rather, it was related to a change in the Chinese world-views from the Han dynasty onwards.6 From the perspective of the official version of the world-views, the model of radiating squares became the core content of imperial Chinese cosmology. Conversely, the standardizing of calendar became the Son of Heaven's authority to regulate the empire.

The mountain-residences of divinities were fixed first in the Qin dynasty (221-207 BC) and later in the Wudi reign of the Han dynasty (204BC-24 AD) as nature-made altars for the Son of Heaven to communicate with Heaven. The divinities in the mountain-residences were turned into magician-assistants (fangshi) to the emperor (Gu 1998), and in later dynasties, ministries were established to house them as specialist-officials who told the Son of Heaven what to do in accordance with cosmological traces in Heaven.

The hierarchically defined zones and their rules of relationship were consolidated as the orthodox model, in which empire was "cosmological conceived as a territorial realm with tributary rulers at its fringes." The countries where the outer zones of civilization had their own distinctive lifestyles and world-views were "tamed" into "lands of princes", although their different styles of life were retained as contrasts to the orthodoxy of the imperial court's ceremonial space.

PASSAGE FROM THE TRIBUTARY MODE TO THE "TURN OF FORTUNE"

By the Tang Dynasty (618-907 AD), a perspective of the world with China as a non-center had become possible. Along with the ascending influences of Buddhism in China, the orthodox cosmology of All Under Heaven was for a period of time seriously disrupted. Monk Xuanzang or simply the "Tang Monk" (602-664 AD) from the capital city, Chang'an (now Xi'an) departed from his temple to conduct a journey to the "West" (India). Being dissatisfied with Chinese perspectives of ontology and cosmology, the Tang Monk. Waited to gain the real truth in India, he threw himself in 627 AD onto a sequence of adventures toward his destination.

After 19 years of travel, he returned to the Chinese capital with 657 sacred books and numerous Buddha statues and plant seeds. In Chang'an, he was assigned by the Tang emperor to implement a grand project of translation. Within a year, he also completed a book known as Datang Xiyu Ji (Notes on the Western Territories of the Great Tang).

The 12 volumes of the book described 150 city-states and tribes that he visited. Monk Xuanzang's Notes on the Western Territories of the Great Tang was a comprehensive system of travelogues. It presented the politics, warfare, local produces, and religiosities of different countries along his journey. Paying special attention to Buddhist spirituality that attracted Xuanzang himself, the book created a mental map in which the Truth among the Other (India) was disposed as a good alternative to secular Confucian ideology.

However, not long after the Tang monk published his book, in the later dynasties of the Song and Yuan (10th to 13th centuries), a tributary mode of reproducing human relationships emerged and it replaced the Other-centered view of the Tang Monk. The tributary mode was partly a result of the development of China's maritime trade on the Southeast and South coasts, which facilitated the creation of a China-centered tributary world system (Wang 1999: 50-84). In a Marxian treatise on the "tributary mode", Gates has identified it instead as a China-bound state, official, and peasant relationships in the sphere of economic production (Gates 1995).

Paying no attention to the fact that its more important aspect was a civilizing process whereby Chinese perspectives of China's position in the world was presented and made real, Gates mistakes taxation and levies such as salt and grain as "tributes" from the peasants. Human capital within the dynastic confines was indeed an important component of the system. But an even more important component was the relationship with "overseas countries" (haiguo) or the "foreigners" (fan) about which many Chinese scholar-officials throughout the periods of Song, Yuan, Ming, and Qing were keenly gathering "ethnographic" (zhi) data.

Therefore, in the Song dynasty, around 1180, Zhou Qufei who lived in Guangxi wrote a book entitled Lingwai Daida (Some Answers from Outside the Southern Hills) in which he described the legal institutions, produces, tribal life, and trade among the frontier peoples of China and in Southeat Asian countries. An emergent tributary mode was applied as one of the main plots of his narrative. In 1225, Zhao Rukuo, a customs inspector on the Southeast Coast published his Gazetteer of All Foreigners (Zhufan Zhi), on the basis of details supplied by Chinese and foreign merchants. A century later, Wang Dayuan, who traveled right round the Indian Ocean on two merchant voyages in the 1330s and reached as far as East Africa Coast, published his Brief Gazetteer of Island Savages (Daoyi Zhilue). Both works focused upon the non-Chinese territories and peoples in Southeast Asia, India, Middle East, and, to a much lesser extent, East Africa. The two most important aspects of description were peoples and products.

From the classical scriptures to these later gazetteers, Chinese representations of the outer zones of humanity and the world had undergone important changes. For instance, the classical Scriptures of Rites and its Han imitations confused the urban design of the dynastic capital with the design of the whole world. The zones of civilization and its lesser kinds were also mapped onto the city of the King or the Emperor. By contrast, in the gazetteers compiled in the Song (960-1279 AD) and the Yuan (1271-1368 AD) dynasties, the centers of tributary stations such as maritime trade harbors on the coast were emphasized as the point of reference for measuring distances between China and other countries.

Nonetheless, the emphasis on the transitional points in space did not lead to the emergence of "cultural relativism". Quite like Western Orientalism (Said 1978), such gazetteers of foreign countries" were imperialist by character.

They were discourses framed by discursive institutions that were produced by the "Chinese world system". They jointly created a structure of center-periphery relationship that culminated in the cosmology of the Heaven. In all these works, the subjectivity of the Other were only recognized as representations of local produces, mountain monsters, ocean chieftains, and half-humans. The gazetteers paid a lot of attention to local produces. They thus involved certain perspectives of trade relationship in the world. But the trade relationships were placed under the tributary system. The exchange between China as the center of the world and peripheries of other countries was defined in terms of the Son of Heaven's obligation to pay greater gifts to the tribal chieftains what he as Father to these "sons" owed them.

We may thus say that the ancient sino-centric world system projected the world into a hierarchy, within which the "civilizing process'" departed from the central zone and extended into the zones of the savages. The zones of the savages were the peripheries that produced materials and fancy products such as exotic spices to be extracted by the center. All these zones were not excluded from the Chinese world. They were instead disposed in a hierarchy of humans, animals, moral types, monsters, and so on, whose co-presence was in turn defined as All Under Heaven. In the hierarchy, the Heaven, the ultimate power and judge of morality and civilization was both the highest authority and divinity.

The role of the gazetteers was assisting the center in its extraction of "surplus value'" in the name of tribute (gongpin) and its self-portrait of Chinese civilization (organized in the order of rite-rewards for the tribute). Meanwhile, unequal exchanges also existed especially in the situations in which the Son of Heaven gave more rewards to what he gained from the tribal chieftains who paid him tributes. In terms of both "tributes" and "rewards" (bao), the gazetteers of All Under Heaven was hierarchically disposed instead of being reciprocally arranged. Such a hierarchy was composed of a square-map-cosmography of the centripetal zones in the Scripture of Rites, and it had remained significant even though explorers such as Zheng He might have discovered a quite different shape of the world.

It was in the later half of the 16th century that the world was shaped by the Lord of Heaven (Tianzhu, the God) into a Ball (Globe). During this short period, knowledge about China exploded in Europe. Adventurers and Catholic missionaries such as Galeote Pereira, Gaspare da Cruz, Mendes Pinto, Matteo Ricci, and so on had woven what they read and heard with what they saw into European narratives of China (Spence 1998: 19-40). Meanwhile, in the Ming Court, the wrong understanding of the world as Square gave way to a Catholic "scientific" view of the world, the world as Globe. Matteo Ricci himself not only combined his science with Chinese cosmology but also painted with a Chinese brush his version of the Globe. In the early 17th century, the Italian Jesuit Giulios Aleni-known in China as Ai Lilue-completed, with his Chinese Jesuit associate Yang Yingjun a Chinese book Zhifang Waiji (An Extra-Register of Geogrophy) (written in 1623 AD) which supposedly "opened" the Chinese eyes to the outside world.

But the new Jesuit knowledge of the world was in the later centuries domesticated by Chinese into a new sino-centric world-view. So in the late 18th century, when George Lord Viscount Macartney brought to British embassy to China, the Qianlong and his Manchu Court still received him merely as representative of a tributary "cheifdom". Meanwhile, in the "Garden and Perfect Brilliance" (Yuanming Yuan) where much foreign elements were included in the display as complementary to All Under Heaven's cultural diversity foreign embassies were received in the universe of Chinese civilization which was still presented as a perfect squared "tribute system" (Hevia 1995). The same domesticated world was further re-enlivened in later Chinese visional encounters with the "modern world system".

Commenting on the royal gardens where the re-enlivened synthesis was made visually real, Sahlins said that "these imperial gardens and hunting lodges signified a cultural politic, encompassing an economics that was likewise inclusive and exclusive and could thus adapt appropriately to the practical situation" (1988:24). In other words, "the synthesis of diversity and conquest made these imperial retreats perfect microcosms. They represented the whole world as the work of the Emperor and within his power."

In line with the "gardening" of civilization, by the mid-19th century, the court's negligence of the maritime world was in the end critiqued by Wei Yuan. In 1842, four months after the Chinese defeat in the Opium War, Wei published his Mapped Gazetteer of the Sea States (Haiguo Tuzhi).

The Book devoted 43 chapters to 6 oceans in the world. Wei already knew a lot about Western geography. Wei read both Matteo Ricci and Jiulios Aleni's maps of the world. He also read and translated many other maps in Western languages. While being fully aware of the geographic divisions of continents, he thought that the Western maps of the world were nothing good, because as barbarians' products, they did not live up to the Chinese spirituality of the Heaven. Thus, to fit the maps into the Heaven-Scape of China, he arranged the continents in the world into oceans that surround China. With the "central kingdom" as the center of the world, Wei's portrait sought to enlighten the rulers of the change of the world order. He paid much attention to the Western powers. However, strategically composed, his book argued for a regional world system that could benefit China. The oceans included in his view of the Chinese maritime empire included Southeast Asia. The China-Southeast Asian Civilization excludes Europe, Russia and America.

As expressed in Wei Yuan and other's anxious efforts of revitalization, such a world-scape came into crises when another kind of world-scape arrived on the Chinese horizon. The consequence has been that even though it has seemed the case that a sort of relatively open anthropological cosmology had originated in ancient China, many Chinese anthropologists have expressed their gratitude to Western anthropologists for revealing much of their Enlightenment to them. None of them refutes the now widely shared view that modern Chinese-speaking anthropology only emerged in the late 19th century translations of social Darwinism, a kind of foreign philosophy that the Chinese intellectuals regarded as what defeated their civilization. However, did the Chinese version of evolutionism make up a cosmology of the Other that turned China's relationship with the "outer world" upside down?

As a very important branch of the Chinese Enlightenment and modernity, works by evolutionist anthropologists were absorbed into Chinese ideas of dynastic reformation. The translators were the first generation of modern Chinese nationalists who viewed European biological metaphors for inter-societal conflicts as the medicine to cure Chinese cultural illnesses.10 Intellectual prophecies of the remade All Under Heaven in the new world-order dominated most of the intellectual and political discussions of China's fate throughout the 19th century. In the 1880s, Kang Youwei first sought to revitalize Confucian Scriptiture of Rites whereby the ideas of "turn of rites" (liyun) and "Great Unity" (Datong) were turned into a native cosmology of progress. In his vision, the renewal of Zhou ideal of civilization and cultural integrity was combined with Hegel's conception of history.

In the last three decades of the 19th century, Kang Youwei and his disciples, Yan Fu, Liang Qichao, and many others began to engage themselves in synthesizing Western evolutionist doctrines and Chinese cosmological concepts. Social Darwinism became the focus of their attention. Yan Fu was the creative introducer of Darwin and evolution theory. Kang Youwei was both China's first prophet of progress and critique of Darwin. Liang Qichao was a Chinese Huxley.

They departed from different perspectives to interpret Western evolutionism. However, the concern that first encouraged them to write about Darwin and evolution was not complex--it was simply China's weakness and peril that drove them to look for the evolutionist way out. "How can we be strong?'" "How can we survive?" These were questions that they in common sought to answer.

To revitalize China, Kang's generation of Chinese thinkers traveled a lot in Europe, America, and Japan. Along their journeys, they kept diaries and later wrote these into systematic travelogues in which advanced Western institutions of civilization and politics were commented. In 1904, Kang Youwei himself visited Italy. In Rome, he paid a special tour in the Roman Senate. He sighed at the observation that "all European cultures stemmed from the

Roman empire." But "if we compare the Roman civilization to ours, we will find that it is a much lesser kind." Kang said that European nation-states that had come to have mature shapes were consequences of the degeneration of ancient civilization. So there is little in Rome for Chinese to learn. The problem seemed to him to be that Europe gained its utility of Heaven's Way (Tiandao) just a hundred years before China. Had China done the same, it would have been much more advanced than Europe. In 1905, Kang visited Paris. Two years later, he published Travelogue in France. He looking backwards into the French Revolution, he suggested that the definite consequence of any revolution was bound to be despotism because revolution, as he saw it, was entirely based on the principle of violence. The best model for China's progress was its own ancient civilization, consisting in the politics of the classical dynasties such as the Zhou and the teachings of Confucius which, to him, was a perfect civilization (wenming meibei) with profound methods for the development of freedom and peace.

Similar interests in European scribes of civilization were manifested in the conceptions put forward by the fathers of modern Chinese anthropology who were involved in the critique of their own culture by means of subjecting ideas of the European social philosophical Other to the native trajectory of modernity. Similarly, in so doing, Chinese cross-cultural translators were not uncreative. In their translations, evolutions was termed "the Argument about the Heaven's Change" (tianyan lun). In the footnotes that they made to the translated texts, many comments were made to interpret evolution into "the turn [or conjuncture] of fortune" (yunhui).

Evolutionism was, to them, not simply a bio-medicine that was prescribed for the "East Asian Sick Men" (dongya bingfu), a self-name for the Chinese. It was, more importantly, an explanation of how Heaven that once shifted to Europe had by the late 19th century returned to its home in China. In the 20th century, Chinese-speaking anthropology has served as an instrument whereby the shift of Heaven from Europe to China has been made more or less a mytho-history. And it is to this special sort of anthropology that we now turn.

THE SELF-CONFINING PROJECTS

By now, a well-known example for our analysis of traditional Chinese world-views has been the late 18th century "mutual disposition" between the Qing and the British. In 1793, two expansive empires-the Qing dynasty of China and the maritime empire of Great Britain met formally for the first time. The occasion was the mission of Lord Macartney sent by the British crown and sponsored by the East India Company to the court of the Qianlong emperor. The history of this encounter could be narrated in terms of its political economic significance. But the event itself involved more interactions between Qing imperial guest ritual and British diplomatic protocals. Macartney insisted to the Qing court that one should distinguish between the homage of tributary princes and the respects of " a great and independent sovereign" such as his own. But from the mandarins' point of view the mission of Macartney was not a mission per se but was an act of the barbarians bringing tributes to China, expressing their sincere desire to turn to civilization. In a historical analysis of this event, James Hevia thus makes the remark:

> ...both the Qing court and members of the British embassy could take a certain amount of satisfaction from the fact that their mode of producing relations of power had uncovered or detected strengths and weaknesses in the other. Neither party, however, was able to move very far outside its own particular version of world-constituting practices...(Hevia 1995:210)

As a post-colonialist historian, Hevia views the Qing court's guest ritual as unfolding the Chinese mode of producing relations of power that encompassed an equally valid approach to world affairs to its Western counterparts. To him, behind what we defined in terms of hospitality, there was in the Qing a historical force of "cherishing men from afar" (huairou yuanren), which to me is better seen as what satisfied Chinese cosmologies of the world or the emperor's "world-constituting virtue." Because both Hevia and Sahlins limit their consideration to the earlier period of the Qing dynasty, they has not answered the question as to whether the perspective of "cherishing men from afar" as a possible way of "mutual disposition" has continued to play an important role in contemporary Chinese cultural politics of "cultural" anthropology. In this regard, I would think that a consideration of modern Chinese-speaking anthropology as a good example of changing Chinese world-views in the later stages of development.

In the late Qing, and particularly in Wei Yuan, Kang Youwei, and their associates' perspectives of the world, the quest for the European Other for the sake of rescuing China from its misfortune was essential. In the early 20th century, it was further radicalized in the New Cultural Movement (1915) and the May Fourth Movement (1919). For the neo-Confucians who are still now active in Chinese studies, these two movements paved the way for the "murder of the great Chinese civilization" in later stages such as the Cultural Revolution (1966-1976). But we should not forget that the long 20th century has also been a century of China's quest for its national identity, and in this quest both modernity and Chinese tradition have been emphasized. The consequence of this synthetic pursuit has been the domestication of Western modernity in China's Heaven and Mind. Modern Chinese-speaking anthropology has fitted into the movement of domestication. In the light of the fact that such new anthropological cosmologies have necessarily involved some perspectives of "mutual disposition", it is important to examine how they have developed their own "mode of producing relations of power".

Relevant to this point, around 1926, two articles were published in Chinese to signal the beginning of domesticating anthropology in China. Cai Yuanpei's "Saying something about ethnology" (shuo minzuxue) (Cai 1926) looked at the issue of how ethnology was important to China and could be associated culturally with Chinese tradition. The core content of Cai's article was about the ways in which ethnology could contribute to Chinese understandings of indigenous ethnic diversity and Chinese civilization. Emphasis was also placed upon how ancient Chinese scholars had provided sound ethnographies of a Culture of cultures in China. Evolutionism was not the central theme of the article. Instead, drawing mostly on German diffusionism, Cai Yuanpei was interested in presenting a historical geography of China to illustrate a new relationship between the center and periphery of the Chinese imperial prefectures (shenzhou). The use of Chinese materials for anthropological theorization was emphasized too, so far as they would serve the reconstruction of the central kingdom's "time-before".

The other article was published in the Journal for Chinese Scholars in the US in the same year. Written by Wu Wenzao, it was entitled "Nationalities and State" (minzu yu guojia) (Wu 1926; Wang 1999-2000). Wu Wenzao, the teacher of the first generation of professional field anthropologists in China, Fei Xiaotong, Francis Hsu, Lin Yuehua, and Tian Rukang, at that time was still a graduate student at Columbia University, learning anthropology and sociology. This earliest piece of his work focused upon the interrelationship between nationality and state, as its title suggests. Reviewing German, French, and British mainstream theories of national states, Wu Wenzao suggested a different line for Chinese state-building. To him, the European idea of "one nation one state" was inapplicable to the Chinese context. Instead, Wu Wenzao suggested that the Chinese modern state should learn from the lesson of European nation-building and concern itself with tolerating and incorporating a diversity of nationalities and cultures. Culture should be separated from politics to the effect that the ancient civilization could be preserved in a modern form. Anthropology enabled China to find a national path distinct from the dominant European model of "one nation one state".

In the years between 1927 and 1948, Chinese anthropology advanced to equal the international standard. The key players in this arena were able to write both English and Chinese. Encouraged by what was conveyed in Cai Yuanpei and Wuwenzao's articles, Luo Xianglin, Ling Chunsheng, Fei Xiaotong, Lin Yaohua, Francis Hsu, Yang Kun, Tian Rukang, Lin Huixiang and others forged forums of anthropological studies in various parts of China. It has been noted that Chinese anthropology during that period prospered in two major camps. The Southern Forum was centered in Academia Sinica in Nanjing. Drawing upon Cai Yuanpei's article and many translations of German and, later, American anthropological works, the group of Southern anthropologists were mainly concerned with historical studies of ethnic cultures. The Northern Forum was centered in Yanjing University and led by Wu Wenzao who had become a professor of sociology after his return to Beiping-now Beijing--in the late 20s. The Yanjing

School of Sociology and Anthropology was centered on two lines of inquiry of which rural ethnographies of small villages and their social change was the most famous. The Northern Forum also promoted the study of ethnic minorities. Contrasting with the Southern Forum, the members of the Northern Forum were less historical and more political. Consequently, the study of ethnic groups was actually termed "bianzhengxue" or the "Political Study of China's Frontiers".

"International" could indeed be the word to describe Chinese anthropology during that period. It should be noted, however, that Chinese anthropology in these two forums was international mainly in the sense that it used many European and American social science concepts. By domesticating the idea of the Other into visions of the internal ethnic and cultural diversity in China, Chinese-speaking anthropologists became concerned mainly with the identity politics and state-building projects within the boundaries of China. An important exception seems to have been Fei Xiaotong's work on American culture. In 1938, when his first English book Peasant Life in China was published in London, Malinowski praised Fei's work as a landmark, one that made a paradigmic shift in anthropology.

By opening up the scope of the Easterners' studying Easterners themselves, he also made it possible for natives to study native anthropology. However, in the late 1940s, when Fei was invited to the University of Chicago, he was no longer satisfied with what he did in London. He wrote a book called America and Americans (1948). In the book, he reversed Margaret Mead's Samoa into America. The American open-mindedness about training children was envisaged as what could salvage China from its educational pitfalls. As Fei suggests, China's sufferings derive from all its imperial educational system that made our people obedient to the despots' rule. Now, the children's culture of the United States demonstrates a new possibility. It allows children to evolve into independent and strong adventurous spirits and such spirits are important for China's self-salvation.

While Fei's work on American culture was forgotten, the domestication of the anthropological Other into an empire of cultures between the 1930s and 1940s paved the way for the emergence of ethnic minority and social reform policy studies between the 1950s and 1970s. Skipping the empty chapter of the Cultural Revolution, from 1950 onwards, most anthropologists have been involved in the research work known as "nationality identification" (minzu shibie). This is policy work aimed at classifying other cultures within China. Using Stalin's criteria for nationality identification, Chinese ethnologists accepted only 15 % of the more than 400 applications from ethnic groups seeking to be recognized as official ethnic minorities (shaoshu minzu). The job was a tough one, as Fei Xiaotong recently reflected (Fei 1997). It was necessary, however, for the new government's attempt to impose a great socialist reconstruction on the Chinese nation.

To facilitate social reform in the ethnic regions, social histories of ethnic cultures were created to fit into the five-staged theory of human history of Stalinist Marxism. Like colonial governments in the 19th century, the Chinese government in the 1950s provided funds for ethnologists to describe ethnic cultures in detail, for the sake of rescuing the disappearing cultures within the socialist modernizing nation. Up to the 1980s, the rural ethnographies of the Yanjing School were denounced for their functionalist opposition to Marxist historical materialism. However, the methodology of small community studies, which combine Mao's own class analysis ethnography of Hunan peasant movements and functionalist anthropological studies of villages, was adopted in case descriptions of land reform and model village promotion including Dazhai. The interpretive framework was a Sinified version of Soviet readings of German social philosophy rather than a native viewpoint or the non-Marxist stand of Euro-American cultural theory.

Our problem with the past achievements in Chinese-speaking anthropology emerges when we compare this type of anthropological production with other [foreign] anthropologies. In a recent publication, The Savage Within: The Social History of British

Anthropology 1922-1972, Henrick Kuklich (1992) argues that much of social anthropology was created out of cross-cultural contrasts that anthropologists were making to reflect upon European totalitarianist nation-state building. The "ordered anarchy" of Africa aptly provided certain opposing features to European conceptions of the nation. The advancement of political anthropology between the 1940s and 60s offered a mirror in which European anthropologists looked at the national "savages within".

Kuklich's point of view about the cross-cultural mirroring of nation is also useful in our consideration of a wider range of Western intellectuals with sometimes self-designated marginal identities (Goody 1995). In continental Europe, for example, the history of ethnology in a similar period of time was situated in a larger history, in which tribes outside the narrow circle of Aryanism were used to challenge intellectual and ideological orthodoxies attaching to Indo-German doctrine. As Martin Thom argues with reference to French sociology: A finer-grained study of Durkheim and of the annee Sociologique would, I think, show just how urgent task it was for republican or socialist intellectuals, especially Jewish, to respond to the anti-Semitism of fin-de-siecle Europe by locating an elementary form of the religious life (totemism) beyond, or prior to that of Roman, Greek, or ancient Indian society (ancestor worship) (Thom 1990).

To make a comparison, our brief discussion above now points to the fact that, as in European social anthropology, modern Chinese-speaking anthropology to the 1960s was related to the projects of nation-state building and modernity. However, in contrast to its European counterpart, Chinese anthropology did not engage in setting up a mirror in which to reflect the "savages within". Instead, Chinese anthropological ethnographies have treated the savages as the enemies of the "great tradition" of modernity and the state. The significance of anthropology has been understood for its bearing on the re-making of Chinese civilization and nation. It is by pushing anthropology of the Other toward the nationalization of cultural diversity and urban-rural differences that Chinese anthropologists in the past had become rather "innovative". Most Chinese anthropologists did not believe that the empire should dissolve into national states in which to create new citizenship and borders of modern sociological totality. Alternatively, as Cai Yuanpei and Wu Wenzao were proposing in the 1920s, it was believed that Chinese nation should be built upon the basis of ancient multi-culturalism of the empire. It so followed that anthropology of other cultures should be domesticated into anthropology of "internal enemies" but not "external noble savages". In the same way, anthropology as a meaningful enterprise was targeted at the social transformation of "people without selves", namely the ethnic minorities and the producers of "little traditions" in the countryside.

For the past twenty years, many regional traditions of Chinese anthropology have been re-established. In Guangzhou, Xiamen, Beijing, and Kunming, anthropologists converged into units with their distinctive local scholarly traditions. Cultural anthropology, sociology and social anthropology, ethnology, and ethnic minority studies developed in earlier periods have their contemporary counterparts. Meanwhile, more and more Western works have been translated and published in Chinese. Exchanges with foreign scholars have become possible. Many students have been able to go abroad and study anthropology. Conferences, seminars, and workshops on anthropology have become part and parcel of the new academic life in Chinese universities and attracted many old and young scholars. As an active element in the movement of promoting anthropology in China, I have been most delighted to observe the gradual return of other voices in Chinese anthropological circle. But looking at it from the historical comparative perspective, I see the current stage as an equally problematic time in the history of Chinese anthropology.

Since the late 1980s, village studies have become an important part of Chinese anthropology and sociology both within and outside China. In the United States, Yan Yunxiang and Jing Jun, both from mainland China, have studied at Harvard University and published their studies of Chinese rural life. Trained in the Western anthropological tradition, they provide two very creative styles of ethnographic decipherment. Working in the village Xiajia, Yan Yunxiang has been most intrigued by the "flow of gifts" in that location. Drawing upon existing anthropological interpretations of gift economy and culture, Yan Yunxiang reflects on the ways in which state socialist hierarchy and the processes of a popular gift economy interact.

To Yan Yunxiang, what is so interesting in Xiajia is the fact that new and old forms of sociality and life style have jointly created a site for a theory of unequal exchange which has not been sufficiently interpreted in existing anthropological theories of reciprocity. Yan Yunxiang's case study is both local and comparative. Therefore, it is specifically about the "native's point of view" because such a view illustrates a general point of social interaction (Yan 1996). Jing Jun's study of a Northwestern Chinese village concerns itself with the politics of memory in opposition to the politics of forgetting. In his vivid description, memories of bitterness coincide with efforts to forget the eras of socialist modernization (Jing 1996).

In a recent article on a similar theme, Jing Jun takes us to a place where a hydro-electric dam was replacing the village. Unlike those without the third eye, he successfully reveals a different viewpoint, that is, the local indifference to modernist visions of development. He highlights how social memories of the past are reconceived as a vision for the future. Critically composed, Jing Jun's study sheds light on our understanding of state-peasant relations in modernizing China and in the dominion of the state's discourse (Jing 1999). Neither of Yan Yunxiang and Jing Jun's studies is aimed at the intellectual facilitation of economic reform. Neither of them seeks to promote modernization projects. Instead, both seek to discover an alternative trajectory of history, a "mental Other" for the critique of dominant "native ideology" of the modernizing state.

So far, internally, there are also several village studies in Chinese sociology and anthropology. These internal studies of village life have mostly been concerned with modernization. For example, some village studies conducted in South China have been solely concerned with the concept of urbanization. In these studies, village communities seem to be important only in the sense that they provide examples of disappearing villages and of emerging small towns and big industries. Modernization is emphasized at the expense of examining possible spaces of cultural difference. One other type of study shares some of Yan Yunxiang and Jing Jun's concerns. Such studies entertain as much local detail as an ethnographic account. However, the "remaking of the village" (cunzhuang de zaizhao) seems to be their central theme. All villages have transformed somewhat since reform. Therefore, even though these two kinds of studies have academic outlooks, they are deeply rooted in the projects of modernization. Scholars within these studies are hardly distanced from the official accounts. On the contrary, "attesting the taste" of the state is their prime concern.

More serious problems exist in ethnic minority studies. In France, Cai Hua from Yunnan has produced two good studies of the Naxi or what he has called "Na People". In his description, the Naxi is interesting in the sense that their lives are so different they offer an alternative perspective of gender relations and kinship to the modern ones that have limited modern anthropological thinking about kinship. Cai's attention is paid especially to the absence of marriage among the Naxi. The absence of a familiar institution that used to provide conceptual framework for Levi-Strauss' "alliance theory" in kinship studies becomes interesting primarily as an ethnographic example with which our past understandings and conclusions could be critiqued. In his work, the Marriage Law that was imposed among the Naxi by the Chinese state in the 1950s is reflected as what has failed to change a structure of its own kind. This political failure is further reflected in his visual representation of the return of the magician among the Naxi, Cai Hua reflects on the limit of linear historicity, similar to Jing Jun's line of argument.

Writing within China, most Chinese anthropologists have produced their works in a very different way from Cai Hua. Many Ethnology Institutes have now been restored in different parts of China. For the purpose of attracting foreign funds, some of these institutes have added the name 'anthropology' to their title. However, the studies that they have conducted have been confined to ethnic policy inquiries. Good relations between the Han and the minority are always the central theme of the works. Alternatively, some local flowers of the national garden may be emphasized to highlight the cultural value of ethnic minorities to the state. To be frank, I look at such studies as something much worse than those conducted in Southwest China in the 1940s concerning "Bianzhengxue", the political study of China's frontiers.

In Western academia, problematic assumptions about Chinese civilization still exert a powerful influence. For the Europeans who have spent long years in "the search for the perfect language", Chinese representations of things and worlds are not perfect. So as Umberto Eco has noted, Leibniz had to "void the Chinese symbols of whatever meaning was assigned to them by previous interpretations", in order to construct his "perfect encyclopedia" of "blind symbols'" (Eco 1995: 286). Paradoxically, seeking to deconstruct structuralist binary opposition of West and Non-West, the anthropologist Jack Goody, unlike Leibniz, has instead forged an argument for the existence of "forms of logic and sequential reasoning'" in "Eastern culture'", which exempts China African mode of non-rational thought.

While living under the condition of epistemological predicaments could be difficult, a lot of Chinese scholars have insisted on the envisioning of a uniquely Chinese culture with reference to what the foreigners have said about our own civilization. To them, European ideas of China as a middle realm--a space or possibility in-between rationality and mythology--will automatically render an evidence of our cultural greatness. For this pursuit, near the end of the 20th century, the Chinese anthropologist Fei Xiaotong proposed the concept of "self-awareness of culture" (wenhua zijue).

This concept called for Chinese anthropologists to study the position of Chinese culture in the world. In his vocation, Fei did not refer to Lebnitz; instead he sought a dynamic of culture change in Malinowski's works. In world situation for Fei has been one in which Western culture dynamicized most civilizations in the world. To him, the lesson of the 20th century has been one that tells us that the long century has been a Western one, since Malinowki discovered the fact. However, in the 21st century, the Western impacts on non-Western cultures will give way to an alternative. The Chinese culture, with all its greatness, its writing systems, and its mixtures and rationality and mythology, will in the end exert its important influences in the world. Yet, as he signs, many "natives" are not yet aware of the fact. The task of "cultural self-awareness'" (wenhua zijue) thus lies in gaining a sort of consciousness of our own culture.

When Fei made his calling, "self-awareness of culture" was becoming the core concern of many Chinese social scientists. To those who have paid attention to contemporary Chinese academia, an important shift of focus in scholarly debates among the new liberal Chinese intellectuals is easily observable. About two years ago, the new generation of intellectuals in Beijing, Shanghai, and other central places of China were still engaged in the controversy over whether great Chinese tradition encompassed a culture of capitalist spirit and democratic modernity. By 1999, small showers of debates between liberal economists, political scientists and culture researchers had evolved into a veritable storm.

A group of intellectuals who would soon lead cultural studies in China came to realize the importance of the critical spirit of Neo-Marxism for China. Arguing that the China Problem was no longer that of socialism but of globalizing capitalism, the Chinese New Left, as they were sometimes called, sought to rethink the modernity of China. For them, culture, or the great tradition of Confucianism and Neo-Confucianism, or all the good syn-texts of rationality and mythology, was no longer important. The issue now was the spirit of modernity that had infiltrated dominant modern discourse and continued to exert its influences upon post-reform state ideological apparatus and political economy. Such influences in turn reduce the possibilities of Chinese culture to maintain its unique position in the world.

The young generation of Chinese intellectuals jointly fought for the national dignity of China from the same stance as some liberal economists and political scientists responded to the "New Left". These enthusiastic scholars critique the condemnation of modernity and development. They argue that Chinese New Culture Movements of the early 20th century are not yet completed. The May Fourth Movement of 1919, together with its rejection of tradition, is still perceived desirable. Critical of "official accounts" of history, the liberal economists postulate that the real danger behind the underdeveloped state constitutional apparatus is the lack of "spontaneously evolved modernity". The liberal political scientists argue that Western critiques of modernity are either premature for China to imitate or already too out-of-date to be adopted. The China Problem is the Chinese reality. It is a reality of the necessary struggles against the ideological justification of a feigned social justice that hinders constitutional development of political economy and market.

To a great extent, Chinese anthropologists have distanced themselves from the political debates over the issue of culture. But we should not forget that even though the two camps says little about culture, both are engaged in certain teleological struggles for China in which the issue of culture is at the core. What is contended here is whether the globalizing modernity has "civilized" us to such an extent that the boundaries of our culture-or what has been seen as the middle realm between rationality and mythology--are no longer obstacles to future advancements. This is the archetypal Chinese anthropological question that our disciplinary ancestors have tried to answer.

Although sometimes insiders' views about China may have been closer to our historical consciousness and political sensibility than outsiders' views, they are also the most close to locally taken-for-granted conceptions which are in turn inseparable from modern politics of national revitalization. In fact, contrasting the internal and external anthropology of China has alerted us to the fact that "self-awareness of culture" should always be gained by posing the Other against the question of the Self, and by distancing the intellectual debate from political teleology. If external sinological anthropological studies have made their contribution to the "self-awareness" of Chinese culture, then this contribution has mainly consisted of the point that Chinese culture should not be studied in isolation as a fixed totality. It could be analyzed in terms of orthodox cosmology as de Groot, Marcel Granet, Maurice Freedman, Katherine Bell, and Steven Sangren have done from their different perspectives. It could also be analyzed in terms of the lasting interactions between state cults, specialist religious systems, and folk traditions as James Watson, Stephan Feuchtwang, Kenneth Dean and many others have done (Ibid.). In fact, the new generation of Chinese anthropologists like Yan Yunxiang, Jing Jun, and others have developed certain novel perspectives from which traditional perceptions of "Chinese culture" are less important than the particular ways of life, exchange, and memories of the common people.

But what does all this mean to our consideration of "general" anthropology? In contemporary Europe and America, recent historical studies of anthropological subjects within and outside the discipline have engaged a great number of anthropologists in revising the arbitrary aspects of contrasting cultural discourse. For example, in a part of Marcus and Fischer's "experimental moment" (1986) and a part of Rabinow's "anthropology of reason" (1997), they even call for a "repatriation of anthropology". In these two different patterns, the expansion of the Western-centered world system into "small communities" (xiao shequ) of the Other and the universality or globalization of Occidental Reason are seen as the modern world politico-economic and discursive formations that have determined the disappearing of the Other.

The task of anthropology, as it is called for in these two reflections, becomes that of divorcing the discipline from the pursuit of specific forms of life that was associated with reflection on cultural difference, and thus with reflection on the envisioned universal progress of Reason and History. However, the question of how to derive alternative cosmologies and social practice from afar, or from outside anthropologists' own societies and cosmologies, remains the central practice of anthropological narratives. To me, the advantage of anthropology over other humanities and social sciences lies in the fact that this particular discipline has cultivated such sophisticated styles of learning. Viewing the cultural Self in the mirror of the Other or, alternatively, seeking common humanity among plural forms of life has enabled Western anthropologists to transcend ethnocentric cosmologies and facilitate transcultural reciprocation of knowledge (Wang 2000).

As some Chinese anthropologists have recently tried to prove, certain Chinese anthropologists also started their profession with a concern with non-Chinese cultures. 19 Indeed, a Chinese sense of Other can be found in Li Anzhai's study of the Zuni and Francis Hsu's comparative study of Indian, American, and Chinese cultures, as well as Fei Xiaotong's travelogues of America. However, an examination of the history of modern Chinese-speaking anthropology validates the argument that the Chinese anthropological circle has been overwhelmingly concerned with the Chinese cultural Self. The Chinese cultural Self has seldom been viewed in relation to other cultures. Even in the exceptions mentioned above, the distinctiveness of Chinese culture is anxiously expressed without much reference to the Other.

After several years of personal involvement in Chinese academic debates, I have become "embodiedly aware" (tihui) of the lasting nativist concern with self-awareness of culture and its futuristic "progress" in China. To the advocates of "anthropology of the south", national development may be an encouraged endeavor, an alternative to "anthropology of the north" that focuses mainly on reflexivity. As Quinlan suggests with reference to "applied anthropological research", " 'Southern' anthropologists' concerns about the logic and practice of development, in contrast, dictate consideration of how the axiom of reflexivity, and the discipline itself, might be woven into the practices of the engineering professions..." To me, this nativist concern, be it conveyed in the engineering of national development or expressing a politic of civilization, has emerged from the particular histories of inter-cultural contacts and mutual influences and our reflections on it should be encouraged to create a sense of conscience towards cross-cultural relationship that has not been finely defined in the contemporary world-systems and nations.

CONCLUSION

In the 20th century, anthropological debates in the West have focused on the issue of the Other. What has now been defined in terms of "modern anthropology" has broadly been reflected as a disciplinary space in which co-present contemporary cultures are studied as counterparts to and reflexive mirrors to and for each other. In such an academic space, cultures "surviving" in different parts of the world have been viewed as what are lived as valuable heritages of mankind, and making good translations of other cultures has been what anthropologists do. So any good anthropology is an exit for our professional scholars to "escape" from the "building" of political economic and power constrains that has limited our quest for knowledge.

Nonetheless, as we have by now come to realize, what anthropologists have done has bifurcated the world into the "West and the rest". Thus, to some post-modernists, anthropology can be seen as the legitimacy of the center (Self) and periphery (Other) division in the modern world system. Reciprocal anthropology has been part of the particular endeavor aiming at transcending the limit. As its advocates, we do not necessarily refute all of what our disciplinary forerunners did; but we are keen to know whether certain possible "third spaces" exist for us to discover and utilize. It is in this wish that Chinese civilization has entered into our horizon. But a problem exists and it is that although anthropological studies of China have existed for more than a century, they have not caught the so-called "general anthropologists" ' attention. It is not that anthropologists who have studied China have written bad ethnographic inquiries or constructed inadequate theoretical frameworks. Chinese civilization has seemed to many theoreticians in anthropology a culture that is not "strangely tribal" enough for purpose of our "mutual knowledge" (Wang 1997). With a rather reversed perspective, in "reciprocal anthropology", China has been rated highly for the same reason that failed Western sinological anthropologists in their efforts to become general anthropologists. Our hope is that Chinese cosmology and patterns of social life may be a "third kind" in-between European Civilization and the "Savage Mind", and as such it may serve as a good means whereby we rethink our cultural relations. With the quest for the disposition of the "third kind", in the above contents, we briefly reviewed several important historical transformations in Chinese perspectives of the world and humanity. Our original project was to reconstruct the historical trajectories of the transmission of anthropological theories in China as an illustration of our point of understanding with multi-lateral cultural correspondence.

But throughout the paper, we have, admittedly in a rather unusual way, examined it with reference to the history of All Under Heaven in ancient China. The historical cosmological approach has in turn allowed us to observe how an empire-turned nation has constructed the relationship between itself and the others. By the end, we have become less easy with the latent conception that our anthropological reflections should be defined as what merely reflects "colonial situations". We have found alternatively that if a distinctively Chinese world-view and cosmology of Self-Other relationship exists, then we may say that such a system of knowledge has undergone the following changes that should not be taken for granted as a ready-made alternative model for cross-cultural co-presence:

1. The model emerged in classical periods as a system encompassing some diverse world-scapes in which the hierarchies and conjunctures of humans, lesser humans, and non-humans were set up in accordance to Chinese ethno-centrism, and in which a sense of "mutual disposition" could only be discovered in the heterodoxies of the mountain-residences and the country songs;

2. In later imperial dynasties of the Tang, Song, Yuan, Ming, and the Qing, a possible breakthrough was made possible in the Tang Monk's voyage-pilgrimage to India; but it soon gave way to a cosmography of a China-centered tributary system in which the Chinese empire defined both "world-trade" and civilization;
3. From the mid-19th century onwards, Chinese scholars had come to understand that there had been counterparts of their empire in the world, and that some of these were stronger than the "central kingdom"; and they made great efforts to revitalize its classical world-scape which was hoped to give to China a renewed vital force;
4. Although in the late 19th century social Darwinism was treated something like a virtuous Other for China, in the later decades, a nation-centered anthropology gradually gained its dominance and has not allowed much space for the performance of transcultural anthropology.

We have somehow taken the point made by Cai Yuanpei and other Chinese anthropological forerunners and sought to "re-discover" the cosmological "roots" (foundations) of Otherness in classical Chinese portraits of the world or what was perceived as "All Under Heaven". Comparing our contemporaries to our ancient ancestors, we find that in the ancient times, certain assortments of representations of the Other did make some impacts on the Chinese conceptions of themselves. The zoning of the universe, the Tang, Song, and Yuan expeditions and discoveries of the world, and the Ming voyages to the Western Oceans are good evidences of what Joseph Needham has called "Chinese anthropological geographies" (Needham 1992). What is more, if we agree with the critiques of intellectual imperialism of the West, we can surely also say that the Chinese anthropological geographies resemble modern Western representations of the Other.

However, we have also found that these senses of Otherness are somehow distinct from Western anthropological ones. With the exception of the Tang Mong's travelogue, all the classical Chinese gazetteers of the savages endeavored to create a universal civilization and a tributary system that is not "culturally ralative". A certain sense of diachronic time was observable in Chinese anthropological geographies. But neither was the contrast one that rendered an inter-subjective retrospection, nor was it serving the purpose of "contrasting to know". Instead, a portrait of tributary mode of material and cultural production or what has since the 1980s been termed the "two civilizations" (liangzhong wenming) in the contemporary regime's reformist ideology was the prime guideline.

As a long-term consequence, there has been little Chinese interest in other cultures in non-Chinese worlds in the past century. Although Africa, Europe, Americas, and Oceania have been targets for Chinese diplomatic politics, they have not been seriously studied as possible alternatives of our world-views. Admittedly, in recent years, debates over issues of globalization and cultural distinction have produced interesting works especially when they juxtapose the Self and the Other in a realm of cultural contacts. But they have been constrained either by the idea of "progress", "institutional change", and "reforms" or by the idea of national independence: so much so that the issue of respecting cultural difference both within and without that nation has hardly received any serious attention.

Such a distinctive Chinese characteristic of anthropology can be illustrated with reference to foreign and Chinese anthropologies about China. Western sinological anthropologists have approached China from several perspectives.22 But they in common seek to discover an ethnographic region. Although not many of them take China as a "cultural lesson" for their own cultures, some have respected Chinese great and little traditions as reflections upon Western-centric modes of institution and ideology and they have done so in the same way as other regional anthropologists have taken tribes as different social formations from Western ones (Beteille 1998). The problem has been that in developing a "China-centered" view of culture, sinological anthropologists have also been tied to their own epistemological and ideological concerns. Some of these concerns have derived from the quest for the "perfect language" for the description of China. For the sake of the quest, a lot of local confusions of categories are organized in such manners that they are dispensed or pressed into something strange to the subjects of their studies-the "Chinese"'.

In China, the quest for a sort of Chineseness has also been made of the inversions of Western concepts. For example, as one of the chapters in the book outlines, between the 1930s and 1940s, a group of Chinese anthropologists were led by Wu Wenzao to formulate a Chinese School of Sociology. They wrote in both Chinese and English. But by applying both Malinowki's ethnographic methodology and sociological perspectives of community, the group of Chinese anthropologists supposedly founded a Chinese School without admitting that it was a Chinese mixture of Anglo-American modern social science (Ibid.:25-64). It is apparent that while Western sinological anthropologists seek to discover a China-centered viewpoint of culture, the native Chinese anthropologists are ready to absorb such a viewpoint into their own school of social science. The difference between Western sinological anthropology and Chinese-speaking anthropology has simply been the difference between the outsider's and insider's anthropologies. But that does not mean that the two are not relateable. For example, after I published my book, on the one hand some Chinese colleagues have said to me that it is a good example of the "nativization of anthropology in China". On the other hand, other colleagues have said that I used Western theories too much to retain my Chinese scholarship. But the two views of the same work have thus shared a common interest: the Chineseness of anthropology.

Some may say that what we just said suggested that like Western anthropology in "colonial situations" Chinese anthropological cosmologies and discipline have been trapped their political and cultural institutions that formated their discourses. But for us, saying that is not enough because we still ought to consider the question of where this critique leads. If we can suggest anything along this line, then we can also say that like Western anthropology, Chinese anthropology needs a sense of reciprocity. It needs to open itself to the whole world and all the different cultures that co-exist. It needs also to develop a system of knowledge and value in which something in-between Self and Other is respected as an important space or arena in which reciprocal understanding is made possible.

Now the project of Transcultural Institute-the prime advocate of reciprocal anthropology--has included, a Chinese partnership, along with European and African ones. Our role is defined in terms of an important component of the multi-lateral cross-cultural perspective. The reason may be simple: any transcultural projects will be unsuccessful without the inclusion of such a large civilization as China whose world-views are, as it were, so different from the others that they provide certain alternative and complementary patterns to the Western learning. Specifically, Chinese involvement in the project has been viewed as highly desirable as a good solution to our common problems of cultural relationship. With an important relevance to what I discussed in the above, in one of the propositions, it is supposed that the Chinese "poetics of hospitality"-the remarkable ways in which the Chinese people receive our guests--could be a good solution to our current transcultural co-presence. No doubt that the "poetics of hospitality" is an important or even the core component of Chinese world-views. But hospitality can better be understood as a sort of "guest ritual" that is part of a larger system-that of "ceremonial order" (lizhi)--with which our ancestors treated the outsiders in their "tributary ways". However, what I have done in this paper is nothing more than pointing to the fact that like the European reification of Chinese symbols, Chinese "ceremonial order" has been embedded in the history of cosmological domestication, whether it has been tributary or nationalistic.

Whether this critique is relevant to other regional anthropologies is another issue for discussion on another occasion. Our hope here is that the discussion can help us detect certain pitfalls in perceiving systems of local knowledge in non-Western contexts as adequate conceptual instruments for epistemological and ontological reflections in the Western contexts. It is also that knowing the problems of learning in a non-Western context should also be an inevitable passage through which our destination of "mutual disposition" can be reached. The ideal is to make multi-directional travels among cultures. But it is still important for Europeans to join in the course of the reciprocation by way of the journey to the "East"-or the "South. Meanwhile, it deems urgent for Chinese to throw ourselves into the voyage towards the "West"-or the "North"-in similar spirituality to, for instance, the Tang Monk's journey to India. When we come across each other in our journeys, we may find something in common, find some sort of space for reciprocal understanding.

Bibliography

Agrawala, S. V.: *The Glorification of the Great Goddess*, All-India Kashray Trust, Varanasi, 1963.

Agrawala, V.: *Shiva Mahadeva: The Great God*, Veda Academy, Varanasi, 1966.

Aiyar, M.K.: *Advaita Vedanta, according to Sankara*, Asia Publishing House, New York, 1965.

Arthur, A.: *Tantrik Texts: Kalivilasa Tantra*, Luzac and Co., London, 1917.

Bhattacharji, Sukumari: *Literature in the Vedic Age*, Kali Ram Press, Calcutta, 1988.

Chakravarti, C.: *The Tantras: Studies on their Religion and Literature*, Punthi Pustak, Calcutta, 1963.

Chaturvedi, M.D.,: *Hinduism, The Eternal Religion*, Bharatiya Vidya Bhavan, Bombay, 1992.

Coomeraswamy, Ananda K.: *Buddha and the Gospel of Buddhism*, MacMillan, London, 1928.

De Bary: *Self and Society in Ming Thought*, Columbia University Press, New York, 1970.

Franco-Maria: *Tantra: Rites of Love*, Rizzoli, New York, 1979.

Furth, H.G. : *The World of Grown-ups: Children's Conceptions of Society*, New York, Elsevier North Holland, 1980.

Goldman, R.: *The Ramayana of Valmiki*, Berkeley Hills Books, New York, 2000.

Holland, D. and Millican, J. : *Adult Literacy, A Handbook for Development Workers*, Oxford, Oxfam, 1995.

Mahendranath, S.: *Comparative Studies in Vedaantism*, Humphrey Milford, Bombay, 1927.

Mearns, David J.: *Shiva's Other Children: Religion and Social Identity amongst Overseas Indians*, Sage, Walnut Creek, 1995.

Michael, J. : *Education Fever: Society, Politics, and the Pursuit of Schooling in South Korea*, Honolulu, University of Hawai Press, 2002.

Michell, George: *The Hindu Temple: An Introduction to Its Meaning and Forms*, University of Chicago Press, Chicago, 1988.

Rao, K. B.: *Ontology of Adavita*, Mulki S. India, Delhi, 1996.

Roderick, R. : *Habermas and the Foundations of Critical Theory*, Basingstoke, Macmillan, 1986.

Rosen, Steven: *Vaisnavi: Women and the Worship of Krishna*, Motilal Banarsidass Publishers, Delhi, 1996.

Sharma, Pushpendra K.: *Hindu Religion and Ethics*, Asian Publication Services, New Delhi, 1997.

Shourie, Arun : *Indian Controversies: Essays on Religion in Politics*, New Delhi, Manohar, 1993.

Simon Coleman: *Pilgrimage: Past and Present in the World Religions*, Harvard University Press, Cambridge, 1995.

Stephens, S. : *Children and the Politics of Culture*, Princeton, Princeton University Press, 1995.

Steven G. Darian: *The Ganges in Myth and History*, Univ. Press of Hawaii, Honolulu, 1978.

Stewart, J. : *Management for the Public Domain*, New York, St, Martin's Press, 1994.

Subhan, John A.: *Sufism: Its Saints and Shrines*, Lucknow, 1938.

Tsultrim, A.: *Women of Wisdom*, MacMillan, London, 1984.

Vidya, D.: *Yogin: Cult and Temples: A Tantric Tradition*, National Museum, New Delhi, 1985.

Wendy, D.: *Karma and Rebirth*. Motilal Banarsidas, Delhi 1993 (1980).

Woods, J.: *The Yoga-System of Patanjali*, Motilal Banarsidass, Delhi, 1966.

Zenith, A.: *The Religion and Philosophy of the Veda and Upanishads*, Harvard University Press, Cambridge, 1925.

Zimmer, Heinrich: *Yogic and Tantric Medicine*, Joseph Campbell, Delhi, 1946.

Zvelebil, Kamil V. : *Companion Studies to the History of Tamil Literature*, Leiden, Brill, 1992.

Index

D

E

F

G

H

I

L

M

N

O

P